ARCO

MASTER THE FEDERAL LAW ENFORCEMENT EXAMS

5th Edition

THOMSON

★

PETERSON'S ™

Australia • Canada • Mexico • Singapore • Spain • United Kingdom • United States

An ARCO Book

ARCO is a registered trademark of Thomson Learning, Inc., and is used herein under license by Thomson Peterson's.

About Thomson Peterson's

Thomson Peterson's (www.petersons.com) is a leading provider of education information and advice, with books and online resources focusing on education search, test preparation, and financial aid. Its Web site offers searchable databases and interactive tools for contacting educational institutions, online practice tests and instruction, and planning tools for securing financial aid. Peterson's serves 110 million education consumers annually.

For more information, contact Thomson Peterson's, 2000 Lenox Drive, Lawrenceville, NJ 08648; 800-338-3282; or find us on the World Wide Web at: www.petersons.com/about.

Previous editions published as *Law Enforcement Exams* © 1992, 2002

Editor: Joe Krasowski; Production Editor: L.A. Wagner; Manufacturing Manager: Ray Golazewski; Composition Manager: Melissa Ignatowski

ISSN: International Standard Serial Number information available upon request.

ISBN: 0-7689-1549-X

Printed in the United States of America

10 9 8 7 6 5 4 3 2 1   07 06 05

Fifth Edition

Contents

Contents

PART III: PRACTICE TEST

APPENDIXES

Petersons.com/publishing

Check out our Web site at www.petersons.com/publishing to see if there is any new information regarding the test and any revisions or corrections to the content of this book. We've made sure the information in this book is accurate and up-to-date; however, the test format or content may have changed since the time of publication.

OTHER RECOMMENDED TITLES

ARCO 24 Hours to the Law Enforcement Exams

ARCO Federal Jobs in Law Enforcement

ARCO Federal Jobs: The Ultimate Guide

ARCO Special Agent/Deputy U.S. Marshal

Before You Begin

HOW THIS BOOK IS ORGANIZED

So you want a career in federal law enforcement. A career in federal law enforcement offers an opportunity to serve your community and to help others. It offers diversity, excitement, and, in most cases, some personal danger. It also offers career security and growth opportunities. Which law enforcement position is for you? Different positions have different requirements for education, experience, medical history, and physical fitness. There are great variations in working conditions, time commitments, travel and relocation requirements, and the work itself. *ARCO Master the Federal Law Enforcement Exams* provides you with the necessary ammunition to help you put your best foot forward, including:

"Top 10 Ways to Raise Your Score" gives you a preview of some of the test-taking strategies you'll learn in the book.

Part I provides basic information about a career in federal law enforcement. You'll learn how the federal government is organized, how to land a federal job, how to write a top-notch application, and how to prepare for the written exam.

Part II profiles the most popular federal law enforcement positions available with the three main branches of government and independent agencies, as well as positions with the Department of Homeland Security.

Part III contains a full-length practice test with detailed answer explanations designed to prepare you for the specific exam you will be required to take.

The **Appendixes** provide information about the Federal Law Enforcement Training Center as well as a listing of important employment resources.

SPECIAL STUDY FEATURES

ARCO Master the Federal Law Enforcement Exams is designed to be as user-friendly as it is complete. To this end, it includes several features to make your preparation much more efficient.

Overview

Each chapter begins with a bulleted overview listing the topics that will be covered in the chapter. This will allow you to quickly target the areas in which you are most interested.

Summing It Up

Each chapter ends with a point-by-point summary that captures the most important points contained in the chapter. They are a convenient way to review key points.

As you work your way through the book, keep your eye on the margins to find bonus information and advice. Information can be found in the following forms:

Note

Notes highlight critical information about a career in federal law enforcement, the application process, and the written exam.

Tip

Tips provide valuable advice for effectively handling the federal law enforcement job-search process.

Alert!

Alerts do just what they say—alert you to common pitfalls or misconceptions.

YOU'RE WELL ON YOUR WAY TO SUCCESS

You have made a decision to pursue a career in federal law enforcement. *ARCO Master the Federal Law Enforcement Exams* will help you select the agencies to which you are most suited and will also guide you in finding, applying for, and landing the job of your dreams. Good Luck!

Top 10 Ways to Raise Your Score

There are concepts you can learn, techniques you can follow, and tricks you can use that will give you the biggest bang for your buck when taking the federal law enforcement exam. Here's our Top 10 list.

1. **Get to the test center early.** Make sure you give yourself plenty of extra time to get there, park your car, if necessary, and even grab a cup of coffee before the test.

2. **Listen to the test monitors and follow their instructions carefully.**

3. **Mark only ONE answer for each question, even if you think that more than one answer is correct.** You must choose only one. If you mark more than one answer, the scoring machine will consider you wrong.

4. **If you change your mind, erase completely.** Leave no doubt as to which answer you mean.

5. **If your exam permits you to use scratch paper or the margins of the test booklet for figuring, don't forget to mark the answer on the answer sheet.** Only the answer sheet is scored.

6. **Check often to be sure that the question number matches the answer space, that you have not skipped a space by mistake.**

7. **If the scoring is "rights only," that is, one point for each correct answer and no subtraction for wrong answers, then by all means you should guess.** Read the question and all of the answer choices carefully. Eliminate those answer choices that you are certain are wrong. Then guess from among the remaining choices. You cannot gain a point if you leave the answer space blank; you may gain a point with an educated guess or even with a lucky guess. In fact, it is foolish to leave any spaces blank on a test that counts "rights only."

8. **Stay alert.** Be careful not to mark a wrong answer just because you were not concentrating.

9. **Do not panic.** If you cannot finish any part before time is up, do not worry. If you are accurate, you can do well even without finishing. It is even possible to earn a scaled score of 100 without entirely finishing an exam part if you are very accurate. At any rate, do not let your performance on any one part affect your performance on any other part.

10. **Check and recheck, time permitting.** If you finish any part before time is up, use the remaining time to check that each question is answered in the right space and that there is only one answer for each question. Return to the difficult questions and rethink them.

PART I

FEDERAL LAW ENFORCEMENT BASICS

CHAPTER 1   All About Federal
             Law Enforcement

All About Federal Law Enforcement

OVERVIEW

- **Structure of the federal government**
- **How to land a federal job**
- **Preparing for the exam**
- **Test format**
- **Summing it up**

To suggest that crime and terrorism are on global upswings is hardly news. Even the most stable governments are affected by the instability and growing fears of the everyday realities posed by such threats. In the United States alone, in addition to the threat of terrorism, a burglary is committed every 6 seconds. While the number of homicides in the United States per capita is four times greater than its nearest competitor, incidents of crime have reached what many consider epidemic proportions in most industrial nations of the world.

Although the United States has experienced a decrease in the accelerated rates of violent crime, two fundamental trends guarantee that almost all types of crime will increase in the coming year. As it does, the demand for competent and effective delivery of security and police service will become a necessity.

The prisons of the world are at or near capacity, and the cost of building new ones is increasing dramatically. As a result, prisoners are receiving shorter sentences and are being paroled earlier. Once back on the street, these individuals must compete with a whole new generation of criminals and criminals in training, which helps to explain why criminals, in general, are becoming bolder and more willing to take risks for less return. Even if these criminals are apprehended, they will be back on the streets sooner next time due to prison overcrowding. The reality is that our jails and prisons have simply been transformed into costly criminal warehouses that really serve as universities of crime, and at best only postpone the problem while backlogging the court system characterized by limitless appeals.

When funding for prisons and jails reaches the point of being politically unreasonable, the system may easily break. If it does, the only deterrence to crime may be the ones we create for ourselves. Until that happens, our various levels of government will be accountable for our collective response. A more security-conscious society and growing concern for terrorism will heighten the need for highly competent and trained security professionals to design and maintain effective law enforcement and security systems for the protection of our social order and institutions. Considering this type of response, federal criminal investigators and security professionals will be hired to respond to the growing threats posed by such activities as illegal drug trafficking, fraud, and threats to national security. Likewise, opportunities for uniformed law enforcement, corrections and security personnel will also be abundant.

STRUCTURE OF THE FEDERAL GOVERNMENT

The first three articles of the Constitution divide the federal government into three branches:

1. Legislative
2. Executive
3. Judicial

This division results in the separation of powers that ensures our democratic system of government. Simply put, the *Legislative* Branch makes the laws, the *Executive* Branch implements them, and the *Judicial* Branch enforces them. With about 3 million employees, the Executive Branch is the largest branch of the federal government.

Salary and Benefits

Federal law enforcement personnel receive very competitive salaries and a wide range of benefits that often surpass those structures provided by many state and municipal agencies as well as organizations in the private sector. Unlike decades past, federal salaries and benefits are superior to those of comparable positions in private industry. Complementing the excellent pay schedules of the federal system are health and life insurance, paid holidays, paid vacation and sick leave, travel expenses, injury compensation, and excellent retirement benefits. Following is a review of the salary structures and primary benefits available to sworn and non-sworn federal law enforcement personnel.

Under the federal system, law enforcement personnel are covered by a number of different pay structures, some established by individual laws and others by administrative authority. The General Schedule for white-collar employees, the Foreign Service, and certain employees in the Veterans Health Administration of the Department of Veterans Affairs are all a part of the statutory pay structures. Salaries under these structures are governed by policies defined in the U.S. Code. The General Schedule pay system covers the majority of federal law enforcement personnel. Special Agents and Regional Security officers of the State Department are covered under the Foreign Service pay plan while the Veterans Health Administration provides pay plans for Veteran Administration medical personnel.

The General Pay Schedule

Nearly three quarters of federal employees are paid under the General Schedule (GS) plan. As such, the General Schedule system is composed of fifteen general grades, each defined in terms of difficulty and responsibilities required for performance, as well as the qualifications required for performance, ranging from GS-1 through GS-15. Within each grade there is a salary range of ten steps where an employee normally starts at step one within a particular grade upon entry. Advancement within grade normally occurs after 52 weeks of service in the first three steps in the specific grade, after 104 weeks service in steps four through six, and after 156 weeks in steps seven and higher. In order to qualify for advancement to the next step, the individual must demonstrate work performance at an acceptable level of competence.

GENERAL PAY SCHEDULE

Effective January 2005

Grade	Step 1	Step 2	Step 3	Step 4	Step 5	Step 6	Step 7	Step 8	Step 9	Step 10
1	$16,016	$16,550	$17,083	$17,613	$18,146	$18,459	$18,984	$19,515	$19,537	$20,036
2	18,007	18,435	19,031	19,537	19,755	20,336	20,917	21,498	22,079	22,660
3	19,647	20,302	20,957	21,612	22,267	22,922	23,577	24,232	24,887	25,542
4	22,056	22,791	23,526	24,261	24,996	25,731	26,466	27,201	27,936	28,671
5	24,677	25,500	26,323	27,146	27,969	28,792	29,615	30,438	31,261	32,084
6	27,507	28,424	29,341	30,258	31,175	32,092	33,009	33,926	34,843	35,760
7	30,567	31,586	32,605	33,624	34,643	35,662	36,681	37,700	38,719	39,738
8	33,852	34,980	36,108	37,236	38,364	39,492	40,620	41,748	42,876	44,004
9	37,390	38,636	39,882	41,128	42,374	43,620	44,866	46,112	47,358	48,604
10	41,175	42,548	43,921	45,294	46,667	48,040	49,413	50,786	52,159	53,532
11	45,239	46,747	48,255	49,763	51,271	52,779	54,287	55,795	57,303	58,811
12	54,221	56,028	57,835	59,642	61,449	63,256	65,063	66,870	68,677	70,484
13	64,478	66,627	68,776	70,925	73,074	75,223	77,372	79,521	81,670	83,819
14	76,193	78,733	81,273	83,813	86,353	88,893	91,433	93,973	96,513	99,053
15	89,625	92,613	95,601	98,589	101,577	104,565	107,553	110,541	113,529	116,517

Administratively Determined Pay Plans

Congress has authorized heads of agencies to establish compensation for the entire agency or for particular groups of positions, without regard to the General Schedule. These plans are called Administratively Determined Pay Plans. Heads of some agencies administratively establish the pay schedules for their agencies while others may not. Although some law enforcement personnel have pay schedules under Administratively

NOTE

Individuals who demonstrate a high-level of performance may advance more rapidly within specific pay grades by being granted quality-step increases.

Determined Pay Systems, most federal law enforcement personnel are not compensated in such manner.

Locality Payments

Federal employees covered under the General Schedule or some other pay systems also may be compensated for the difference between prevailing federal and private-sector salaries in a particular geographic location. Known as Locality Pay, this type of compensation is designed to provide competitive pay within more than thirty metropolitan areas in the United States and may be adjusted on an annual basis.

Law Enforcement Salary Rates

Congress established the Federal Law Enforcement Pay Reform Act of 1990 that set forth special salary rates for law enforcement officers at grades GS-3 through GS-10 and included pay enhancements that range from one to seven salary steps above those found in the General Schedule. Under this pay plan, a law enforcement officer who is appointed at grade GS-5 step one, for example, would receive a starting salary under this enhancement equal to the starting salary of GS-5 step eight in the General Schedule. Salary schedules below GS-3 and above GS-10 are not affected. Special salary rates do not apply to uniform police officers, corrections officers, criminal investigators, certain security specialists, and personnel assigned to military detention and/or rehabilitation facilities.

SALARY TABLE NO. 491
LAW ENFORCEMENT OFFICERS

Effective January 2005

Grade	Step 1	Step 2	Step 3	Step 4	Step 5	Step 6	Step 7	Step 8	Step 9	Step 10
3	$23,577	$24,232	$24,887	$25,542	$26,197	$26,852	$27,507	$28,162	$28,817	$29,472
4	26,466	27,201	27,936	28,671	29,406	30,141	30,876	31,611	32,346	33,081
5	30,438	31,261	32,084	32,907	33,730	34,553	35,376	36,199	37,022	37,845
6	32,092	33,009	33,926	34,843	35,760	36,677	37,594	38,511	39,428	40,345
7	34,643	35,662	36,681	37,700	38,719	39,738	40,757	41,776	42,795	43,814
8	36,108	37,236	38,364	39,492	40,620	41,748	42,876	44,004	45,132	46,260
9	38,636	39,882	41,128	42,374	43,620	44,866	46,112	47,358	48,604	49,850
10	42,548	43,921	45,294	46,667	48,040	49,413	50,786	52,159	53,532	54,905

Special Pay Adjustments

The Federal Law Enforcement Pay Reform Act of 1990 also established special pay adjustments for law enforcement employees. These adjustments are provided for officers who are stationed in selected metropolitan areas and are administered in similar fashion as Locality Pay. However, officers can receive only the higher of the two, not both. These adjustments apply to all grades. Log on to www.opm.gov/oca/05tables/locdef.asp for definitions of Locality Pay areas. Below is an example of a Special Pay Adjustment Schedule.

SALARY TABLE—CHICAGO

Effective January 2005

Grade	Step 1	Step 2	Step 3	Step 4	Step 5	Step 6	Step 7	Step 8	Step 9	Step 10
1	$19,171	$19,810	$20,448	$21,083	$21,721	$22,095	$22,724	$23,359	$23,386	$23,983
2	21,554	22,067	22,780	23,386	23,647	24,342	25,038	25,733	26,429	27,124
3	28,222	29,006	29,790	30,574	31,358	32,142	32,926	33,710	34,494	35,278
4	31,680	32,560	33,439	34,319	35,199	36,079	36,959	37,838	38,718	39,598
5	36,434	37,419	38,405	39,390	40,375	41,360	42,345	43,330	44,315	45,300
6	38,414	39,512	40,609	41,707	42,805	43,902	45,000	46,098	47,195	48,293
7	41,468	42,687	43,907	45,127	46,347	47,566	48,786	50,006	51,226	52,445
8	43,221	44,571	45,922	47,272	48,622	49,972	51,323	52,673	54,023	55,373
9	46,247	47,739	49,230	50,722	52,213	53,705	55,196	56,688	58,179	59,670
10	50,930	52,573	54,217	55,860	57,504	59,147	60,791	62,434	64,078	65,721
11	54,151	55,956	57,761	59,566	61,371	63,176	64,982	66,787	68,592	70,397
12	64,903	67,066	69,228	71,391	73,554	75,717	77,880	80,043	82,206	84,369
13	77,180	79,753	82,325	84,897	87,470	90,042	92,614	95,187	97,759	100,331
14	91,203	94,243	97,284	100,324	103,365	106,405	109,445	112,486	115,526	118,566
15	107,281	110,858	114,434	118,011	121,588	125,164	128,741	132,318	135,894	139,471

Premium Pay
LAW ENFORCEMENT AVAILABILITY PAY

To compensate federal criminal investigators for unscheduled overtime duty and to insure that criminal investigators are available based upon needs of the various agencies, Congress passed the Law Enforcement Availability Pay Act of 1994. Under the authority of this act, a large majority of criminal investigators and game law enforcement receive a salary premium of 25 percent of basic pay. To qualify for this pay, investigators are expected to work, or be available to work, an average of two hours of duty time above every regular eight-hour workday. As long as investigators meet the required conditions, the pay plan is actually an employee entitlement.

OTHER PREMIUM PAY

Another type of premium pay covers work performed beyond the standard workday or service week, such as compensatory time in lieu of overtime pay; Sunday premium pay (when Sunday is part of the service week); and night-shift differential pay.

Death and Disability Benefits

Under the Public Officers' Benefits Act and the Federal Law Enforcement Dependents Assistance Act, Congress provides benefits to the families of officers whose deaths or disabilities occur in the line of duty. This Act was enacted to assist in the recruitment and retention of law enforcement officers and firefighters. In the case of one's death as a result of a traumatic injury sustained in the line of duty, there will be a one-time payment of benefit. For an individual who is totally disabled, and the injury prevents the person from obtaining any gainful work, permanent disability will be awarded. Law enforcement officers eligible for this program include police, corrections, probation, parole, judicial, and other law enforcement officers of federal, state, county, and local public agencies.

Federal Law Enforcement Dependents Assistance Act

The Federal Law Enforcement Dependents Assistance Act provides financial assistance for higher education to spouses and children of federal law enforcement officers killed or disabled in the line of duty. These benefits are intended to pay for education expenses (tuition, room and board, books, supplies and fees) for dependents who attend a qualifying program of education at an eligible institution.

Retirement Benefits

Most commissioned federal law enforcement personnel are covered under special provisions that require voluntary or mandatory retirement at an earlier age than other federal employees. These provisions apply to personnel who serve in certain covered positions that include most criminal investigators, uniformed police officers, corrections officers, personnel assigned to correctional and military detention facilities and certain rehabilitation facilities, and security specialists. Under these provisions qualified personnel may retire after twenty or twenty-five years of service, depending on age. However, retirement is mandatory at age 57. In most cases, personnel appointed to covered positions must receive the appointment prior to their thirty-seventh birthday. Applicants over the age of 37 who have previous service credit under special law enforcement provisions may retire at age 57 with twenty years of creditable service.

FEDERAL THRIFT SAVINGS PLAN

The Federal Thrift Savings Plan, similar to the 401(k) plans offered through private corporations, provides savings and tax benefits for government employees to supplement retirement savings. The plan offers tax-deferred investment earnings as well as choice of investment vehicles. Covered employees may contribute up to 10 percent of their basic pay each pay period and contributions are either partially or fully matched by the government, depending on the percentage of income contributed.

Life Insurance

Most federal civilian employees are eligible to participate in the Federal Employees' Group Life Insurance Program. This is a plan that offers life insurance and accidental death and dismemberment coverage. These policies do not build cash value or loan value, and participants may purchase additional life insurance coverage to cover eligible family members.

Health-Care Benefits

The Federal Employees Health Benefits Program provides health-care insurance coverage to eligible employees. This program offers a wide selection of health plans designed for managed health maintenance. Once appointed, employees are covered without medical exams or restrictions related to age or physical condition and may select coverage for family members. The government contributes between 60 and 75 percent toward the total cost of the premiums depending on the plan selected.

Sick Leave

All full-time federal civilian employees earn thirteen days of paid sick leave per year. Sick leave may be used for medical, dental, or optical treatment or examination; to care for ill family members; or to make arrangements as the result of the death of a family member or attend the funeral of a family member. Under the Family and Medical Leave Act of 1993, federal employees may take up to twelve weeks of unpaid leave for purposes defined under the Act.

Annual Leave

Federal employees accumulate paid annual leave (vacation or other purposes) based upon years of service. Annual leave is earned at a rate of thirteen days per year for employees with fewer than three years of service, twenty days per year for those with three to fifteen years of service, and twenty-six days per year for those with more than fifteen years of service.

Paid Holidays

Federal employees receive ten paid holidays per year, including:

- New Year's Day
- Martin Luther King Jr.'s Birthday
- Washington's Birthday
- Memorial Day
- Independence Day
- Labor Day
- Columbus Day
- Veterans' Day
- Thanksgiving Day
- Christmas Day

HOW TO LAND A FEDERAL JOB

Landing a federal job today is much easier than it was just a short time ago. The notorious centralized "register" system has all but disappeared, so job seekers can now apply directly to the agencies for which they'd like to work. This new system empowers job seekers to choose where they'd like to work and grants agencies the power to choose whom they'd like to hire. Also, many federal examinations have been done away with, so that fewer than 20 percent of all nonpostal service jobs require civil service tests. This speeds up and simplifies the federal hiring process to a great degree. All you need is a little time, a little energy, and a bit of determination to be on your way to a federal career. Following the tips contained in these chapters will help you narrow your focus and give you a solid step-by-step game plan to guide you to the federal job that is right for you.

The Federal Job Search

Most people are painfully familiar with searching for a job in corporate America. They know all about shuffling through the want ads and wandering door-to-door, resume in hand. But how do you go about finding those elusive federal jobs?

Does a federal job search resemble a private-sector search? Consider the typical job search in corporate America. Most job seekers start with the classified ads, a convenient, inexpensive, low-risk way to look for job openings. There is nothing wrong with browsing through the classifieds—people do land jobs this way. Unfortunately, applying to jobs that announced their openings to the general public puts you in the midst of a huge amount of competition. If you are reading the ad, it is likely that many other qualified candidates are reading it too. This "front door" approach to job hunting can be frustrating, because it puts you in the middle of the stiffest competition for the job.

NOTE

Employees who must work on a federal holiday receive double their regular pay.

ALERT!

Don't jump into your job search blindly. It is wise to gather information and develop a strategy before you enter the federal job-search arena.

Other private-sector job seekers try the "back door" approach to job hunting. They try tapping into the "hidden" job market. They search for the jobs that have not yet been advertised, that perhaps have not yet solidified in the minds of the hiring managers. These are the jobs for which they figure they can stand alone as qualified candidates because no one else knows the jobs exist. Tapping into the "hidden" job market involves networking, making telephone and personal contacts, and involves more risk to the ego than simply reading the classifieds.

How do these standard job-hunting approaches compare to a federal job search? Surprisingly, a federal job search is quite similar to a private-sector job search, and in many ways, federal searches are even easier. Although most people don't realize it, both the front door and back door job-search strategies can work in the federal sector just as they do in the private sector. Most people, however, are not sure how to find the "classified ads" for federal jobs (they aren't usually listed in the daily paper), and they are unaware that a "hidden" job market exists for federal jobs.

Surf the Web

When it comes to the federal hiring process, the Internet is tailor-made. While Internet job searches in the private sector may not always yield results, it is the number one place to conduct a job search for federal employment. Why does it work so well? Here are a few reasons:

1. The federal government generally does not advertise its job openings in the local newspaper, as so many private-sector corporations do. Thus, the Internet is nearly a single-source outlet for federal job announcements.

2. Every sizeable agency in the federal government has a Web site, and nearly all provide a list of current vacancies within their agency (or a link to current vacancies).

3. You can find out about openings in a timely manner, rather than having to wait for (and pay for) a biweekly publication of federal job openings.

4. Many agencies even provide online application forms so that the application writing and mailing processes are greatly simplified.

5. You never have to leave your home to find federal job listings.

6. Job announcements are available 24 hours a day, 7 days a week, so you can search for them at your convenience.

7. Since federal jobs are located throughout the nation, the Internet is a great way to reach a national audience easily.

The Job Announcement

When a position is open and an examination is to be given for it, a job announcement is drawn up. This generally contains everything an applicant has to know about the job. The announcement begins with the job title and salary. A typical announcement then describes the work, the location of the position, the education and experience requirements, the kind of examination to be given, and the system of rating. It may also have something to say about veteran preference and the age limit. It tells which application form is to be filled out, where to get the form, and where and when to file it.

Study the job announcement carefully. It will answer many of your questions and help you decide whether you like the position and are qualified for it.

There is no point in applying for a position and taking the examination if you do not want to work where the job is. The job may be in your community or hundreds of miles away at the other end of the state. If you are not willing to work where the job is, study other announcements that will give you an opportunity to work in a place of your choice.

The words **Optional Fields**—sometimes just the word **Options**—may appear on the front page of the announcement. You then have a choice to apply for that particular position in which you are especially interested. This is because the duties of various positions are quite different even though they bear the same broad title. Not every announcement has options. But whether or not it has them, the precise duties are described in detail, usually under the heading, **Description of Work.** Make sure that these duties come within the range of your experience and ability.

Most job requirements give a **deadline for filing** an application. Others bear the words **No Closing Date** at the top of the first page. This means that applications will be accepted until the needs of the agency are met. In some cases a public notice is issued when a certain number of applications have been received. No application mailed past the deadline date will be considered.

Every announcement has a detailed section on **education and experience requirements** for the particular job and for the optional fields. Make sure that in both education and experience you meet the minimum qualifications. If you do not meet the given standards for one job, there may be others open where you stand a better chance of making the grade.

If the job announcement does not mention **veteran preference,** it would be wise to inquire if there is such a provision in your state or municipality. There may be none or it may be limited to disabled veterans. In some jurisdictions, surviving spouses of disabled veterans are given preference. All such information can be obtained through the agency that issues the job announcement.

Applicants may be denied examinations and eligible candidates may be denied appointments for any of the following reasons:

- intentional false statements;

- deception or fraud in examination or appointment;

- use of alcohol or drugs to the extent that ability to perform the duties of the position is impaired; and/or

- criminal, infamous, dishonest, immoral, or notoriously disgraceful conduct.

The announcement describes the **kind of test** given for the particular position. Please pay special attention to this section. It tells what areas are to be covered in the written test and lists the specific subjects on which questions will be asked. Sometimes sample questions are given.

Usually the announcement states whether the examination is to be **assembled** or **unassembled.** In an assembled examination applicants assemble in the same place at the same time to take a written or performance test. The unassembled examination is one where an applicant does not take a test. Instead, he or she is rated on his or her education and experience and whatever records of past achievement the applicant is asked to provide.

In the competitive examination all applicants for a position compete with each other; the better the mark, the better the chance of being appointed. Also, competitive examinations are given to determine desirability for promotion among employees.

The Application Process

Having studied the job announcement and having decided that you want the position and are qualified for it, your next step is to get an application form. The job announcement tells you where to send for it.

On the whole, application forms differ little from state to state and locality to locality. The questions that have been worked out after years of experimentation are simple and direct, designed to elicit a maximum amount of information about you.

Many prospective employees have failed to get a job because of slipshod, erroneous, incomplete, misleading, or untruthful answers. Give the application serious attention, for it is the first important step toward getting the job you want. On the following pages are samples of a New York City Application for Examination and a State of California Application for Employment and/or Examination.

NEW YORK CITY APPLICATION FOR EXAMINATION

FOLLOW DIRECTIONS ON BACK
Fill in all requested information clearly, accurately, and completely.

The City will only process applications with complete, correct, legible information which are accompanied by correct payment or waiver documentation.

All unprocessed applications will be returned to the applicant.

DEPARTMENT OF CITYWIDE ADMINISTRATIVE SERVICES
DIVISION OF CITYWIDE PERSONNEL SERVICES
1 Centre Street, 14th floor
New York, NY 10007

APPLICATION FOR EXAMINATION

(Directions for completing this application are on the *back* of this form. Additional information is on the Special Circumstances Sheet)

Download this form on-line: nyc.gov/html/dcas

Check One:
☐ Open Competitive
☐ Promotion

1. EXAM #:

2. EXAM TITLE:

3. SOCIAL SECURITY NUMBER:

4. LAST NAME:

5. FIRST NAME:

6. MIDDLE INITIAL:

7. MAILING ADDRESS:

8. APT. #:

9. CITY OR TOWN:

10. STATE:

11. ZIP CODE:

12. PHONE:

13. OTHER NAMES USED IN CITY SERVICE:

Questions 14 & 15:
Discrimination on the basis of sex, sexual orientation, age, creed, color, age, disability status, veteran status or religious observance is prohibited by law. The City of New York is an equal opportunity employer. The identifying information requested on the form is to be used to determine the representation of protected groups among applicants. This information is voluntary and will not be made available to individuals making hiring decisions.

14. RACE/ETHNICITY (Check One):
☐ White
☐ Black
☐ Hispanic
☐ American Indian/ Alaskan Native
☐ Asian/Pacific Islander

15. SEX (Check One):
☐ Male
☐ Female

16. ARE YOU EMPLOYED BY HEALTH AND HOSPITALS CORPORATION? (Check One):
☐ YES
☐ NO

17. CHECK ALL BOXES THAT APPLY TO YOU: (Directions for this section are found on the "Special Circumstances" Sheet)
☐ I AM A SABBATH OBSERVER AND WILL REQUEST AN ALTERNATE TEST DATE (Verification required. See Item A on Special Circumstances Sheet)
☐ I HAVE A DISABILITY AND WILL REQUEST SPECIAL ACCOMMODATIONS (Verification required. See Item B on Special Circumstances Sheet)
☐ I CLAIM VETERANS' CREDIT (For qualifications see Item C on Special Circumstances Sheet)
☐ I CLAIM DISABLED VETERANS' CREDIT (For qualifications see Item C on Special Circumstances Sheet)
☐ I CLAIM PARENT LEGACY CREDIT (For qualifications see Item D on Special Circumstances Sheet)
☐ I CLAIM SIBLING LEGACY CREDIT (For qualifications see Item D on Special Circumstances Sheet)

18. Your Signature: _____ Date: _____

MICHAEL R. BLOOMBERG
Mayor

MARTHA K. HIRST
Commissioner

NOTE: You should apply for an examination __only__ if you meet the qualification requirements set forth in the Notice of Examination. Read the Notice of Examination carefully before completing the application form.

Fill in all requested information clearly, accurately, and completely. The City will only process applications with complete, correct, legible information which are accompanied by correct payment or waiver documentation. All unprocessed applications will be returned to the applicant.

Included in this material is a voter registration form. If you take this opportunity to register to vote, please mail the postage-paid form directly to the Board of Elections. The provision of government services is not conditioned on being registered to vote.

When appropriate the City will issue a refund for unprocessed applications after the close of the filing period.

DIRECTIONS FOR SUBMITTING APPLICATION FOR EXAMINATION

FORMS	All required forms which are listed in the upper-right-hand corner of the Notice of Examination must accompany your application. Failure to include these forms may result in your disqualification and you <u>will not</u> receive test scores.
FEE	The amount of the fee is stated in the Notice of Examination. Only a *MONEY ORDER* made out to *D.C.A.S. (EXAMS)* is acceptable payment (check or cash **are not** accepted). On the front of the money order you must clearly write your *full name, social security number* and *the exam number*. Keep your Money Order receipt as proof of filing.
FEE WAIVER	A filing fee is not charged if you are a New York City resident receiving public/cash assistance from the New York City Department of Social Services. To have the fee waived, you **must** be receiving full benefits and not partial benefits. If you are eligible, you must enclose a legible photocopy of your current Benefit Card (**formerly known as the Medicaid Card**) with your application. **The Food Coupon Photo Identification Card is *unacceptable*.** You must write your *social security number* and the *exam number* on the front of the photocopy of the Benefit Card. The name on your application must exactly match the name printed on your Benefit Card. <u>**Fee Waivers are limited to persons who are recipients of Public Assistance at the time of submission of the application.**</u> Any person who falsifies information concerning current receipt of Public Assistance in order to obtain a fee waiver may be banned from appointment to any position within the City of New York, and may be subject to criminal prosecution. All such violations will be referred to the Department of Investigation.
APPLICATION SUBMISSION	Your application must be postmarked no later than the last day of the application period indicated on the Notice of Examination. Mail the completed application, supporting documents, and required filing fee or fee waiver to: DCAS Application Section 1 Centre Street, 14th Floor, New York, NY 10007 *C/O Exam #, Exam Title*

INSTRUCTIONS FOR COMPLETING APPLICATION FORM PROPERLY
To ensure proper processing of Application print all information *CLEARLY*. Failure to do so will delay or disqualify your application.

1. EXAM NO. / EXAM TITLE	See the Notice of Examination prior to filling in the exact exam number and exam title. Check either the Open Competitive (OC) or Promotion (PRO) box to indicate the type of examination you are applying for.
2. - 12. GENERAL INFORMATION	$ The address you give will be used as your mailing address for all official correspondence. $ Only one (1) address for each person is maintained in the files of this Department. $ If you change your mailing address after applying, see the Change Of Address section on Special Circumstances Sheet.
13. OTHER NAMES USED	If you have worked for a New York City agency under another name, write the other name in this section. If you have not used other names, skip this section.
14. - 15. ETHNICITY / SEX	Completing this information is voluntary. This information will <u>not</u> be made available to individuals making hiring decisions.
16. HHC EMPLOYEE	If you are employed by the Health and Hospitals Corporation, check the YES box in this section.
17. SPECIAL CIRCUMSTANCES	(Sabbath/Religious Observers, Special Accommodations because of a Disability, Veterans' or Disabled Veterans' Credit, Parent or Sibling Legacy Credit) Please see the "Special Circumstances" direction sheet for qualifications and definitions associated with this section.
18. SIGNATURE	Signing the application indicates that all statements you provided on this form and all other forms required for this examination are true and subject to the penalties of perjury.

Applicants who do not receive an admission card at least **4 days** prior to the tentative test date must obtain an admission card by coming to the Examining Service Section of the New York City Department of Citywide Administrative Services, 1 Centre Street, 14th Floor, Room 1448.

Rev. 05/2004

DEPARTMENT OF CITYWIDE ADMINISTRATIVE SERVICES
DIVISION OF CITYWIDE PERSONNEL SERVICES

Exam Support Group – Application Section
One Centre Street, 14th Floor
New York, NY 10007
Automated Telephone: (212) 669-1357 • Fax: (212) 669-4734

APPLICATION SUPPLEMENT

Exam Title: _____   Exam No: _____

Section 50-b of the New York State Civil Service Law requires that all applicants for Civil Service examinations be asked the following questions:

1. Do you have any loans made or guaranteed by the New York State Higher Education Services Corporation which are currently outstanding?

   CHECK <u>ONLY</u> ONE: YES ☐   NO ☐

RETURN THIS SUPPLEMENT WITH YOUR APPLICATION FOR CIVIL SERVICE EXAMINATION <u>ONLY</u> IF YOU HAVE CHECKED THE YES BOX.

2. If you checked the YES box in *Question 1,* are you presently in default on such loan?

   CHECK <u>ONLY</u> ONE: YES ☐   NO ☐

SOCIAL SECURITY NUMBER: ☐☐☐ - ☐☐ - ☐☐☐☐

<u>PLEASE PRINT CLEARLY:</u>
FULL NAME: _____
                  (Last Name, First Name, Middle Initial)

ADDRESS: _____
                  (Include the Apartment Number, Floor, and/or In Care of- C/O, if applicable)

CITY, STATE, ZIP: _____

COMPLETE THIS AFFIRMATION: I affirm under penalties of perjury that all statements made on this application and all supplementary information are true.

Signature: _____   Date: ____ / ____ / ____

DP-2512A (Rev. 05/2003)

The Official New York City Web Site
www.nyc.gov

STATE OF CALIFORNIA APPLICATION FOR EMPLOYMENT AND/OR EXAMINATION

STATE OF CALIFORNIA — STATE PERSONNEL BOARD

**EXAMINATION AND/OR
EMPLOYMENT APPLICATION**

Applications will be processed ONLY for classifications where an examination is in progress and the published final filing date has not passed, or for vacant positions where a department requests an application.

STD. 678 (REV. 12/2001) Page 1

PRINT OR TYPE—PLEASE SEE INSTRUCTIONS ON BACK PAGE

APPLICANT'S NAME *(Last)*	*(First)*	*(M.I.)*	SOCIAL SECURITY NUMBER

MAILING ADDRESS *(Number)*	*(Street)*	E-MAIL ADDRESS	WORK TELEPHONE NUMBER

(City)	*(County)*	*(State)*	*(Zip Code)*	HOME TELEPHONE NUMBER

EXAMINATION(S) OR JOB TITLE(S) FOR WHICH YOU ARE APPLYING | PERSONNEL USE ONLY

FOR SPOT EXAMINATIONS, ENTER THE LOCATION WHERE YOU WISH TO WORK.

ANSWER THE FOLLOWING QUESTIONS: (Answer questions 8, 9, 10, and/or 11 only if the examination indicates they are required.)

1. Enter the county in which you would like to take the examination if different from the county of your residence: _____

2. Do you need reasonable accommodation to take an interview or written test? .... ☐ YES ☐ NO

3. Do your religious beliefs prevent you from taking an examination on Saturday? .... ☐ YES ☐ NO

4. Are you now employed by the State of California? (If "YES", fill in the information below.) .... ☐ YES ☐ NO
   Department: _____ Subdivision: _____

5. Have you ever been dismissed or terminated from any position for performance or other disciplinary reasons? (Applicants whose dismissals or terminations were overturned, withdrawn [unilaterally or as part of a settlement] or revoked need not answer "Yes".) If "Yes" to Question #5, give details in Item #12, and refer to the Instructions for further information. ☐ YES ☐ NO

6. In addition to English, list any other languages you:
   a. possess verbal fluency in _____
   b. possess written fluency in _____

7. I certify I can type at a speed of_____words per minute. (For typing applicants only.)

(Answer Questions 8, 9, 10, and/or 11 ONLY if the examination indicates they are required.)

8. Do you meet the minimum and/or maximum age requirements? .... ☐ YES ☐ NO

9. Do you possess a valid California Driver License? (If "YES", fill in the information below.) .... ☐ YES ☐ NO
   License # _____ Class: _____ Restrictions: _____

10. Have you ever been convicted by any court of a misdemeanor crime of domestic violence? .... ☐ YES ☐ NO

11. Have you ever been convicted by any court of a felony? .... ☐ YES ☐ NO

12. EXPLANATIONS

CERTIFICATION–IMPORTANT–PLEASE READ BEFORE SIGNING–If not signed, this application may be rejected.

I certify under penalty of perjury that the information I have entered on this application is true and complete to the best of my knowledge. I further understand that any false, incomplete, or incorrect statements may result in my disqualification from the examination process or dismissal from employment with the State of California. I authorize the employers and educational institutions identified on this application to release any information they may have concerning my employment or education to the State of California.

APPLICANT'S SIGNATURE	DATE SIGNED

APPLICANTS--DO NOT USE THE SPACE BELOW--FOR PERSONNEL USE ONLY

Classes	01	02	03	04	05	06		
WC for Series								
RC/Flag for Series								

Flags _ _ _ _ _ _ _

WC _

FOR PERSONNEL USE ONLY	
STATUS	
☐ ACCEPTED	☐ REJECTED WC _
EXPERIENCE	LICENSE REQUIREMENT
EDUCATION	OTHER
STAFF	DATE PROCESSED

CODES

STATE OF CALIFORNIA — STATE PERSONNEL BOARD

EXAMINATION AND/OR
EMPLOYMENT APPLICATION

STD. 678 (REV. 12/2001) Page 2

APPLICANT'S NAME *(Last)*	*(First)*	*(M.I.)*	SOCIAL SECURITY NUMBER

13. EDUCATION

DID YOU GRADUATE FROM HIGH SCHOOL?   IF NOT, DO YOU POSSESS A GED OR EQUIVALENT?   IF NOT, ENTER THE HIGHEST GRADE YOU COMPLETED

☐ YES   ☐ NO   ☐ YES   ☐ NO

UNIVERSITY OR COLLEGE—NAME AND LOCATION, BUSINESS, CORRESPONDENCE, TRADE OR SERVICE SCHOOL	COURSE OF STUDY	UNITS COMPLETED		DIPLOMA, DEGREE OR CERTIFICATE OBTAINED	DATE COMPLETED
		SEMESTER	QUARTER		

14. LIST BELOW VALID LICENSES, CERTIFICATES OF PROFESSIONAL OR VOCATIONAL COMPETENCE, OR MEMBERSHIP IN PROFESSIONAL ASSOCIATIONS CALLED FOR IN THIS EXAMINATION ANNOUNCEMENT. *(If you are an attorney, please include first Bar date with license information if the examination announcement requires it.)*

LICENSE/CERTIFICATION NUMBER	DATE ADMITTED TO THE BAR	EXPIRATION DATE	IN THE SPACE BELOW, INDICATE SPECIFIC COURSE REQUIREMENTS NEEDED TO SATISFY REQUIREMENTS FOR THIS EXAMINATION

15. EMPLOYMENT HISTORY—*Begin with your most recent job. List each job separately.*

FROM *(M/D/Y)*	TO *(M/D/Y)*	TITLE/ JOB CLASSIFICATION *(Include Range or Level, if applicable)*	
HOURS PER WEEK	TOTAL WORKED (Years/Months)	COMPANY/STATE AGENCY NAME	SUPERVISOR
SALARY EARNED $	PER	ADDRESS	

DUTIES PERFORMED

REASON FOR LEAVING

FROM *(M/D/Y)*	TO *(M/D/Y)*	TITLE/ JOB CLASSIFICATION *(Include Range or Level, if applicable)*	
HOURS PER WEEK	TOTAL WORKED (Years/Months)	COMPANY/STATE AGENCY NAME	SUPERVISOR
SALARY EARNED $	PER	ADDRESS	

DUTIES PERFORMED

REASON FOR LEAVING

STATE OF CALIFORNIA — STATE PERSONNEL BOARD

**EXAMINATION AND/OR
EMPLOYMENT APPLICATION**

STD. 678 (REV. 12/2001) Page 3

APPLICANT'S NAME *(Last)*	*(First)*	*(M.I.)*	SOCIAL SECURITY NUMBER

15. EMPLOYMENT HISTORY—*(Continued)*

FROM *(M/D/Y)*	TO *(M/D/Y)*	TITLE/ JOB CLASSIFICATION *(Include Range or Level, if applicable)*	
HOURS PER WEEK	TOTAL WORKED (Years/Months)	COMPANY/STATE AGENCY NAME	SUPERVISOR
SALARY EARNED $	PER	ADDRESS	

DUTIES PERFORMED

REASON FOR LEAVING

FROM *(M/D/Y)*	TO *(M/D/Y)*	TITLE/ JOB CLASSIFICATION *(Include Range or Level, if applicable)*	
HOURS PER WEEK	TOTAL WORKED (Years/Months)	COMPANY/STATE AGENCY NAME	SUPERVISOR
SALARY EARNED $	PER	ADDRESS	

DUTIES PERFORMED

REASON FOR LEAVING

FROM *(M/D/Y)*	TO *(M/D/Y)*	TITLE/ JOB CLASSIFICATION *(Include Range or Level, if applicable)*	
HOURS PER WEEK	TOTAL WORKED (Years/Months)	COMPANY/STATE AGENCY NAME	SUPERVISOR
SALARY EARNED $	PER	ADDRESS	

DUTIES PERFORMED

REASON FOR LEAVING

STATE OF CALIFORNIA — STATE PERSONNEL BOARD

**EXAMINATION AND/OR
EMPLOYMENT APPLICATION**

STD. 678 (REV. 12/2001) Page 4

APPLICANT'S NAME (Last)	(First)	(M.I.)	SOCIAL SECURITY NUMBER

15. EMPLOYMENT HISTORY—(Continued)

FROM (M/D/Y)	TO (M/D/Y)	TITLE/ JOB CLASSIFICATION (Include Range or Level, if applicable)	
HOURS PER WEEK	TOTAL WORKED (Years/Months)	COMPANY/STATE AGENCY NAME	SUPERVISOR
SALARY EARNED $	PER	ADDRESS	

DUTIES PERFORMED

REASON FOR LEAVING

FROM (M/D/Y)	TO (M/D/Y)	TITLE/ JOB CLASSIFICATION (Include Range or Level, if applicable)	
HOURS PER WEEK	TOTAL WORKED (Years/Months)	COMPANY/STATE AGENCY NAME	SUPERVISOR
SALARY EARNED $	PER	ADDRESS	

DUTIES PERFORMED

REASON FOR LEAVING

FROM (M/D/Y)	TO (M/D/Y)	TITLE/ JOB CLASSIFICATION (Include Range or Level, if applicable)	
HOURS PER WEEK	TOTAL WORKED (Years/Months)	COMPANY/STATE AGENCY NAME	SUPERVISOR
SALARY EARNED $	PER	ADDRESS	

DUTIES PERFORMED

REASON FOR LEAVING

STATE OF CALIFORNIA — STATE PERSONNEL BOARD

**EXAMINATION AND/OR
EMPLOYMENT APPLICATION**

STD. 678 (REV. 12/2001) Page 5

EQUAL EMPLOYMENT OPPORTUNITY
(For Examination Use Only)

APPLICANT: To assist the State of California in its commitment to Equal Employment Opportunity, applicants are asked to voluntarily provide the following information. This questionnaire will be separated from the application prior to the examination and will not be used in any employment decisions. Government Code Section 19705 authorizes the State Personnel Board to retain this information for research and statistical purposes.

SOCIAL SECURITY NUMBER

AGE
☐ (1) UNDER 21   ☐ (3) 21 - 39   ☐ (6) 40 - 69   ☐ (7) 70 AND OVER

GENDER
☐ MALE   ☐ FEMALE

Ethnic Category (Please check the box that best describes your race/ethnicity.):

☐ (7) AMERICAN INDIAN OR ALASKAN NATIVE-- Persons having origins in any of the tribal peoples of North America, and who maintain cultural identification through tribal affiliation or community recognition.

ENTER TRIBAL IDENTIFICATION OR AFFILIATION

☐ (2) ASIAN-- Persons having origins in any of the original peoples of the Far East, Southeast Asia, or the Indian Subcontinent. This includes China, Japan, and Korea.

☐ (1) BLACK-- Persons having origins in any of the black racial groups of Africa.

☐ (8) FILIPINO-- Persons having origins in any of the original peoples of the Philippine Islands.

☐ (4) HISPANIC-- Persons of Mexican, Puerto Rican, Cuban, Central or South American, or other Spanish culture or origin, regardless of race.

☐ (8) PACIFIC ISLANDERS-- Persons having origins in the Pacific Islands, such as Samoa.

☐ (5) WHITE-- Persons having origins in any of the original peoples of Europe, North Africa, or the Middle East.

Check if:
☐ (9) OTHER *(Specify)*

☐ (7) DISABLED -- A person with a disability is an individual who: (1) has a physical or mental impairment or medical condition that limits one or more life activities, such as walking, speaking, breathing, performing manual tasks, seeing, hearing, learning, caring for oneself or working; (2) has a record or history of such impairment or medical condition; or (3) is regarded as having such an impairment or medical condition.

☐ MILITARY--A military veteran; a widow or widower of a veteran; or a spouse of a 100% disabled veteran.

How did you learn of this Examination?
☐ TELEPHONE JOB LINE   ☐ WORD OF MOUTH   ☐ INTERNET

☐ ADVERTISEMENT IN _____   ☐ EXAMINATION BULLETIN LOCATED AT _____

THANK YOU FOR COMPLETING THIS QUESTIONNAIRE

FEDERAL APPLICATION FORMS

On January 1, 1995, the federal government began to give applicants an option: to submit a federal employment application form such as the OF 612 or the older SF 171, or to submit a self-designed federal resume instead.

OF 612: This is the federal application form that replaces the SF 171. It's a bit shorter than its predecessor and a bit less involved in the general information areas, but it still requires a lot of time and energy to get it done right. Much to the delight of all federal job seekers, this form is now available in screen-fillable, printable form (the Adobe® Acrobat® PDF/F format) at The Office of Personnel Management (OPM) Web site at www.opm.gov. An example of an OF 612 follows.

OF 612

Instructions for Optional Application for Federal Employment - OF 612

You may apply for most Federal jobs with a resume, an Optional Application for Federal Employment (OF 612), or other written format. If your resume or application does not provide all the information requested on this form and in the job vacancy announcement, you may lose consideration for a job. Type or print clearly in black ink. Help speed the selection process by keeping your application brief and sending only the requested information. **If essential to attach additional pages, include your name and Social Security Number on each page.**

• For information on Federal employment, including alternative formats for persons with disabilities and veterans' preference, contact the U.S. Office of Personnel Management at 478-757-3000, TDD 478-744-2299, or via the Internet at www.USAJOBS.opm.gov.

• If you served on active duty in the United States Military and were separated under honorable conditions, you may be eligible for veterans' preference. To receive preference, if your service began after October 15, 1976, you must have a Campaign Badge, Expeditionary Medal, or a service-connected disability. Veterans' preference is not a factor for Senior Executive Service jobs or when competition is limited to status candidates (current or former career or career-conditional Federal employees).

• Most Federal jobs require United States citizenship and also that males over age 18 born after December 31, 1959, have registered with the Selective Service System or have an exemption.

• The law prohibits public officials from appointing, promoting, or recommending their relatives.

• Federal annuitants (military and civilian) may have their salaries or annuities reduced. Every employee must pay any valid delinquent debt or the agency may garnish their salary.

• Send your application to the office announcing the vacancy. If you have questions, contact the office identified in the announcement.

Privacy Act Statement

The U.S. Office of Personnel Management and other Federal agencies rate applicants for Federal jobs under the authority of sections 1104, 1302, 3301, 3304, 3320, 3361, 3393, and 3394 of title 5 of the United States Code. We need the information requested in this form and in the associated vacancy announcements to evaluate your qualifications. Other laws require us to ask about citizenship, military service, etc. In order to keep your records in order, we request your Social Security Number (SSN) under the authority of Public Law 104-134 (April 26, 1996). This law requires that any person doing business with the Federal government furnish an SSN or tax identification number. This is an amendment to title 31, Section 7701. Failure to furnish the requested information may delay or prevent action on your application. We use your SSN to seek information about you from employers, schools, banks, and others who know you. We may use your SSN in studies and computer matching with other Government files. If you do not give us your SSN or any other information requested, we cannot process your application. Also, incomplete addresses and ZIP Codes will slow processing. We may confirm information from your records with prospective nonfederal employers concerning tenure of employment, civil service status, length of service, and date and nature of action for separation as shown on personnel action forms of specifically identified individuals.

Public Burden Statement

We estimate the public reporting burden for this collection will vary from 20 to 240 minutes with an average of 40 minutes per response, including time for reviewing instructions, searching existing data sources, gathering data, and completing and reviewing the information. Send comments regarding the burden statement or any other aspect of the collection of information, including suggestions for reducing this burden to the U.S. Office of Personnel Management (OPM), OPM Forms Officer, Washington, DC 20415-7900. The OMB number, 3206-0219, is currently valid. OPM may not collect this information and you are not required to respond, unless this number is displayed. Do not send completed application forms to this address. Follow directions provided in the vacancy announcement(s).

THE FEDERAL GOVERNMENT IS AN EQUAL OPPORTUNITY EMPLOYER

OPTIONAL APPLICATION FOR FEDERAL EMPLOYMENT – OF 612

Form Approved
OMB No. 3206-0219

Section A – Applicant Information

★ Use Standard State Postal Codes (abbreviations). If outside the United States of America, and you do not have a military address, type or print "OV" in the State field (Block 6c) and fill in the Country field (Block 6e) below, leaving the Zip Code field (Block 6d) blank.

1. Job title in announcement	2. Grade(s) applying for	3. Announcement number

4a. Last name	4b. First and middle names	5. Social Security Number

6a. Mailing address ★	7. Phone numbers (include area code if within the United States of America)
	7a. Daytime

6b. City	6c. State	6d. Zip Code	7b. Evening

6e. Country (if not within the United States of America)

8. Email address (if available)

Section B – Work Experience

Describe your paid and nonpaid work experience related to this job for which you are applying. Do not attach job description.

1. Job title (if Federal, include series and grade)

2. From (mm/yyyy)	3. To (mm/yyyy)	4. Salary per	5. Hours per week
		$	

6. Employer's name and address	7. Supervisor's name and phone number
	7a. Name
	7b. Phone

8. May we contact your current supervisor?   Yes ☐   No ☐
If we need to contact your current supervisor before making an offer, we will contact you first.

9. Describe your duties and accomplishments

Section C – Additional Work Experience

1. Job title (if Federal, include series and grade)

2. From (mm/yyyy)	3. To (mm/yyyy)	4. Salary per	5. Hours per week
		$	

6. Employer's name and address	7. Supervisor's name and phone number
	7a. Name
	7b. Phone

8. Describe your duties and accomplishments

U.S. Office of Personnel Management
Previous edition usable

NSN 7540-01-351-9178
50612-101

Page 1 of 2

Optional Form 612
Revised December 2002

Section D – Education

1. Last High School (HS)/GED school. Give the school's name, city, state, ZIP Code (if known), and year diploma or GED received:

2. Mark highest level completed: Some HS ☐ HS/GED ☐ Associate ☐ Bachelor ☐ Master ☐ Doctoral ☐

3. Colleges and universities attended. Do not attach a copy of your transcript unless requested.			Total Credits Earned		Major(s)	Degree (if any), Year Received
			Semester	Quarter		
3a. Name						
City	State	Zip Code				
3b. Name						
City	State	Zip Code				
3c. Name						
City	State	Zip Code				

Section E – Other Qualifications

Job-related training courses (give title and year). Job-related skills (other languages, computer software/hardware, tools, machinery, typing speed, etc.). Job-related certificates and licenses (current only). Job-related honors, awards, and special accomplishments (publications, memberships in professional/honor societies, leadership activities, public speaking, and performance awards). Give dates, but do **not** send documents unless requested.

Section F – General

1a. Are you a U.S. citizen? Yes ☐ No ☐ ➜ 1b. If no, give the Country of your citizenship

2a. Do you claim veterans' preference? No ☐ Yes ☐ ➜ If yes, mark your claim of 5 or 10 points below.
2b. 5 points ☐ ➜ Attach your *Report of Separation from Active Duty* (DD 214) or other proof.
2c. 10 points ☐ ➜ Attach an *Application for 10-Point Veterans' Preference* (SF 15) and proof required.

3. Were you ever a Federal civilian employee? No ☐ Yes ☐ ➜ If yes, list highest civilian grade for the following:

3a. Series	3b. Grade	3c. From *(mm/yyyy)*	3d. To *(mm/yyyy)*

4. Are you eligible for reinstatement based on career or career-conditional Federal status? No ☐ Yes ☐
   If requested in the vacancy announcement, attach *Notification of Personnel Action* (SF 50), as proof.

Section G – Applicant Certification

I certify that, to the best of my knowledge and belief, all of the information on and attached to this application is true, correct, complete, and made in good faith. I understand that false or fraudulent information on or attached to this application may be grounds for not hiring me or for firing me after I begin work, and may be punishable by fine or imprisonment. I understand that any information I give may be investigated.

1a. Signature	1b. Date *(mm/dd/yyyy)*

U.S. Office of Personnel Management
Previous edition usable

NSN 7540-01-351-9178
50612-101

Page 2 of 2

Optional Form 612
Revised December 2002

Print Form   Save Form   Clear Form

SF 171: For years, the Standard Form 171 was the ruling king of the federal application process. It is no longer printed or distributed by the feds, but it is still accepted by personnel offices as an official government application form. Since it has now been out of print for many years, the newer form may be a better bet at striking a familiar chord with personnel specialists.

The Federal Resume

The resume is a tempting substitute for the preprinted application forms since you can design it yourself. You must make it much longer and more detailed than a traditional resume, however, so it may not save as much time as you think. Federal resumes work well when they are the requested format used by the agency, but they can be confusing to staffing specialists who are familiar with standardized forms and must search varied resume formats for the information they seek. Resumes do have the advantage of being available online at the USAJOBS Web site online resume builder (www.USAJOBS.opm.gov). This allows you to store, edit, and print your resume from the system as needed or to submit it electronically for specific positions at federal agencies. Both the OF 612 and the federal resume format require basically the same information. The most important thing to note is that whatever form you choose, all applications to the federal government *must* include the following information, or you may lose consideration for the job:

Job Information

- Announcement number, and title and grade(s) of the job you are applying for.

Personal Information

- Full name, mailing address (with ZIP Code), and day and evening phone numbers (with area code)
- Social security number
- Country of citizenship (Most Federal jobs require U.S. citizenship.)
- Veterans' preference

   (If you served on active duty in the U.S. Military and were separated under honorable conditions, you may be eligible for veterans' preference. To receive preference if your service began after October 15, 1976, you must have a Campaign Badge, Expeditionary Medal, or a service-connected disability. For further details, call OPM at 912-757-3000. Select "Federal Employment Topics" and then "Veterans." Or, dial the electronic bulletin board at 912-757-3100.)

- Reinstatement eligibility (If requested, attach SF 50 proof of your career or career-conditional status.)
- Highest federal civilian grade held (Also give job series and dates held.)

Education

- High School
  - ○ Name, City, and State (ZIP Code if known)
  - ○ Date of diploma or GED
- Colleges or universities
  - ○ Name, City, and State (ZIP Code if known)
  - ○ Majors
  - ○ Type and year of any degrees received (If no degree, show total credits earned and indicate whether semester or quarter hours.)
- Send a copy of your college transcript only if the job vacancy announcement requests it.

Work Experience

- Give the following information for your paid and nonpaid work experience related to the job you are applying for. (Do not send job descriptions.)
  - ○ Job title (include series and grade if federal job)
  - ○ Duties and accomplishments
  - ○ Employer's name and address
  - ○ Supervisor's name and phone number
  - ○ Starting and ending dates (month and year)
  - ○ Hours per week
  - ○ Salary
- Indicate if we may contact your current supervisor.

Other Qualifications

- Job-related training courses (title and year)
- Job-related skills, for example, other languages, computer software/hardware, tools, machinery, typing speed
- Job-related certificates and licenses (current only)
- Job-related honors, awards, and special accomplishments; for example, publications, memberships in professional or honor societies, leadership activities, public speaking, and performance awards (Give dates but do not send documents unless requested.)

KSA Supplement

Knowledge, Skills and Abilities (KSAs) are of vital importance. Let's take a closer look at them.

The KSA requirement is a growing trend in the world of federal employment. In fact, there are very few vacancy announcements that do not request a KSA supplement from the applicant. What is it?

The KSA is a request on the vacancy announcement for the applicant to address—independently of the OF 612, SF 171, or federal resume—several questions or important factors regarding career experience as it relates to the vacancy duties. The applicant simply uses a blank piece of paper that he or she attaches to the resume or application and, in paragraph form, answers the KSA questions.

KSA questions can be as general as requesting the applicant to "Address your experience regarding written and oral communication skills." Or, they can be very specific, such as "Describe your ability to oversee procurement and contracting procedures as well as grant activities." In other cases, they may not be posed in question format at all, but simply listed as important qualification factors.

While the resume or application is used merely to determine that the applicant meets the basic qualifications ("rated for eligibility"), the KSAs are used to determine the strength of the applicant in the most important areas of the job. The hiring office has already determined exactly what factors should be evaluated on incoming applications and how much weight each factor should be given, and the KSAs are numerically scored ("ranked") against these factors. Therefore, do not scrimp on your KSA supplement. Give examples from past work or nonwork experiences that lend credence to your having the qualities the hiring officials are searching for. Use the full-length allowance given. If no length is specified, each KSA answer should be about two full paragraphs, or one-half to one full page. When in doubt, don't leave anything out. Refer your examples back to the OF 612 or resume to help the staffing specialists cross-reference.

Tips for a Well-Written KSA

Here are four tips to help you write an outstanding KSA supplement:

1 **For each KSA, provide several examples of your experience as it relates to the responsibilities of the position for which you are applying.** Describe your experience in terms of the context of your responsibilities, the challenges you faced, the action that you took in response to these challenges, and the results of your actions. Your narrative should contain enough representative examples to provide a sound basis for staffing specialists and hiring officials to assess the breadth and depth of your qualifications.

ALERT!

Often, the final hiring decision comes down to the KSA supplemental answers you supply.

2 **Don't generalize.** Address each KSA with as much detail as possible. Describe your experience in terms of specific job-related activities, focusing on key skills and strengths such as leadership, budgeting, researching, and writing.

3 **Each KSA answer should include the context or environment in which you performed your job duties.** Was it a large office setting? How many people were involved? What was the volume of sales? How many regions or districts were involved? Quantify whenever possible.

4 Demonstrate your competence not only through professional experience, but also through volunteer experience, education, training, special accomplishments, awards, and potential for growth.

The Inside Scoop

Have you ever wondered what happens to your application once it enters the federal personnel office? From an outsider's perspective, federal personnel offices can seem inefficient and rigidly uncommunicative. What in the world takes them so long to review your application? It is wise to take a peek at what goes on behind the scenes in the federal application process, because if you know the rules of the game, you know how to play to win. The following sections explain the new federal application process in general terms from the point at which the screening process begins.

Rating

After the closing date of a particular position, when all the applications have been collected by the agency announcing the job, the personnel specialist who has been handling this particular vacancy makes an initial review of all applications to ensure that applicants meet the minimum qualifications. Thus, the applications are initially rated, and those that are not minimally qualified are screened out. Some agencies send the candidates a notice at this stage, advising them of their rating. Either they have passed the initial screening or they haven't.

This rating is based upon a numerical scoring process that staffing specialists use to compare your application to a job standard. Do you have the level of education that you need to qualify for the job? Do you have enough years of related or general experience (paid or unpaid)? Do you have related training? Do you have special accomplishments that apply? Are you a veteran? These are the terms that actually earn you points, and if you chalk up enough of them you pass the initial screening. It is vital, therefore, to write a very complete and thorough application. If you leave off important information, you won't get the credit you deserve, and you might not pass the screening.

If you don't hear from an agency right away after sending in an application, don't be alarmed. It could be that the position has been put on hold, or things are moving along slowly. If you want to call the personnel office to check on the status of your application, you can, but don't waste time trying to "sell yourself" to personnel employees as a winning candidate since they typically don't have the power to influence the hiring decision. Generally, staffing specialists simply write vacancy announcements, screen incoming applications, and assist in upholding federal hiring policy. They do not decide who will get the job.

Ranking

After the initial screening, the personnel office or the hiring office may name a number of people to form a "panel of experts" to review the applications in depth. These experts should have at least the same grade level as the announced job and are usually in the same field. The panel reviews the information on each application and any supplements (such as the KSA) and considers it in relation to the announced criteria for the job. In this way, the panel comes up with a "best qualified" list, again assigning numerical scores. This is called ranking.

The hiring office has determined in advance exactly what factors should be evaluated and specifically what weight the panel should give to each factor. This is very different from the way a private-sector organization reviews job applications. The private-sector hiring process is not usually as specific, allowing hiring officials to fill a position based more on gut instinct and personal rapport with the candidates in the initial interviews. The federal job search usually does not involve interviewing until the final three "best qualified" candidates have already been selected. Choosing the top three most highly ranked job candidates is called the "rule of three."

Because of this detailed numerical evaluation system, federal job applicants have a tough time standing out from the crowd of other applicants. Since large numbers of qualified candidates are likely to apply for an advertised federal vacancy, and because only the top three candidates are likely to be interviewed, it is difficult to land an interview with the hiring official and to impress him or her with intelligence and charm. Federal applicants who are going through the front door must rely heavily on their paperwork—their federal application—to win the job for them.

Eight Keys to the Federal Application System

Before getting into the details of applying, there are a few key points to remember about the federal application system:

1 **If the job you are applying for is a current job opening, be sure to read the vacancy announcement before sending any employment forms to the agency.** The vacancy announcement tells you the preferred method of submitting your application and what additional information they require.

2 If the vacancy announcement lists KSAs, be sure to address them very carefully and thoroughly—these are often the "make or break" points for federal job candidates.

3 **OPM's Web site, www.usajobs.opm.gov, allows you access to electronic and hard copy application forms, and it provides a resume builder that lets you edit, save, and print a federal-style resume.** The key is not to write

one good resume or OF 612 and then send it away without saving it. Either save it on the computer or make hard copies of it first, so that you don't have to redo all that work to fill out another. If you plan to use the postal service, remember that a copy of a federal application will be accepted just as quickly as an original, so make several copies of your completed application before you send it off in the mail (each copy must be *signed* in ink, however).

4 **Some people argue that they want to individualize each resume or application to the particular job for which they are applying.** But, after you've filled out one OF 612 or federal resume, you won't want to fill out another. To work efficiently, write one good application template and then customize your credentials to fit a particular job via the KSA supplement (more on that later in this chapter). If you are working with a hard copy that you plan to send through the mail, leave certain spaces on your template blank.

5 **Besides the federal government's USAJOBS site, which provides free fillable OF 612 forms in Word or Adobe® Acrobat® PDF, there are software programs available for a fee that provide additional services.** For example, the *Quick and Easy Federal Jobs Kit Version 6.0* (put out in 2001 by the Federal Research Service, Vienna, Virginia) allows you to search for a job, fill out application forms or resumes, then print, fax, or e-mail the application from within the program. *Quick and Easy* handles Resumix resumes and includes additional application formats used by various agencies. The cost is $49.94 plus shipping. Call 800-782-7424 or log on to www.fedjobs.com. You can also check with your local library or community college to see if either has this program available for public use.

6 **Federal agencies generally do not accept unsolicited applications.** They simply don't know what to do with them. Certain job openings are assigned to certain staffing specialists, and if an application comes in that doesn't belong to a particular opening, no one knows where it should go. The chances of sending in an application to a federal agency out of the blue and landing a chance job slot are pretty slim. Also, you should not expect to be considered for a wide range of positions at an agency based on a single application submission. Unless you see information that specifically states otherwise, your application will probably be considered only for the particular job opening for which you are applying, and then it will be discarded.

7 **Federal staffing specialists place you into a salary or grade category according to an "eligibility system."** They review your experience, education, etc., to determine what grade you are qualified for within a certain job series. So if you wish to be a soil scientist with the U.S. Soil Service, a staffing specialist will review your background according to that job standard and will qualify you as a GS-5, GS-7, GS-9, etc. You can find these job standards in the book *Qualification Standards Operating Manual*, which can be accessed from the OPM Web site at www.opm.gov. A look at these standards helps you determine which jobs you qualify for and at what grade level. These standards are also often spelled out on the vacancy announcement.

8 **Again, read the vacancy announcement before you send in your application.** Often the vacancy announcement lists supplemental information that you must submit along with your application. Your application will be dismissed as incomplete without it, no matter how qualified you are.

The Federal Application: Acceptable vs. Exceptional

While you can probably write an acceptable application simply by following the directions on the form, below are several bits of "inside information" that will help your federal application be exceptional. When writing the OF 612, consider these guidelines.

1 **Never stay within the allotted space on the Work Experience blocks.** On the current OF 612 form, there is a certain amount of blank or lined space for you to fill in information about a past or current employer. If you fill up the allotted space but do not run beyond it, your job description is probably too short. Be sure to use an additional sheet of paper to give you the space you need to include all the details that can earn you points in the rating and ranking process. Simply type the additional information on a blank sheet of paper and attach it to the form. Make sure each added page includes your name, social security number, and the job title or vacancy announcement number you are applying for. Label it as a "continuation sheet for Job Block —."

Be careful not to let the mind-set of a private-sector job search influence the length of your job description information. While private-sector job searches stress brevity on the resume, federal applications are meant to be very thorough and specific. You can't lose points for a federal application that is too long (unless all the important information gets swallowed up in a bunch of gobbledygook), but you will *not* get points for information that is not on the application form.

2 **Give them the details.** Think of it this way: in the federal hiring process, your application form (or federal resume) serves as the equivalent of the first interview. This is very different from a private-sector job search. In a corporate job search, your resume serves to pique the interest of the hiring officials. They think, "Hmm. This person looks interesting. Let's call her in and interview her to find out if she really is qualified." In the public sector, hiring officials determine whether or not you are qualified from your paperwork alone. There is no initial screening interview, and there are no second chances. Put it all on your application: don't let your application be screened out erroneously simply because you didn't tell them enough about your background!

3 **Do not generalize.** This again is different from the way you write a corporate resume. A good corporate resume can make statements such as "Prepared reports," and the reader can pick up the gist of things and will ask for details if need be in the interview. But a good SF 171, OF 612, or Federal Resume cannot make such a generalized statement without costing the applicant dearly. Suppose the staffing specialist is screening the applications for experience in researching and writing scientific reports. An application that states "I prepared scientific reports" will probably lose significant points, because the word "prepared" does not give the staffing specialist any idea what the applicant actually did. Did he type reports? Edit them? Collate them? Research them? Write them? The word "prepared" is much too vague.

And how did he accomplish his work with reports? If he researched them, did he gather information by telephone? From whom? Did he read trade journals? Did he collect data from other reports? How many? How long did it take him to do this? "Reports" is also too vague. What kind of reports were these that the applicant "prepared"? Were they financial reports? Status reports? Technical reports? And how long were they? One page? Five pages? Fifty pages? How often were they "prepared"? Weekly? Monthly? Daily? Were they computerized? And to whom were they distributed? What was their purpose? As you can see, while "prepared reports" is fine as two words on a resume, it should be about two paragraphs on a federal application. You can be sure your application is detailed enough if you always answer for yourself the question *how*. We recently worked on a federal application with a man who kept writing that he "monitored foreign affairs in target countries." Well, how did he do that? Did he visit the foreign countries? Did he talk to correspondents there? Did he watch CNN? Did he read journals or newspapers? Always answer the question *how*.

TIP

On the OF 612 form, leave blank spaces 1 (job title in announcement), 2 (grade applying for), 3 (announcement number), and 18 (signature and date). This way, you can write in information appropriate to the job for which you are applying and can sign/date the application in original ink.

❹ Add more job blocks. The OF 612 form only offers two job blocks in which you can detail your past experience. Don't be afraid to add extra blocks to include all jobs from your career history that have relevance to the job you are applying for. Simply use an additional sheet of paper and label it a "continuation sheet." Include your name, social security number, and the vacancy announcement number at the top of the page.

❺ Use key words and phrases from the vacancy announcement. Make sure that the information on your application clearly matches the skills and experience that are listed on the vacancy announcement as vital to the job. Remember that agency staffing specialists will be looking for key words and phrases that match the job requirements outlined on the vacancy announcement. The closer the match, the more points you will earn in the evaluation process.

❻ Include volunteer work and military experience. A staffing specialist reviews your application to see if you have accrued a certain amount of time doing or learning things related to the job for which the agency is hiring. The staffing specialist does not care whether or not you got paid while you were doing or learning those things. In many cases, *volunteer experience is equivalent to paid experience.* This same theory applies to active-duty military experience and experience in the military reserves.

❼ Pay attention to sections on Training Courses and "Special Skills." These sections ask the applicant to list any training courses taken or special skills, awards, honors, certificates, etc., that are job related. These items are very important to almost all federal applications and they are often point-getters. The rule to follow: Do not stay within the allotted space when answering these questions. It is fine to run on to an additional page in order to include all of the courses and awards you have taken or received.

List all training courses, even if they were very informal. Don't overlook informal awards and special recognition. All special accomplishments inside and outside of the job should be listed briefly here.

Do not be modest. This is your chance to let it be known how hard you've worked and what a talented person you are. If you don't say it here, you may miss your chance at the job.

PREPARING FOR THE EXAM

There are two main types of exams: competitive and noncompetitive. About 80 percent of federal jobs fall under the Competitive Service and are filled on the basis of an applicant's education and work experience. An applicant's qualifications are assessed based on a standard application form (such as an OF 612 or SF 171), an applicant's resume, or a written examination required for particular positions.

Federal law enforcement positions are filled through a number of different examinations. Most of these have been developed over the years by the Office of Personnel Management (OPM). Some exams are administered by the OPM for the agencies at their request. Others are administered directly by the agencies. Some of these exams are known by their distinctive names such as the Treasury Enforcement Agent (TEA) Exam, given to Special Agent candidates in a number of agencies and departments. Other OPM exams have descriptive titles such as the Federal Clerical Examination, or are simply known by the job titles for which they test, as in the Border Patrol Agent Exam. Still other exams are tailor-made for specific positions. These exams tend to draw questions from the whole gamut of OPM exams.

Many factors enter into a test score. The most important factor should be the ability to answer the questions, which in turn indicates the ability to learn and perform the duties of the job. Assuming that you have this ability, knowing what to expect on the exam and familiarity with techniques of effective test-taking should give you the confidence you need to do your best on the exam.

There is no quick substitute for long-term study and development of your skills and abilities to prepare you for doing well on tests. However, there are some steps you can take to help you do the very best that you are prepared to do. Some of these steps are done before the test, and some are followed when you are taking the test. Following these steps may help you feel more confident as you take the actual test.

Don't make the test harder than it has to be by not preparing yourself. You are taking a very important step in preparation by reading this book and taking the sample test that is included. This will help you to become familiar with the tests and the kinds of questions you will have to answer.

On examination day, allow the test itself to be the main attraction of the day. Do not squeeze it in between other activities. Be sure to bring your admission card, a form of

NOTE

Only a relative handful of federal jobs require applicants to take a written examination.

identification, and pencils. Gather these the night before so that you are not flustered by a last-minute search. Arrive rested, relaxed, and on time. In fact, plan to arrive a bit early. Leave plenty of time for traffic tie-ups or other complications that might upset you and interfere with your test performance.

In the test room, the examiner will hand out forms for you to fill out. He or she will give you the instructions that you must follow in taking the examination. The examiner will tell you how to fill in the grids on the forms. Time limits and timing signals will be explained. If you do not understand any of the examiner's instructions, ASK QUESTIONS! It would be ridiculous to score less than your best because of poor communication.

At the examination, you must follow instructions exactly. Fill in the grids on the forms carefully and accurately. Misgridding may lead to loss of veteran's credits to which you may be entitled or misaddressing of your test results. Do not begin until you are told to begin. Stop as soon as the examiner tells you to stop. Do not turn pages until you are told to do so. Do not go back to parts you have already completed. Any infraction of the rules is considered cheating. If you cheat, your test paper will not be scored, and you will not be eligible for appointment.

The answer sheet for most multiple-choice exams is machine scored. You cannot give any explanations to the machine, so you must fill out the answer sheet clearly and correctly.

Avoid Careless Errors

Don't reduce your score by making careless mistakes. Always read the instructions for each test section carefully, even when you think you already know what the directions are. It's why we stress throughout this book that it's important to fully understand the directions for these different question types before you go into the actual exam. It will not only reduce errors, but it will save you valuable time.

If you have time, reread any complicated instructions after you do the first few questions to check that you really do understand them. Of course, whenever you are allowed to, ask the examiner to clarify anything you don't understand.

Other careless mistakes affect only the response to particular questions. This often happens with arithmetic questions, but can happen with other questions as well. This type of error, called a "response error," usually stems from a momentary lapse of concentration.

Example

The question reads: "The capital of Massachusetts is …." The answer is (D) Boston, and you mark (B) because "B" is the first letter of the word "Boston."

Example

The question reads: "8 – 5 = …." The answer is (A) 3, but you mark (C) thinking "third letter."

A common error in reading comprehension questions is bringing your own information into the subject. For example, you may encounter a passage that discusses a subject you know something about. While this can make the passage easier to read, it can also tempt you to rely on your own knowledge about the subject. You must rely on information within the passage for your answers—in fact, sometimes the "wrong answer" for the questions are based on true information about the subject not given in the passage. Since the test makers are testing your reading ability, rather than your general knowledge of the subject, an answer based on information not contained in the passage is considered incorrect.

Manage Your Time

Before you begin, take a moment to plan your progress through the test. Although you are usually not expected to finish all of the questions given on a test, you should at least get an idea of how much time you should spend on each question in order to answer them all. For example, if there are sixty questions to answer and you have 30 minutes, you will have about 30 seconds to spend on each question.

Keep track of the time on your watch or the room clock, but do not fixate on the time remaining. Your task is to answer questions. Do not spend too much time on any one question. If you find yourself stuck, do not take the puzzler as a personal challenge. Either guess and mark the question in the question booklet or skip the question entirely, marking the question as a skip and taking care to skip the answer space on the answer sheet. If there is time at the end of the exam or exam part, you can return and give marked questions another try.

TEST FORMAT

Multiple-Choice Questions

Almost all federal law enforcement exams are multiple-choice. This means that you normally have four or five answer choices. But it's not something that should be overwhelming. There is a basic technique to answering these types of questions. Once you've understood this technique, it will make your test-taking far less stressful.

First, there should only be one correct answer. Since these tests have been given time and again, and the test developers have a sense of which questions work and which questions don't work, it will be rare that your choices will be ambiguous. They may be complex, and somewhat confusing, but there will still be only one right answer.

The first step is to look at the question, without looking at the answer choices. Then select the correct answer. That may sound somewhat simplistic, but it's usually the case that your first choice is the correct one. If you go back and change it, redo it again and again, it's more likely that you'll end up with the wrong answer. Thus, follow your instinct. Once you have come up with the answer, look at the answer choices. If your answer is one of the choices, you're probably correct. It's not 100 percent infallible, but it's a strong possibility that you've selected the right answer.

With math questions you should first solve the problem. If your answer is among the choices, you're probably correct. Don't ignore things like the proper function signs (adding, subtracting, multiplying, and dividing), negative and positive numbers, and so on.

But suppose you don't know the correct answer. You then use the "process of elimination." It's a time-honored technique for test-takers. There is always one correct answer. There is usually one answer choice that is totally incorrect—a "distracter." If you look at that choice and it seems highly unlikely, then eliminate it. Depending on the number of choices (four or five), you've just cut down the number of choices to make. Now weigh the other choices. They may seem incorrect or they may be correct. If they seem incorrect, eliminate them. You've now increased your odds at getting the correct answer.

In the end, you may be left with only two choices. At that point, it's just a matter of guessing. But with only two choices left, you now have a 50 percent chance of getting it right. With four choices, you only have a 25 percent chance, and with five choices, only a 20 percent chance at guessing correctly. That's why the process of elimination is important.

How to Mark Your Answer Sheet

1. Answer each question in the correct place. If you should skip an answer space and mark a series of answers in the wrong places, you must erase all those answers and do the questions over, marking your answers in the proper places. You cannot afford to waste time due to incorrectly marking your answer sheet. Therefore, as you answer each question, look at its number and check that you are marking your answer in the space with the same number.

2. Blacken your answer space firmly and completely.

3. Mark only one answer for each question. If you mark more than one answer, you will be considered wrong, even if one of the answers is correct.

4. If you change your mind, you must erase your mark. Attempting to cross out an incorrect answer will not work. You must erase any incorrect answer completely. An incomplete erasure might be read as a second answer.

5. All of your answering should be in the form of blackened spaces. The machine cannot read English. Do not write any notes in the margins.

Should You Guess?

You may be wondering whether or not it is wise to guess when you are not sure of an answer (even if you've reduced the odds to 50 percent) or whether it is better to skip the question when you are not certain. The wisdom of guessing depends on the scoring method for the particular examination part. If the scoring is "rights only," that is, one point for each correct answer and no subtraction for wrong answers, then by all means you should guess. Read the question and all of the answer choices carefully. Eliminate those answer choices that you are certain are wrong. Then guess from among the remaining choices. You cannot gain a point if you leave the answer space blank; you may gain a point with an educated guess or even with a lucky guess. In fact, it is foolish to leave any spaces blank on a test that counts "rights only." If it appears that you are about to run out of time before completing such an exam, mark all the remaining blanks with the same letter. According to the law of averages, you should get some portion of those questions right.

If the scoring method is "rights minus wrongs," DO NOT GUESS. A wrong answer counts heavily against you. On this type of test, do not rush to fill answer spaces randomly at the end. Work as quickly as possible while concentrating on accuracy. Keep working carefully until time is called. Then stop and leave the remaining answer spaces blank.

In guessing the answers to multiple-choice questions, take a second to eliminate those answers that are obviously wrong, then quickly consider and guess from the remaining choices. Once you have decided to make a guess, do it right away and move on; don't keep thinking about it and wasting time. You should always mark the test questions at which you guess so that you can return later. For those questions that are scored by subtracting a fraction of a point for each wrong answer, the decision as to whether or not to guess is really up to you. A correct answer gives you one point; a skipped space gives you nothing at all, but costs you nothing except the chance of getting the answer right; a wrong answer costs you $\frac{1}{4}$ point. If you are really uncomfortable with guessing, you may skip a question, but you must then remember to skip its answer space as well. The risk of losing your place if you skip questions is so great that we advise you to guess even if you are not sure of the answer. Our suggestion is that you answer every question in order, even if you have to guess. It is better to lose a few $\frac{1}{4}$ points for wrong guesses than to lose valuable seconds figuring where you started marking answers in the wrong place, erasing, and re-marking answers. On the other hand, do not mark random answers at the end. Work steadily until time is up.

One of the questions you should ask in the testing room is what scoring method will be used on your particular exam. You can then guide your guessing procedure accordingly.

Scoring

If your exam is a short-answer exam, such as those often used by companies in the private sector, your answers will be graded by a personnel officer trained in grading test questions. If you blackened spaces on the separate answer sheet accompanying a multiple-choice exam, your answer sheet will be machine scanned or will be hand scored using a punched card stencil. Then a raw score will be calculated using the scoring formula that applies to that test or test portion—rights only, rights minus wrongs, or rights minus a fraction of wrongs. Raw scores on test parts are then added together for a total raw score.

A raw score is not a final score. The raw score is not the score that finds its way onto an eligibility list. Raw scores are converted to scaled scores according to an unpublicized formula of its own. The scaling formula allows for slight differences in difficulty of questions from one form of the exam to another and allows for equating the scores of all candidates. The score you receive is not your number right, not your raw score, and, despite being on a scale of 1 to 100, not a percentage. It is a scaled score. If you are entitled to veterans' service points, these are added to your passing scaled score to boost your rank on the eligibility list. Veterans' points are added only to passing scores. A failing score cannot be brought to passing level by adding veterans' points. The score earned plus veterans' service points, if any, is the score that finds its place on the rank-order eligibility list. Highest scores go to the top of the list.

SUMMING IT UP

- With the growing concern over national security, law enforcement opportunities with the federal government are at an all-time high.

- Federal law enforcement personnel receive very competitive salaries and a wide range of benefits that often surpass those offered by many state and municipal agencies as well as organizations in the private sector.

- Don't be intimidated by the seemingly daunting task of preparing your application.

- The process of writing your application will boost your confidence and increase your self-awareness, making you a more articulate interviewer and a stronger candidate for the federal job you choose to pursue.

- To score high on your exam, it is important that you are prepared, avoid careless errors, manage your time, and understand the pros and cons of guessing.

PART II

WHERE THE JOBS ARE

Executive Branch

OVERVIEW

- **Department of Agriculture**
- **Department of Defense**
- **Department of Energy**
- **Department of Health and Human Services**
- **Department of the Interior**
- **Department of Justice**
- **Department of State**
- **Department of the Treasury**
- **Department of Veterans Affairs**
- **Summing it up**

The federal government offers a variety of opportunities to persons considering a career in federal law enforcement. While the goals of federal agencies differ and their authorities cover broad geographic areas, the scope of most agencies is specific and limited. Some have enforcement duties that deal with criminal or regulatory matters; others deal with security or military affairs. Many federal law enforcement positions require extensive travel, and most require relocation at some time during the officer's career. Federal law enforcement positions offer glamour overlaid with hard work, long hours, and, in many cases, personal danger. A clearer picture of law enforcement activities at the federal level is possible if the functions of some of the major federal agencies are examined. Specific positions within the most popular federal departments are described in detail in the next four chapters.

DEPARTMENT OF AGRICULTURE

The U.S. Department of Agriculture (USDA) enforces numerous laws designed to protect farmers, the public, and the national forests. These include laws relating to animal disease, quarantine, meat inspection, and the entry and spread of insects.

U.S. Forest Service

The U.S. Forest Service, one of the agencies within the Department of Agriculture, enforces federal forest-related laws and regulations. Typical violations involve stealing or damaging trees, setting fires, and operating vehicles that are hazardous to fire safety.

The Forest Service is dedicated to the management, protection, and efficient use of the National Forests and Grasslands, ensuring that they continue to provide sustainable yields of renewable resources such as water, forage, wildlife, timber, and outdoor recreation. The Forest Service protects lands and resources within its jurisdiction from wildfires, diseases, and forest insects, and from unfortunate instances of theft and vandalism.

Law enforcement is essential to the management, use, and protection of National Forest lands and associated resources. The Forest Service currently employs more than 800 law enforcement personnel nationwide.

Forest Service law enforcement personnel work outdoors in an interesting and exciting environment. Learning about ecosystem management and the diversity of natural resources can be personally rewarding. Patrolling in public areas, protecting the nation's flora and fauna, and responding to crisis situations on National Forest lands help to make Forest Service agents and officers some of the most visible and respected members of the federal law enforcement service.

Special Agent

Special Agents are criminal investigators who plan and conduct investigations concerning possible violations of criminal and administrative provisions of the Forest Service and other statutes under the U.S. Code. Special Agents are required to carry firearms; make arrests; prepare investigative reports; present cases for prosecution to U.S. Attorneys; maintain liaison with local, state, and federal agencies; and work independently with little or no supervision.

- **Training and Promotion:** Initial appointments are generally made at grade GS-5. Career progression to grades GS-7 and GS-9 generally requires a minimum of one year at each grade level and a supervisor's recommendation that the employee is ready for advancement to the next level. Promotions to higher grade levels and supervisory levels are made through the competitive procedures of the federal Merit Promotion System.

- **Basic Qualifications:** Applicants must have a bachelor's degree or three years' experience in criminal law enforcement, criminal investigation, and/or related professions. An equivalent combination of education and experience may be substituted; one academic year of full-time undergraduate study is equivalent to nine months of experience. Persons age 37 or older are not eligible for appointment unless they are presently in a federal civilian law enforcement position or have served in such a position in the past.

  In addition, Special Agents must:

  ○ meet basic educational and experience prerequisites.

  ○ successfully complete a basic law enforcement course and pass the Physical Efficiency Battery of tests.

  ○ pass a special background investigation conducted initially and periodically.

  ○ pass a drug urinalysis test.

  ○ pass a qualifying test in the use of firearms.

  ○ successfully complete one year of field training.

  ○ demonstrate emotional and mental stability.

  ○ be in excellent physical condition.

  ○ possess a valid driver's license.

Uniformed Law Enforcement Officer

Uniformed Law Enforcement Officers enforce federal laws and regulations governing National Forest lands and resources. They establish a regular and recurring presence on vast amounts of public land, roads, and campgrounds, taking appropriate action when illegal activity is observed. In addition, Uniformed Law Enforcement Officers:

- work closely and maintain liaison with local, state, and federal law enforcement officials.

- conduct informational and educational programs.

- provide emergency medical aid.

- eliminate hazardous situations.

- enforce drug-control laws on National Forest lands.

- assist outside agencies in conducting search and rescue missions on National Forest lands.

- assist Special Agents in executing search warrants.

- **Training and Promotion:** Initial appointments are generally made at grade GS-5. Promotions to higher grade levels and supervisory levels are made through the competitive procedures of the federal Merit Promotion System.

- **Basic Qualifications:** Applicants must have a bachelor's degree or one year of experience in criminal law enforcement or related professions. An equivalent combination of education and experience may be substituted.

In addition, Uniformed Law Enforcement Officers must:

- O meet basic educational and experience prerequisites.
- O successfully complete a basic law enforcement course and pass the Physical Efficiency Battery of tests.
- O pass a special background investigation conducted initially and periodically.
- O pass a drug urinalysis test.
- O pass a qualifying test in the use of firearms.
- O successfully complete one year of field training.
- O demonstrate emotional and mental stability.
- O be in excellent physical condition.
- O possess a valid driver's license.

Agricultural Research Service

The Agricultural Research Service (ARS) is the main scientific research agency of the USDA. Its job is to find solutions to agricultural problems that affect Americans every day. These problems include protecting crops and livestock from pests and disease, improving the quality and safety of agricultural products, determining the best nutrition for people from infancy to old age, sustaining the soil and other natural resources, ensuring profitability for farmers and processors, keeping costs down for consumers, and providing research support to other federal agencies.

Physical Security Specialist

The Agricultural Research Service of the USDA is responsible for conducting research to develop new information and technology directed toward solving technical agricultural problems that have a national priority. ARS Physical Security Specialists support the USDA Beltsville Agricultural Research Center that consists of more than 500 buildings located in Beltsville, Maryland. Their specific responsibilities include conducting on-site security surveys, analyses, and evaluation of the performance and effectiveness of physical security structures and devices such as fences, locks, barriers, lighting, intrusion detection systems, and access control systems. Members are also responsible for preparing written reports describing actions engaged to correct security deficiencies; overseeing and coordinating contracts with vendors of the monitoring and maintenance of intrusion alarm and access control systems; reviewing access control information concerning operational effectiveness; assisting with the maintenance and repair of electronic monitors and access control systems; controlling access codes for employee, both issuance and removal; and acting as liaison with other divisions and organizations concerning physical security and fire protection.

Generally, unless special assignments are issued, ARS Physical Security Specialists are assigned to the 6,800-acre site in Beltsville. Work schedules may include shift work as well as holidays due to the nature of the security concerns.

- **Training and Promotion:** Physical Security Specialists are trained in specialties that cover agency policies and directives, intrusion detection systems and devices, access control, crime prevention, federal law and regulations, report writing, investigative techniques, conduct of security surveys, and agency-specific issues.
- **Basic Qualifications:** U.S. citizenship is required of all applicants who receive appointment. Those appointed at the GS-5 level must hold a bachelor's degree or have three years of general experience, one year of which is equivalent to GS-4. Although advanced degrees are beneficial in GS-level appointments and salary advancement, promotions are based on available openings, performance evaluations, and recommendations of supervisors.

For specific information about working conditions, training and promotional opportunities, and application requirements, log on to the Department of Agriculture Web site at www.usda.gov/wps/portal/usdahome.

DEPARTMENT OF DEFENSE

The Department of Defense (DoD) is responsible for providing the military forces needed to deter war and protect the security of the United States. The major elements of these forces are the Army, Navy, Air Force, and Marine Corps. The Secretary of Defense exercises authority, direction, and control over the Department, which includes the Office of the Secretary of Defense, the Chairman of the Joint Chiefs of Staff, three Military Departments, nine Unified Combatant Commands, the DoD Inspector General, fifteen Defense Agencies, and seven DoD Field Activities.

National Security Agency

The principle responsibilities of the National Security Agency (NSA) personnel are to develop and secure cryptology. The agency coordinates, directs, and performs highly specialized activities to protect U.S. information systems and produce foreign intelligence information. A high-technology organization, the NSA is on the cutting edge of communications and data management. It is also one of the most important centers of foreign language analysis and research within the federal government.

Investigator

If one thrives on discovering clues that uncover hidden truths, a career as an NSA Investigator may be rewarding. NSA Investigators conduct background investigations and prepare reports on their findings. Discoveries and recommendations are used to improve the NSA's ability to provide accurate intelligence and perform critical national security missions. Specific job duties include, but are not limited to, preparing reports of investigations that are factually accurate, grammatically correct, and completed in a timely manner; and conducting interviews/interrogations.

- **Training and Promotion:** To perform its investigative mission, prior investigative experience is not required. NSA investigators learn to use techniques through a formal investigative training period that lasts ten to twelve weeks. Through formal NSA training and rotational assignments, investigators are exposed to a variety of security disciplines.

- **Basic Qualifications:** Applicants must be U.S. citizens, and hold a bachelor's degree from an accredited college or university. Investigators are expected to learn the use of interrogative techniques to resolve adjudicative issues and gain knowledge of significant suitability issues, counterintelligence indicators, and NSA policies and regulations.

Investigators should present a mature, professional, businesslike appearance and possess the capability to interview people of varied backgrounds. Excellent verbal and written communication, interpersonal, and problem-solving skills are required. Ability to work well independently in a deadline-driven environment is essential. Candidates must possess a valid driver's license, responsible driving record, and the ability to qualify to carry a firearm. Some travel is required.

U.S. Naval Criminal Investigative Service

The Naval Criminal Investigative Service (NCIS) is the primary law enforcement and counterintelligence arm of the U.S. Navy. It works closely with other local, state, federal, and foreign agencies to counter and investigate the most serious crimes: terrorism, espionage, computer intrusion, homicide, rape, child abuse, arson, procurement fraud, and more.

Special Agent

Special Agents are among the most adept and resourceful law enforcement professionals anywhere. Never restricted to a narrow specialty, even relatively junior agents are expected to handle a wide variety of criminal, antiterrorism, and counterintelligence matters with equal skill. Special Agents travel the globe and may even be stationed aboard ship. In-depth training, critical assignments, and excellent benefits are offered to attract the most qualified candidates.

NCIS Special Agents enjoy one of the most challenging and fulfilling careers in law enforcement. World travel and life abroad—in locations such as Italy, Japan, England, and Bahrain and aboard ship—are part of the NCIS Special Agent's experience. NCIS is considered an ideal agency for work in law enforcement specialties such as computer investigations, forensic science, threat assessment analysis, economic crimes, and electronic countermeasures.

- **Training and Promotion:** NCIS provides extensive training for special agents—from the nineteen-week NCIS Basic Agent Course held at the Federal Law Enforcement Training Center to in-service training on subjects ranging from death investigations to crime scene processing, domestic security, unarmed self-defense, and critical incident stress debriefing to multimonth programs on technical surveillance countermeasures, polygraph, procurement fraud, protective service, and yearlong graduate programs in forensic science, foreign counterintelligence, and language studies. Promotional opportunities are based on availability of positions and individual performance evaluations. Pay increases are in line with other federal law enforcement pay structures and scales.

- **Basic Qualifications:** Applicants must be at least 21 years old but under the age of 37, have an accredited baccalaureate degree, have vision correctable to 20/20 with normal color vision, be a U.S.-born or naturalized citizen, and be able to pass a background screening investigation. Applicants are not required to enlist in the Navy or Marine Corps, but may have preexisting military or law enforcement experience, which is often very desirable.

For specific information about working conditions, training and promotional opportunities, and application requirements, log on to the Department of Defense Web site at www.defenselink.mil.

DEPARTMENT OF ENERGY

The Department of Energy (DOE) has four overriding national security priorities:

1. Ensuring the integrity and safety of the country's nuclear weapons
2. Promoting international nuclear safety
3. Advancing nuclear nonproliferation
4. Continuing to provided safe, efficient, and effective nuclear power plants for the U.S. Navy

The DOE has stewardship of vital national security capabilities, from nuclear weapons to leading-edge research and development projects. The DOE must ensure the security of these critical programs through the application of an effective and coordinated counterintelligence program. Department activities are also focused on protecting the nation's nuclear weapons secrets, maintaining sensitive scientific secrets, and defeating terrorism. The DOE is an integral part of the national efforts to reduce global danger from weapons of mass destruction.

National Nuclear Security Agency

The Department of Energy works to enhance national security through the military application of nuclear energy through the National Nuclear Security Agency (NNSA). The NNSA also maintains and enhances the safety, reliability, and performance of the U.S. nuclear weapons stockpile—including the ability to design, produce, and test—in order to meet national security requirements.

The NNSA has four missions with regard to national security:

1. To provide the U.S. Navy with safe, militarily effective nuclear propulsion plants and to ensure the safe and reliable operation of those plants
2. To promote international nuclear safety and nonproliferation
3. To reduce global danger from weapons of mass destruction
4. To support U.S. leadership in science and technology

Special Agent

The DOE Office of Inspector General (OIG) Special Agents investigate fraud, waste, abuse, and mismanagement in these and other programs and operations of the Department that require large budget outlays and may be victim of fraudulent activity. Program fraud investigators will often focus on DOE contractors or grantees and include offenses such as falsification of contractor certified payrolls, overcharging for goods and services, misappropriation of funds, violation of project construction permits, and theft of government property. Special Agents also investigate DOE personnel misconduct, including violations such as embezzlement, theft of government property and supplies, and fraudulent claims. Special Agents are authorized to conduct surveillance and undercover operations, carry firearms, make arrests, execute search warrants, and serve subpoenas. Investigations may be conducted jointly with other federal agencies as well as state and local governments.

- **Training and Promotion:** Candidates attend an eight-week Criminal Investigator Training Program at the Federal Law Enforcement Training Center. In-service training may include courses in DOE program investigations, legal issues and updates, DOE regulations, investigative techniques, criminal and civil law, first aid and CPR, arrest techniques, defensive tactics, and firearms proficiency. Promotional opportunities are determined by availability and performance evaluations.

- **Basic Qualifications:** Applicants must be U.S. citizens and at least 21 years old but under the age of 37. Eyesight requirements include "sufficiently good vision in each eye, with or without correction." New agents are generally appointed at the GS-5 level while having completed a four-year course of study leading to a bachelor's degree, or three years' general experience, one year of which is equivalent to GS-4. Appointment at the GS-7 level requires one year of graduate education, or superior academic achievement during undergraduate studies.

For specific information about working conditions, training and promotional opportunities, and application requirements, log on to the Department of Energy Web site at www.energy.gov.

DEPARTMENT OF HEALTH AND HUMAN SERVICES

The Department of Health and Human Services (HHS) has among its responsibilities the task of protecting the country's health. Three agencies within the department that enforce laws related to this goal are the Centers for Disease Control and Prevention (CDC), the Food and Drug Administration (FDA), and the Environmental Protection Agency (EPA).

Centers for Disease Control and Prevention

The CDC is one of the thirteen major operating components of the Department of Health and Human Services. Since it was founded in 1946 to help control malaria, CDC has remained at the forefront of public health efforts to prevent and control infectious and chronic diseases, injuries, workplace hazards, disabilities, and environmental health threats. Today, CDC is globally recognized for conducting research and investigations and for its action-oriented approach. CDC applies research and findings to improve people's daily lives and responds to health emergencies—something that distinguishes CDC from its peer agencies.

Special Agent

Because the CDC is under the authority of the HHS, Special Agents of the HHS Office of Inspector General (OIG) conduct investigations of fraud, waste, abuse, and misman-agement in these and other programs and operations of the Center that require large budget outlays and may be victim of fraudulent activity. Program fraud investigators will often focus on CDC contractors or grantees, and include offenses such as falsifica-tion of contractor certified payrolls, overcharging for goods and services, misappropria-tion of funds, violation of project construction permits, and theft of government property. Special Agents also investigate CDC personnel misconduct, including viola-tions such as embezzlement, theft of government property and supplies, and fraudulent claims. Special Agents are authorized to conduct surveillance and undercover opera-tions, carry firearms, make arrests, execute search warrants, and serve subpoenas. Investigations may be conducted jointly with other federal agencies as well as state and local governments.

- **Training and Promotion:** Candidates attend an eight-week Criminal Investiga-tor Training Program at the Federal Law Enforcement Training Center. In-service training may include courses in DOE program investigations, legal issues and updates, DOE regulations, investigative techniques, criminal and civil law, first aid and CPR, arrest techniques, defensive tactics, and firearms proficiency. Promo-tional opportunities are determined by availability and performance evaluations.

- **Basic Qualifications:** Applicants must be U.S. citizens and at least 21 years old but under the age of 37. Eyesight requirements include "sufficiently good vision in each eye, with or without correction." New agents are generally appointed at the GS-5 level while having completed a four-year course of study leading to a bachelor's degree, or three years' general experience, one year of which is equivalent to GS-4. Appointment at the GS-7 level requires one year of graduate education, or superior academic achievement during undergraduate studies.

Food and Drug Administration

The FDA is a scientific, regulatory, and public health agency that oversees most food products (other than meat and poultry); human and animal drugs; therapeutic agents of biological origin; medical devices; radiation-emitting products for consumer, medical, and occupational use; cosmetics; and animal feed. The FDA is responsible for protecting the public health by assuring the safety, efficacy, and security of human and veterinary drugs, biological products, medical devices, our nation's food supply, cosmetics, and products that emit radiation. The FDA is also responsible for advancing the public health by helping to speed innovations that make medicines and foods more effective, safer, and more affordable; and helping consumers get the accurate, science-based information they need to use medicines and foods to improve their health.

Special Agent

Violations of federal law relating to FDA programs and operations—such as those pertaining to the Food, Drug and Cosmetic Act; Federal Anti-tampering Act; Prescription Drug Marketing Act; and the Safe Medical Device Act—are investigated by Special Agents of the FDA Office of Criminal Investigations (OCI). The FDA-OCI has the primary responsibility for criminal investigation of tampering and threat incidents involving products regulated by the FDA. The objective of such investigations is to determine whether tampering has occurred, the seriousness of the problem, the quantity of affected products on the market, the source of the tampering, and the removal of contaminated products from consumers or commerce. Special Agents also investigate misconduct and violations of laws by FDA personnel related to Administration programs and operations, including offenses such as bribery, conflict of interests, embezzlement, or misappropriation of federal funds. Special Agents are authorized to conduct surveillance and undercover operations, carry firearms, make arrests, execute search warrants, and serve subpoenas. Likewise, investigations may be conducted jointly with other federal agencies as well as state and local governments.

- **Training and Promotion:** FDA-OCI Special Agents attend the eight-week Criminal Investigator Training Program at the Federal Law Enforcement Training Center. In-service training may include courses in FDA program investigations, legal issues and updates, FDA regulations, investigative techniques, criminal and civil law, first aid and CPR, arrest techniques, defensive tactics, and firearms proficiency. Promotional opportunities are determined by availability and performance evaluations.

- **Basic Qualifications:** Applicants must be U.S. citizens and at least 21 years old but under the age of 37. Eyesight requirements include "sufficiently good vision in each eye, with or without correction." New agents are generally appointed at the

GS-5 level while having completed a four-year course of study leading to a bachelor's degree, or three years' general experience, one year of which is equivalent to GS-4. Appointment at the GS-7 level requires one year of graduate education, or superior academic achievement during undergraduate studies.

Environmental Protection Agency

The mission of the EPA is to protect human health and the environment. Since 1970, the EPA has been working for a cleaner, healthier environment for the American people. The EPA works to develop and enforce regulations that implement environmental laws enacted by Congress. The EPA is responsible for researching and setting national standards for a variety of environmental programs, and delegates to states and tribes the responsibility for issuing permits and for monitoring and enforcing compliance. Where national standards are not met, the EPA can issue sanctions and take other steps to assist the states and tribes in reaching the desired levels of environmental quality.

At laboratories located throughout the United States, the Agency works to assess environmental conditions and to identify, understand, and solve current and future environmental problems; integrate the work of scientific partners such as nations, private-sector organizations, academia and other agencies; and provide leadership in addressing emerging environmental issues and in advancing the science and technology of risk assessment and risk management.

Special Agent

Special Agents of the Environmental Protection Agency Office of Inspector General (EPA-OIG) conduct investigations that focus on fraud, waste, and abuse in programs and operations administered or financed by the EPA. Often complex and sensitive in nature, EPA-OIG investigations revolve around violations of federal statutes pertaining to large interstate corporate entities and subsidiaries, grants, and contracts; violations of the Federal Clean Air Act standards and asbestos removal projects; bribery of EPA personnel; and complex conspiracies. Investigations may also focus on official misconduct by Agency personnel involving conflict of interests, kickbacks, and embezzlement of federal funds. Special Agents are authorized to conduct surveillance and undercover operations, carry firearms, make arrests, execute search warrants, and serve subpoenas. Investigations may be conducted jointly with other federal agencies as well as state and local governments.

- **Training and Promotion:** EPA-OCI Special Agents attend the eight-week Criminal Investigator Training Program at the Federal Law Enforcement Training Center. In-service training may include courses in EPA program investigations, legal issues and updates, EPA regulations, investigative techniques, criminal and civil law, first aid and CPR, arrest techniques, defensive tactics, and firearms proficiency. Promotional opportunities are determined by availability and performance evaluations.

- **Basic Qualifications:** Applicants must be U.S. citizens and at least 21 years old but under the age of 37. Eyesight requirements include "sufficiently good vision in each eye, with or without correction." New agents are generally appointed at the GS-5 level while having completed a four-year course of study leading to a bachelor's degree, or three years' general experience, one year of which is equivalent to GS-4. Appointment at the GS-7 level requires one year of graduate education, or superior academic achievement during undergraduate studies.

For specific information about working conditions, training and promotional opportunities, and application requirements, log on to the Department of Health and Human Services Web site at www.os.dhhs.gov.

DEPARTMENT OF THE INTERIOR

Since its inception in 1789, the Department of the Interior (DOI) has had a wide range of responsibilities entrusted to it, including the construction of the national capital's water system; the colonization of freed slaves in Haiti; exploration of western wilderness; oversight of the District of Columbia jail; regulation of territorial governments; management of hospitals and universities; management of public parks; and the basic responsibilities for Indians, public lands, patents, and pensions.

The Department manages one of every five acres of land in the United States, providing opportunities for wilderness, wildlife protection, recreation, and resource development; supplies water for much of the West so that farmers can grow food and people can turn on their taps; provides access to energy and minerals so that people can warm and cool their homes, and drive to their jobs; honors the special responsibilities to American Indians, Alaska Natives, and affiliated Island communities; and protects wildlife and improves the environment. Further, the Department is committed to building partnerships to encourage conservation and preservation of natural and cultural resources; to bringing innovative approaches to solving land management and water disputes; and to developing energy, including renewable sources of energy, in the most environmentally protective manner.

Office of Inspector General

Violations of federal law relating to DOI programs and operations—such as those pertaining to the nation's public lands and minerals, national parks, national wildlife refuges, western water resources, and federal trust responsibilities to Indian tribes—are investigated by Special Agents of the DOI Office of Inspector General (OIG). The DOI-OIG has the primary responsibility for criminal investigation of tampering and threat incidents involving DOI programs and operations.

Special Agent

The objective of Special Agent investigations is to determine whether contractors have committed fraud or embezzlement, the seriousness of any such problems, violations of the Migratory Bird Treaty Act and other environmental laws, and workers' compensation fraud. Special Agents also investigate misconduct and violations of laws by DOI personnel relating to Administration programs and operations, including offenses such as bribery, conflict of interests, embezzlement, or misappropriation of federal funds. Special Agents are authorized to conduct surveillance and undercover operations, carry firearms, make arrests, execute search warrants, and serve subpoenas. Likewise, investigations may be conducted jointly with other federal agencies such as the FBI, Bureau of Land Management Law Enforcing Branch, U.S. Fish and Wildlife Service, Defense Criminal Investigative Service, and Environmental Protection Agency as well as state and local governments.

- **Training and Promotion:** Special Agents attend the eight-week Criminal Investigator Training Program at the Federal Law Enforcement Training Center. In-service training may include courses in program investigations, legal issues and updates, regulations, investigative techniques, criminal and civil law, first aid and CPR, arrest techniques, defensive tactics, and firearms proficiency. Promotional opportunities are determined by availability and performance evaluations.

- **Basic Qualifications:** Special Agent applicants must be U.S. citizens and at least 21 years old but under the age of 37. Eyesight requirements include "sufficiently good vision in each eye, with or without correction." New agents are generally appointed at the GS-5 level while having completed a four-year course of study leading to a bachelor's degree, or three years' general experience, one year of which is equivalent to GS-4. Appointment at the GS-7 level requires one year of graduate education, or superior academic achievement during undergraduate studies.

Bureau of Indian Affairs

The Bureau of Indian Affairs (BIA) is the principle bureau within the federal government responsible for the administration of federal programs for organized Indian tribes, and for promoting Indian self-determination. The Bureau also has responsibilities emanating from treaties and other agreements with Native groups.

Special Agent

Operating from BIA offices nationwide, Special Agents investigate violations of federal, state, tribal, and local laws on Indian reservations, such as assault, burglary, auto theft, child sexual abuse, murder, robbery, rape, drug trafficking, fraud, and criminal activity related to gaming operations and other legitimate businesses operating within Indian country. Investigations involve surveillance and undercover operations, often under hazardous conditions. Special Agents are authorized to carry firearms, make arrests, execute search warrants, and serve subpoenas.

- **Training and Promotion:** Special Agents attend the eight-week Criminal Investigator Training Program at the Federal Law Enforcement Training Center. In-service training may include courses in program investigations, legal issues and updates, regulations, investigative techniques, criminal and civil law, first aid and CPR, arrest techniques, defensive tactics, and firearms proficiency. Promotional opportunities are determined by availability and performance evaluations.

- **Basic Qualifications:** Under the Indian Reorganization Act of 1934, qualified Indian applicants are given hiring preference for BIA positions, although applications from non-Indian candidates are encouraged. Special Agent applicants must be U.S. citizens and at least 21 years old but under the age of 37. Eyesight requirements include "sufficiently good vision in each eye, with or without correction." New agents are generally appointed at the GS-5 level while having completed a four-year course of study leading to a bachelor's degree, or three years' general experience, one year of which is equivalent to GS-4. Appointment at the GS-7 level requires one year of graduate education, or superior academic achievement during undergraduate studies.

Bureau of Land Management

The Bureau of Land Management (BLM) administers public lands within a framework of the Federal Land Policy and Management Act of 1976 and other laws. The surface acres under the Bureau management comprise one-eighth of America's land surface and amount to 41 percent of the land under federal ownership.

Special Agent

BLM Special Agents are responsible for the investigation of criminal activities relating to 270 million acres of public lands and resources managed by the Bureau as well as 300 million acres where mineral rights are owned by the federal government. Bureau investigations focus on offenses such as timber theft, destruction or theft of archaeological artifacts, unlawful sale or treatment of wild horses or burros, violation of conservation laws, marijuana cultivation, and other criminal acts that occur on Bureau-managed forests and ranges. Special Agents are authorized to conduct surveillance and undercover operations, carry firearms, make arrests, execute search warrants, and serve subpoenas.

- **Training and Promotion:** BLM Special Agents attend the eight-week Criminal Investigator Training Program at the Federal Law Enforcement Training Center. In-service training may include courses in BLM program investigations, legal issues and updates, BLM regulations, investigative techniques, criminal and civil law, first aid and CPR, arrest techniques, defensive tactics, and firearms proficiency. Promotional opportunities are determined by availability and performance evaluations.

- **Basic Qualifications:** Applicants must be U.S. citizens and at least 21 years old but under the age of 37. Eyesight requirements include "sufficiently good vision in each eye, with or without correction." New agents are generally appointed at the

GS-5 level while having completed a four-year course of study leading to a bachelor's degree, or three years' general experience, one year of which is equivalent to GS-4. Appointment at the GS-7 level requires one year of graduate education, or superior academic achievement during undergraduate studies.

National Park Service

Created by Congress on August 25, 1916, the National Park Service (NPS) preserves the natural and cultural resources and values of the National Park System for the enjoyment, education, and inspiration of this and future generations. The National Park System of the United States comprises 388 areas covering more than 84 million acres in forty-nine states, the District of Columbia, American Samoa, Guam, Puerto Rico, Saipan, and the Virgin Islands. These areas are of such national significance as to justify special recognition and protection in accordance with various acts of Congress. The Park National Service cooperates with partners to extend the benefits of natural and cultural resource conservation and outdoor recreation throughout this country and the world.

Park Police Officer

The U.S. Park Police provide law enforcement services to designated areas within the National Park Service (primarily the Washington, D.C., New York, and San Francisco metropolitan areas). The force consists of highly-trained and professional police officers who work to prevent and detect criminal activity; conduct investigations; apprehend individuals suspected of committing offenses against federal, state, and local laws; provide protection to the president of the United States and visiting dignitaries; and provide protective services to some of the most recognizable monuments and memorials in the world.

Police officers may work different hours of the day, all days of the week, including holidays. Schedules are subject to change, and overtime is required at times. Officers must be adaptable and willing to adjust to frequent compulsory changes in work shifts, work locations, and other factors. Police officers must be able to work under a great deal of pressure, yet still maintain a clear head and a positive attitude and work ethic.

- **Training and Promotion:** Upon appointment, the recruit officer receives approximately nineteen weeks of intensive training at the Federal Law Enforcement Training Center. While assigned to the Federal Law Enforcement Training Center, starting salary is $40,758. Upon graduation, the recruit officer receives on-the-job training under the guidance of an experienced Field Training Officer.

- **Basic Qualifications:** Applicants must be U.S. citizens and at least 21 years old but under the age of 37. They must have completed at least 60 college credits or two years of military service at the time of appointment. Upon completion of training, officers are initially assigned to the Washington, D.C., area, where the largest contingent of Park Police is located.

Park Ranger

NPS Park Rangers are responsible for law enforcement and natural resources management duties at more than 300 locations that are part of the National Park System and other managed locations. Park Rangers supervise, manage, and perform work in the conservation and use of resources in national parks and other federally managed areas. Park Rangers carry out various tasks associated with forest or structural fire control; protection of property; gathering and dissemination of natural, historical, and scientific information; development of interpretive material for the natural, historical, and cultural features of an area; demonstration of folk art and crafts; enforcement of laws and regulations; investigation of violations, complaints, trespass/encroachment, and accidents; search and rescue; and management of historical, cultural, and natural resources, such as wildlife, forests, lakeshores, seashores, historic buildings, battlefields, archaeological properties, and recreation areas. They also operate campgrounds, which includes such tasks as assigning sites, replenishing firewood, performing safety inspections, providing information to visitors, and leading guided tours. Differences in the exact nature of duties depend on the grade of position, the site's size, and specific needs.

Park Rangers work in urban, suburban, and rural areas. More than half of the Park Rangers work in areas east of the Mississippi River. Much of their work is performed outdoors. However, Rangers must also work in offices, especially as they advance and assume more managerial responsibilities. During their careers, most Rangers can expect to be assigned to several different parts of the country.

- **Training and Promotion:** The orientation and training a Park Ranger receives on the job is sometimes supplemented with formal training courses. Training for duties that are unique to the Park Service is available at the Horace M. Albright Training Center at Grand Canyon National Park, Arizona, and the Stephen T. Mather Training Center at Harpers Ferry, West Virginia. Rangers also attend the twelve-week Land Management Law Enforcement Training Program at the Federal Law Enforcement Training Center. Park Rangers also receive a minimum of 40 hours of in-service training annually, including courses in subjects such as traffic and accident investigation, search and seizure, criminal law, patrol techniques, defensive tactics, and firearms proficiency.

  Depending upon qualifications, Park Rangers begin their service at various grades. From the entry, Rangers may move through the ranks to become District Rangers, Park Managers, and Staff Specialists in interpretation, resource management, park planning, and related areas. At upper levels, Rangers' responsibilities and independence increase as their influence covers more staff and area. Upper-level managers in the Park Service are recruited primarily for their managerial capabilities. Competition exists for Park Ranger positions in all grade levels. The starting salary for summer Ranger hires with a college degree is a GS-4 ($18,687); permanent Ranger hires are GS-5 ($20,908) to GS-9 ($31,680) depending on college degrees and experience.

- **Basic Qualifications:** Applicants for NPS Ranger positions must be U.S. citizens, at least 21 years old but under the age of 37, and possess a high school diploma. Appointees to full-time law enforcement status must be under the age of 37. Requirements also include two years of progressively responsible experience that has demonstrated the ability to learn and apply complex regulations and procedures, or two years of active-duty military experience, or two years of education above high school.

Special Agent

Special Agents are responsible for the investigation of a wide range of criminal offenses and civil matters pertaining to NPS programs and operations. Investigations focus on incidents that occur on the grounds of national parks and monuments, scenic parkways, preserves, trails, campgrounds, battlefields, seashores, lakeshores, recreational areas, and historic sites that encompass the NPS. Offenses investigated include violations of the Archaeological Resources Protection Act, Endangered Species Act, and Migratory Bird Treaty Act; NPS recreation and use violations; hazardous waste disposal and other environmental crimes; marijuana cultivation and other drug offenses; assault; rape; homicide; robbery; weapons offenses; vandalism; arson; and other property and personal crimes. NPS Special Agents are authorized to carry firearms, conduct surveillance and undercover operations, make arrests, execute search warrants, and serve subpoenas.

- **Training and Promotion:** NPS Special Agents attend the eight-week Criminal Investigator Training Program at the Federal Law Enforcement Training Center. In-service training may include courses in NPS program investigations, legal issues and updates, NPS regulations, investigative techniques, criminal and civil law, first aid and CPR, arrest techniques, defensive tactics, and firearms proficiency. Promotional opportunities are determined by availability and performance evaluations.

- **Basic Qualifications:** Applicants must be U.S. citizens and at least 21 years old but under the age of 37. Eyesight requirements include "sufficiently good vision in each eye, with or without correction." New agents are generally appointed at the GS-5 level while having completed a four-year course of study leading to a bachelor's degree, or three years' general experience, one year of which is equivalent to GS-4. Appointment at the GS-7 level requires one year of graduate education, or superior academic achievement during undergraduate studies.

For specific information about working conditions, training and promotional opportunities, and application requirements, log on to the Department of the Interior Web site at www.doi.gov.

U.S. Fish and Wildlife Service

The U.S. Fish and Wildlife Service (FWS) is responsible for the conservation, protection, and enhancement of fish and wildlife and their habitat, including migratory birds, endangered species, certain marine mammals, and inland sport fisheries.

Special Agent

Special Agents investigate violations of federal fish and wildlife laws covered under the Federal Endangered Species Act, Convention on the International Trade in Endangered Species, Migratory Bird Treaty Act, Marine Mammal Protection Act, Wild Bird Conservation Act, Eagle Protection Act, Airborne Hunting Act, and other laws. Special Agents engage in surveillance and undercover operations, are authorized to carry firearms, make arrests, execute search warrants, and serve subpoenas. Investigations may be conducted jointly with the National Marine Fisheries Service, Customs Service, FBI, USDA Animal and Plant Inspection Service, Food and Drug Administration, and other agencies.

- **Training and Promotion:** FWS Special Agents attend the eight-week Criminal Investigator Training Program at the Federal Law Enforcement Training Center. In-service training may include courses in FWS program investigations, legal issues and updates, FWS regulations, investigative techniques, criminal and civil law, first aid and CPR, arrest techniques, defensive tactics, and firearms proficiency. Promotional opportunities are determined by availability and performance evaluations.

- **Basic Qualifications:** Applicants must be U.S. citizens and at least 21 years old but under the age of 37. Eyesight requirements include "sufficiently good vision in each eye, with or without correction." New agents are generally appointed at the GS-5 level while having completed a four-year course of study leading to a bachelor's degree, or three years' general experience, one year of which is equivalent to GS-4. Appointment at the GS-7 level requires one year of graduate education, or superior academic achievement during undergraduate studies.

DEPARTMENT OF JUSTICE

The overriding mission of the Department of Justice is to enforce the law and defend the interests of the United States according to the law; to ensure public safety against foreign and domestic threats; to provide federal leadership in preventing and controlling crime; to seek just punishment for those guilty of unlawful behavior; to administer and enforce the nation's immigration laws fairly and effectively; and to ensure fair and impartial administration of justice for all Americans.

Bureau of Alcohol, Tobacco and Firearms

The Department of the Treasury established the Bureau of Alcohol, Tobacco and Firearms (BATF) to enforce laws relating to alcohol, tobacco, firearms, and explosives. The objective of the BATF is to enjoin voluntary compliance with these laws and to minimize willful violations. To do so, the BATF has two enforcement units—criminal and regulatory. The criminal enforcement unit seeks to eliminate illegal possession and use of firearms and explosives, reduce traffic in illicit alcohol, and assist state and local law enforcement agencies in reducing crime and violence. The regulatory enforcement unit helps ensure full collection of revenues due from legal alcohol and tobacco industries and aids in preventing commercial bribery, consumer deception, and improper trade practices.

Inspector

An important part of the BATF law enforcement effort is its inspection force. BATF Inspectors must constantly be alert to the possibility of fraud, negligence, or illegal activities. When they uncover evidence of criminal activities, Inspectors turn it over to the BATF Special Agents responsible for criminal investigations. BATF Inspectors carry out their duties in a variety of work settings. Inspections might take place at breweries; wineries; distilleries; plants that manufacture distilled spirits for industrial, scientific, and medical use; and laboratories conducting scientific research projects. BATF Inspectors' work may also take them to wholesale liquor establishments, cigar and cigarette manufacturing plants, firearms and explosives retailers, and manufacturers and importers.

BATF Inspectors visit business establishments alone or as part of an inspection team. They contact and interview company representatives and gather basic data about procedures and operations. They acquire financial statements as well as business and public records to verify information and to make certain that required taxes have been paid. In addition, they determine that the business has the various special licenses, permits, and other authorizations required by federal law. They are also responsible for judging whether facilities and equipment meet legal standards and if manufacturing processes and operations are being conducted in accordance with the law. If violations are detected, company representatives are advised to correct those conditions. In cases of criminal violations such as fraud, tax evasion, or falsified inventories, Inspectors prepare detailed summaries of evidence to assist Special Agents in preparing cases for criminal prosecution. Inspectors prepare written reports of their activities, may serve legal papers in violation of federal laws, and sometimes testify as government witnesses during court proceedings. BATF Inspectors may be assigned to workstations anywhere in the United States and are required to travel when performing field inspections. Working hours are usually regular and average 40 hours per week.

- **Training and Promotion:** BATF Inspectors are chosen from the top of the list of eligible candidates meeting the entry standards of the Bureau of Alcohol, Tobacco, and Firearms. Prospects for advancement are generally favorable. Promotions are not automatic but rather are based on satisfactory performance and the recommendations of supervisory staff. An alternative advancement route is to become a BATF Special Agent. Many of the experience requirements for Special Agents give preferential treatment to job applicants from within the agency.

- **Basic Qualifications:** Applicants must be a U.S. citizen; be registered with selective service or be exempt from having to do so under selective service law; be between the ages of 21 and 37 at the time of appointment, unless the applicant has had previous service in a federal civilian law enforcement position covered by special civil service retirement provisions, including early or mandatory retirement (Maximum age limitations may not be waived for any applicant, including those entitled to veterans' preference.); possess a current and valid driver's license; complete a BATF Special Agent applicant questionnaire; pass the Treasury Enforcement Agent Examination; pass the BATF Special Agent applicant assessment test; successfully complete a field panel interview, including a writing sample; pass a polygraph examination and successfully complete a background investigation for a top-secret clearance; be in compliance with BATF's drug policy for Special Agent applicants; pass a medical examination by an authorized government physician and meet medical requirements; meet uncorrected distant vision of at least 20/100 in each eye, and corrected distant vision of 20/20 in one eye and 20/30 in the other; and pass a drug test.

Special Agent

BATF Special Agents, stationed in hundreds of offices throughout the United States, contribute greatly in the battle against crime and violence in our country. Major responsibilities of Special Agents are to:

- investigate criminal violations of federal laws within the enforcement jurisdiction of the Department of Justice.

- investigate violations relating to explosives, firearms, arson, and alcohol and tobacco diversion.

- analyze evidence through investigative leads, seizures and arrests, execution of search warrants, and a variety of other means.

- prepare concise criminal investigative case reports.

- testify for the government in court or before grand juries.

Special Agents can assume other identities and work undercover. They associate with criminals, purchase contraband, observe illegal activities, and gather intelligence information through these investigative methods. After sufficient evidence is gathered, it is evaluated by other BATF Special Agents to determine what actions should follow. Where indicated, Special Agents seize, search, and arrest suspects and gather contraband and other evidence as authorized by appropriate legal warrants. In carrying out these tasks, Special Agents work in teams or as part of a larger group of Special Agents conducting raids of suspected locations.

BATF Special Agents are trained in self-defense tactics as well as in the use of various types of firearms, and they employ these skills as needed during the course of an investigation. Special Agents prepare detailed, written summaries of all facts and evidence assembled in each investigation. They assist the U.S. Attorney in preparing the case before trial and in presenting it before the court. BATF Special Agents often make court appearances to testify for the prosecution during criminal proceedings.

Special Agents must sign a geographic mobility agreement with BATF that makes them subject to relocation at any time. Special Agents may be assigned to work in locations anywhere in the United States and travel frequently during the course of their investigations. They are also subject to transfers and work assignments based on the needs of the Bureau. The working hours of Special Agents are often irregular and in excess of 40 hours a week. In addition to working under stressful and dangerous conditions, the work is often physically strenuous and is performed in all kinds of environmental conditions.

- **Training and Promotion:** Selected applicants shall be appointed in the excepted service and must satisfactorily complete a three-year trial period that includes but is not limited to successful completion of the Criminal Investigator training program, Special Agent basic training, and qualifying and maintaining firearms proficiency.

  Newly hired Special Agents usually enter duty at the GS-5 level. Promotions are contingent on satisfactory work performance at each level and require the recommendations of supervisory personnel.

  The journeyman level for a Special Agent is GS-11. Selections for promotion to positions above the GS-11 level are made as vacancies occur in accordance with the Bureau's merit promotion procedures.

- **Basic Qualifications:** Applicants must be U.S. citizens; registered with the selective service or be exempt from having to do so under selective service law; be between the ages of 21 and 37 at the time of appointment, unless the applicant has had previous service in a federal civilian law enforcement position covered by special civil service retirement provisions, including early or mandatory retirement (Maximum age limitations may not be waived for any applicant, including those entitled to veterans' preference.); possess a current and valid driver's license; complete a BATF Special Agent applicant questionnaire; pass the Treasury Enforcement Agent Examination; pass the BATF Special Agent applicant assessment test; complete a field panel interview, including a writing sample; pass a polygraph examination and successfully complete a background investigation for a top-secret clearance; be in compliance with BATF's drug policy for Special Agent applicants; pass a medical examination by an authorized government physician and meet medical requirements; meet uncorrected distant vision of at least 20/100 in each eye, and corrected distant vision of 20/20 in one eye and 20/30 in the other; and pass a drug test.

Drug Enforcement Administration

The Drug Enforcement Administration (DEA), an agency of the U.S. Department of Justice, has the leading role in the fight against drug abuse in our country. The DEA's mission is to control narcotic and dangerous drug abuse effectively through law enforcement, education, training, and research activities. It is responsible for enforcing statutes and laws relating to the unlawful distribution and use of such products as heroin, opium, cocaine, hallucinogens, marijuana, synthetic narcotics that can be addictive (such as Demerol and methadone), and dangerous nonnarcotic drugs (such as amphetamines and barbiturates). The aim is to bring to justice those individuals and organizations, at home and abroad, engaged in growing, manufacturing, or distributing controlled, dangerous substances destined for illegal traffic in the United States. The efforts of this agency are directed at the highest level of suppliers and toward the confiscation of the greatest quantity of illegal drugs before they reach the street pushers. In line with these responsibilities, the DEA develops overall federal drug enforcement strategies and leads the way in developing narcotic and dangerous drug suppression programs at national and international levels. The DEA also regulates legal trade in narcotics and dangerous drugs.

Special Agent

Special Agents are the backbone of the DEA and represent half of its total workforce. A Special Agent's career within the DEA represents an opportunity for diversified experience, international posts of duty, and assignments at numerous posts of duty within the United States. The primary mission of DEA Special Agents is to enforce laws dealing with narcotics and dangerous drugs by investigating the alleged or suspected criminal activities of major drug traffickers on both the national and international scenes. They concentrate their efforts on locating and eliminating illegal sources of supply and distribution that quite often involve secret manufacturers of drugs and sources of drugs diverted from legitimate channels.

When a case assignment is received from DEA supervisory personnel, Special Agents, working alone or in teams, review and analyze all the available data the agency has on file and make preliminary plans about the ways in which the investigation will be conducted. Additional facts and evidence are obtained by interviewing, observing, and interrogating witnesses, suspects, and informants with knowledge of the case. In many instances, Special Agents must carefully examine and evaluate financial and inventory records or other sources of information to verify facts previously obtained or to uncover new evidence indicating criminal activities. Very often, hard facts and evidence about activities of illegal drug dealers cannot be obtained by traditional investigative methods. In such cases, Special Agents undertake the very risky job of assuming other identities and working undercover.

An important part of the Special Agent's job involves surveillance activities. This is done in a number of ways, such as on stakeouts, in vehicles, or on foot, and may involve the use of electronic methods authorized by appropriate court orders. Information concerning illegal drug trafficking by individuals and organized groups is collected, analyzed, and distributed as intelligence data so that investigations may be conducted in a systematic fashion and duplication of effort may be avoided. These data are also used in the planning and development of DEA strategies and in the continuous exchange of information among federal, state, and local law enforcement agencies and appropriate foreign governments. When investigations have been concluded, Special Agents evaluate all the available facts and evidence and consult with supervisory personnel to determine what legal actions should follow. Special Agents have full police power to enforce all federal laws anywhere in the United States. When sufficient evidence exists, they arrest, take suspects into custody, and seize evidence and contraband as authorized by appropriate legal warrants. These actions are carried out by teams of Special Agents or by groups of Special Agents who are part of a strike force unit. DEA Special Agents are well trained in the use of firearms and self-defense methods and employ these skills as needed during arrests. Special Agents prepare detailed, written reports of each case in which they take part. These reports include all data, evidence, statements of witnesses and defendants, and other relevant information useful during court proceedings. They assist government attorneys in trial preparations and testify for the prosecution during trials and grand jury proceedings.

The Drug Enforcement Administration is also responsible for regulating the legal trade in narcotic and dangerous drugs, and Special Agents must have the versatility to conduct accountability investigations of drug wholesalers, suppliers, and manufacturers. Activities include establishing import-export and manufacturing quotas for various controlled drugs, registering all authorized handlers of drugs, inspecting the records and facilities of major drug manufacturers and distributors, and investigating instances in which drugs have been illegally diverted from legitimate sources. In addition to their enforcement responsibilities, DEA Special Agents use methods of training and education in their fight against narcotics and drug abuse. In overseas operations, for example, DEA activities are aimed at developing international awareness of the criticality of the illegal drug problem and obtaining support for drug trafficking suppression measures. Special Agents also work to secure cooperation between nations in sharing information and intelligence about drug-related activities. On the domestic scene, Special Agents train federal, state, local, and foreign law enforcement officers in drug identification techniques and narcotic and dangerous drug control methods. Special training is also available through the DEA in forensic drug chemistry for chemists employed by law enforcement agencies and for key personnel in the legal drug industry. Special Agents give lectures; make speeches; and serve as panel members for civic, social, community, and other types of organizations expressing concern and interest in the drug abuse problem.

Special Agent positions are located in most major cities throughout the United States and in certain large cities overseas. The work involves frequent travel as well as irregular hours and overtime. Special Agents work a considerable amount of administratively uncontrollable overtime for which they are well compensated. Special Agents must be available for assignment at any time; they are usually required to transfer to different locations, at government expense, based on workload requirements and the needs of the agency. Special Agents must be willing to accept assignment to duty stations anywhere in the United States upon appointment and at any time thereafter, including foreign assignments. In fact, applicants are required to sign a statement to this effect prior to appointment. This job involves hazardous duty, working under stress, and the possibility of physical injury during dangerous assignments.

- **Training and Promotion:** The training program that DEA Special Agents must undergo is so rigorous that many applicants do not make it to the first cut. Candidates must sign a statement of understanding prior to appointment that continued employment with DEA is contingent upon successful completion of this training.

  Most Special Agents are given special appointments approved for the DEA by the Office of Personnel Management. Special Agents given these appointments may be converted to career appointments after three to four years of fully satisfactory service. Once hired, prospects for upward mobility are generally good.

  Special Agents are eligible for promotion after one year of satisfactory work performance at the entry level. Promotions are not automatic and are based on the Agent's job performance, demonstrated ability to perform the duties of the higher-level job, and the recommendations of supervisory personnel.

  Most Special Agents are appointed at GS-7. A limited number of appointments may be made at GS-9. The Special Agent position has promotion potential to GS-12. Promotions beyond GS-12 are made through the DEA's Merit Promotion Plan.

- **Basic Qualifications:** Applicants must be U.S. citizens; be registered with the selective service or be exempt from having to do so under selective service law; be between the ages of 21 and 37 at the time of appointment, unless the applicant has had previous service in a federal civilian law enforcement position covered by special civil service retirement provisions, including early or mandatory retirement (Maximum age limitations may not be waived for any applicant, including those entitled to veterans' preference.); possess a current and valid driver's license; complete a BATF Special Agent applicant questionnaire; pass the Treasury Enforcement Agent Examination; pass the BATF Special Agent applicant assessment test; successfully complete a field panel interview, including a writing sample; pass a polygraph examination and successfully complete a background investigation for a top-secret clearance; be in compliance with BATF's drug policy for Special Agent applicants; pass a medical examination by an authorized government physician and meet medical requirements; meet uncorrected distant vision of at least 20/100 in each eye, and corrected distant vision of 20/20 in one eye and 20/30 in the other; and pass a drug test.

Federal Bureau of Investigation

The Federal Bureau of Investigation (FBI) is responsible for investigating violations of all federal laws except those specifically within the jurisdiction of other federal agencies. The FBI handles violations such as sabotage, treason, and espionage as well as other internal security matters. Although the jurisdiction of the FBI is limited, the Bureau has the responsibility for enforcing numerous federal laws, including:

- kidnapping, extortion, and bank robbery
- offenses involving interstate transportation
- civil rights violations
- assaulting or killing a U.S. president or federal officer
- violating the security of personnel employed by the federal government and property owned by the government

In addition, the FBI maintains a centralized system of fingerprint identification, the National Crime Information Center to supply information on known or suspected criminals; crime laboratory services; and training programs to increase law enforcement effectiveness at all levels of government.

Special Agent

A Special Agent's most important function is gathering evidence in cases where specific federal laws have been violated and then presenting findings to the office of a U.S. Attorney. Special Agents plan, coordinate, and conduct investigations using the considerable resources of the Bureau. Working alone or in teams, Special Agents conduct surveillance, work undercover, and seize and arrest individuals as authorized by legal warrants. FBI Special Agents must be skilled in the use of several types of firearms as well as hand-to-hand defensive tactics. They're also required to prepare detailed, written reports on all aspects of cases in which they're involved. They assist the staff of U.S. Attorneys' offices in preparing cases for trial and appear as witnesses during trials and grand jury hearings.

FBI Special Agents are assigned to one of fifty-nine divisional offices located in cities throughout the United States and Puerto Rico. They may also work in FBI headquarters in Washington, D.C., or in FBI resident agencies scattered across the country. Travel and work weeks in excess of 40 hours are routine. Agents must be available for assignments at any time and are subject to call 24 hours a day. In addition, transfer to different locations is usually required at some point during one's career.

- **Training and Promotion:** Once chosen, applicants must complete an intensive, four-month training program at the FBI Academy in Quantico, Virginia. This training program teaches new Special Agents the basic skills they will need to conduct effective investigations in all the FBI's investigative programs, such as:
  - counterterrorism
  - ethics with practical law enforcement applications

- ❍   computer intrusions and fraud
- ❍   communications and interviewing
- ❍   informant development
- ❍   evidence collection and handling
- ❍   equal opportunity employment and cultural sensitivity
- ❍   counterintelligence
- ❍   computer search and seizure
- ❍   human behavior
- ❍   communications and interviewing
- ❍   constitutional criminal procedure
- ❍   physical fitness and defensive tactics
- ❍   firearms
- ❍   practical problems

- **Basic Qualifications:** Special Agents are specially trained personnel, chosen from an extensive pool of applicants because they possess specific areas of expertise. To be an FBI Special Agent, an individual must be a U.S. citizen; be at least 23 but not yet have reached his or her 37th birthday on appointment; have at least a bachelor's degree from an accredited, four-year program at a college or university; pass a written examination; complete several in-person interviews; and pass a comprehensive medical examination, including vision and hearing tests.

Applicants with these qualifications will be chosen if they have specific experience or expertise needed by the FBI. The criteria change over time according to the FBI's current priorities. Traditionally, the FBI seeks applicants with backgrounds in law enforcement, law, or accounting. Today, the FBI not only seeks applicants with these backgrounds, but also with expertise in languages, computers, and the sciences. For information on what specific skills the FBI is looking for today, log on to the FBI Web site at www.fbi.gov.

Due to the FBI's responsibilities in criminal law enforcement and in the Intelligence Community, all FBI employees, whether they are Special Agents or Professional Support, must qualify for a top-secret security clearance before they can begin their service. This qualification includes an extensive background investigation. The FBI does not make a final decision to hire an individual until all the information gathered during the background investigation is assessed. Once hired, all FBI employees must maintain their eligibility for a top-secret security clearance, undergo a limited background check every five years, and submit to random drug tests throughout their careers.

The FBI's Applicant Program manages background investigations on all persons who apply for positions with the Department of Energy, the Nuclear Regulatory Commission, the Department of Justice, and the FBI. The program also oversees background checks for presidential appointees, White House staff candidates, and

U.S. Court candidates. Background investigations involve interviewing neighbors and coworkers of applicants and checking criminal and credit records.

U.S. Marshals Service

The U.S. Marshals Service is the nation's oldest and most versatile federal law enforcement agency. Since 1789 federal Marshals have served the nation through a variety of vital law enforcement activities. Ninety-four U.S. Marshals, appointed by the president or the U.S. attorney general, direct the activities of ninety-four district offices and personnel stationed at more than 350 locations throughout the fifty states, Guam, Northern Mariana Islands, Puerto Rico, and the Virgin Islands. A U.S. Marshal heads each district and the District of Columbia Superior Court.

Deputy U.S. Marshal

Deputy U.S. Marshals perform a variety of duties, primarily of a law enforcement nature. Deputies are charged with the primary responsibility of providing security to the federal courts and for ensuring the personal safety of judges, jurors, and attorneys as well as the physical security of court buildings and facilities. They remove disorderly spectators from court premises and, in some cases, repel attempted attacks by intruders during federal judicial proceedings. During crucial court cases, Deputies conduct surveys of federal court buildings to determine the adequacy of security and, where necessary, recommend the use of fixed and mobile security units. Specially trained Deputies furnish 24-hour protection to federal judges and their immediate families when threats, whether real or apparent, are made as a result of decisions rendered by the court. The Marshals Service has primary responsibility for investigating violations of certain federal fugitive statutes. Deputies perform investigative duties in the execution of arrest warrants for federal probation, parole, mandatory release, and bond default violators, and in the apprehension of federal escapees. Under the Organized Crime Act of 1970, the U.S. Marshals Service provides protection to state and federal witnesses who testify for the government in cases against organized crime. The protection of these witnesses, and members of their families whose lives may be jeopardized by court testimony, can extend from the initial court appearance through the completion of the trial and includes the use of modern electronic communication and security equipment. Deputy U.S. Marshals have the added responsibility of maintaining custody of federal prisoners from the time of arrest to their sentencing or release from confinement. They also transport federal prisoners between court and prison facilities as directed by legal warrants and the Bureau of Prisons.

Newly hired Deputy Marshals must be willing to accept an initial assignment to any duty location and must be available for transfer to different work locations based on the needs of the U.S. Marshals Service. This work involves frequent travel for extended periods of time as well as irregular work schedules and overtime. It also may involve personal risk, working under both physical and mental stress, and the possibility of physical injury during the performance of duties.

- **Training and Promotion:** Applicants are required to undergo a rigorous ten-week basic training program at the U.S. Marshals Service Training Academy. Promotional opportunities depend on availability and performance evaluations. All Deputy U.S. Marshals enter the service at grade GS-5. Once appointed, they may progress to the GS-9 level. Positions above this level are filled through servicewide competition. These higher-level jobs often require reassignment to another district at government expense.

- **Basic Qualifications:** Applicants must have a minimum of three years of responsible volunteer or paid experience or a four-year degree from an accredited college or university. In addition to the GS-5 experience requirement above, applicants must have one year of responsible law enforcement experience that required the exercise of tact, courtesy, and the ability to deal effectively with associates, subordinates, the general public, and prisoners. This experience must demonstrate an applicant's abilities as a competent law enforcement officer, including the ability to make arrests and use firearms proficiently.

  If an applicant cannot qualify based on education or experience alone, the service will combine education and experience in an attempt to satisfy the minimum general experience requirements at the GS-5 level for Deputy U.S. Marshal positions.

For specific information about working conditions, training and promotional opportunities, and application requirements, log on to the Department of Justice Web site at www.usdoj.gov.

DEPARTMENT OF STATE

The U.S. Department of State uses diplomacy to promote and protect American interests by:

- managing diplomatic relations with other countries and international institutions
- promoting peace and stability in regions of vital interest
- supporting U.S. businesses at home and abroad
- helping developing nations establish stable economic environments
- providing information and services for citizens traveling and living abroad
- issuing visas for foreigners

The United States maintains diplomatic relations with nearly 180 of the 191 countries in the world. It maintains nearly 265 diplomatic and consular posts around the world, including embassies, consulates, and missions to international organizations.

Bureau of Diplomatic Security

The Bureau of Diplomatic Security is responsible for providing a safe and secure environment for the conduct of U.S. foreign policy. Every diplomatic mission in the world operates under a security program designed and maintained by Diplomatic Security.

Diplomatic Security trains foreign civilian law enforcement officers in disciplines designed to reduce the threat and repercussions of terrorism throughout the world.

Diplomatic Security's role evolves to meet new challenges. In concert with local security forces, Special Agents are protecting the president of Afghanistan as well as training an Afghan force to take over the full responsibility. Also, the Bureau is currently completing security measures for the U.S. Embassy in Baghdad and training assigned staff to live and work safely in Iraq.

In the United States, Diplomatic Security investigates passport and visa fraud, conducts personnel security investigations, and protects the Secretary of State and high-ranking foreign dignitaries and officials.

Special Agent

Within the U.S. Department of State, Special Agents are charged with conducting criminal and general investigations that concern operations, programs, and personnel of the U.S. Department of State. Criminal investigations will generally focus on fraud in the use and/or issuance of U.S. passports and visas at home and abroad as well as smuggling activities. In terms of personnel, investigations will encompass integrity issues such as bribery, collusion, conflict of interests, kickbacks, embezzlement, and theft or conversion of U.S. property. State Department Special Agents are authorized to conduct surveillance and undercover operations, carry firearms, execute search warrants, serve subpoenas, and make arrests. Investigations may be conducted as single agency operations or jointly with other federal, state, or local government agencies as well as those of foreign governments. Although not generally acknowledged, Special Agents will also provide security and protection services for Department of State officials at home and abroad.

Special Agents spend a substantial portion of their careers abroad serving at diplomatic posts. While assigned abroad, Special Agents are often referred to as Regional Security Officers (RSOs). Overseas assignments offer great opportunity for career growth and usually occur immediately after the initial tour of duty in a domestic field office. Assignment abroad can, however, occur much earlier depending upon needs of the service.

At U.S. embassies and consulates abroad, RSOs develop and implement the various aspects of a comprehensive security program designed to protect personnel, property, and information against terrorists, foreign intelligence agents, and criminals.

Domestic assignments are equally challenging and rewarding. An officer can aspire to managing field office programs or a Department headquarters office responsible for support operations.

- **Training and Promotion:** A substantial training investment is made in each candidate selected for this program. Six months of training begin with an orientation period in Washington, D.C., followed by basic and specialized training at the

Federal Law Enforcement Training Center. Training continues at State Department facilities in the Washington, D.C., area. Candidates must pass all required tests at the Federal Law Enforcement Training Center. Initially, candidates are trained in personal protection techniques, criminal law and investigation, background investigations, first aid, firearms, and defensive driving. To prepare for specific overseas assignments, Special Agents are trained in security management, post operations, counterintelligence, electronic security, and languages. Other instruction includes advanced firearms techniques, explosive devices, ordnance detection, arson investigation, and medical assistance.

With proven aptitudes and on-the-job performance, a Diplomatic Security Special Agent may advance to the position of regional security officer, who is responsible for managing security operations for an embassy or for several diplomatic posts within an assigned area. RSOs work closely with top State Department officials and serve as operational supervisors of U.S. Marine Security Guard detachments.

- **Basic Qualifications:** To be considered for a position as a Special Agent, a candidate must be a U.S. citizen; hold a bachelor's degree; be at least 20 years of age (Candidates must be at least 21 years old but must not have reached their 37th birth date at time of appointment.); be registered, if required, with the selective service; successfully undergo written and oral assessments; successfully undergo a thorough background investigation and qualify for a top-secret security clearance; pass a stringent medical exam; be available for worldwide assignment; qualify for a Department of State Class 01 medical clearance; pass physical fitness tests; possess a valid U.S. driver's license; be willing to carry and use firearms and qualify with firearms throughout career; and successfully complete all aspects of six-month training.

For specific information about working conditions, training and promotional opportunities, and application requirements, log on to the Department of State Web site at www.state.gov.

DEPARTMENT OF THE TREASURY

The Department of the Treasury is the primary federal agency responsible for the economic and financial prosperity and security of the United States, and as such is responsible for a wide range of activities including advising the president on economic and financial issues, promoting the president's growth agenda, and enhancing corporate governance in financial institutions.

In the international arena, the Department of the Treasury works with other federal agencies, the governments of other nations, and the International Financial Institutions to encourage economic growth, raise standards of living, and predict and prevent—to the extent possible—economic and financial crises.

In addition to monetary functions, the Department of the Treasury also oversees critical functions in enforcement, economic policy development, and international treaty negotiation, to name a few.

Internal Revenue Service

The Internal Revenue Service (IRS) is responsible for determining, assessing, and collecting internal revenue in the United States. This revenue consists of personal and corporate income taxes; excise, estate, and gift taxes; as well as employment taxes for the nation's Social Security system.

In addition, the IRS is an important enforcement agency within the Department of the Treasury. There are two law enforcement units within the IRS. The first, Criminal Investigation Internal Security Inspectors, investigate prospective employees' backgrounds and alleged cases of misconduct or illegal activities involving IRS personnel. IRS law enforcement personnel have powers limited by the various federal tax laws, but they cooperate with and assist local enforcement personnel in matters of mutual concern. Criminal Investigation Division Special Agents investigate tax fraud including failure to file tax returns and evasion of income or miscellaneous federal taxes.

Criminal Investigation Internal Security Inspector

The Inspection Service, an essential part of the IRS, carries out responsibilities of great importance to America and its citizens. It has the mission of ensuring that high standards of honesty exist and are maintained at all levels of operation in the Internal Revenue Service.

The Inspection Service's two basic operations are Internal Audit and Internal Security. Staff members in these units are responsible for making sure that the IRS maintains a reputation as one of the most efficient government agencies with personnel who meet high standards of honesty, loyalty, and conduct.

Internal Security Inspectors make up the IRS's own investigative unit, and their duties are varied and often complex. Part of their work requires conducting detailed character and background investigations of prospective IRS employees including applicants or appointees to technical or nontechnical jobs and those involved with handling funds; public accountants and former IRS employees who apply to represent taxpayers at IRS hearings; and those involved in charges of unethical conduct by lawyers, accountants, or others involved in IRS proceedings. Of primary importance to these Inspectors are complaints or information that indicates possible wrongdoing by IRS employees. Attempts made to bribe or corrupt employees to obtain improper advantage in tax matters threaten the integrity of the IRS, and swift action is required to gather evidence, resolve the accusations, and take whatever measures are necessary to protect trust in the agency.

Internal Security Inspectors also investigate attempts to influence or interfere with the administration of IRS statutes through the use of threats, assaults, and similar methods. They are often assigned as armed escorts responsible for protecting IRS employees and government witnesses in legal proceedings. Other duties performed by Inspectors include investigation of cases in which federal tax information was illegally disclosed, either by IRS personnel or by preparers who were given this information in confidence; accidents involving IRS employees or property that result in civil law suits;

and the conduct of special investigations, studies, and inquiries when directed by the Secretary of the Treasury, the Commissioner of the Internal Revenue Service, or other high-level officials. Internal Security Inspectors work cooperatively with law enforcement personnel of other agencies and at times may assist in providing security for the president of the United States and other American or foreign dignitaries.

Internal Security Inspectors may be assigned to workstations at the National Office of the Internal Revenue Service in Washington, D.C., or to one of the regional or district offices found throughout the United States. There are fifty-eight IRS district offices with at least one in each of the fifty states. Regional offices are located in the following cities: San Francisco, Dallas, Cincinnati, Chicago, Atlanta, Philadelphia, and New York. Internal Security Inspectors work irregular schedules in excess of 40 hours a week and may have to travel to carry out their duties. They often work under stress and are subject to personal risks during certain assignments.

- **Training and Promotion:** Special Agent candidates are required to attend a comprehensive training program at the Federal Law Enforcement Training Center. Training begins with an orientation program sponsored by the National Criminal Investigation Training Academy. Generally, the prospects for advancement in this field are favorable, and those who demonstrate the ability to assume more difficult and responsible tasks may compete for higher-level technical, supervisory, and managerial positions.

- **Basic Qualifications:** Applicants must be U.S. citizens and must not have reached their 37th birthday at the time of certification. Applicants must be available to work anywhere in the United States. Applicants must carry and use a firearm. They are required to possess a valid driver's license.

Criminal Investigation Special Agent

Criminal violations of the Internal Revenue Code, with the exception of those relating to alcohol, tobacco, and firearms, are the responsibility of the second law enforcement unit within the IRS—Special Agents of the Criminal Investigation Division (CID). Attempts to evade or defeat a tax and willful failure to file returns are the principal violations with which Special Agents are concerned. Their investigations center primarily on income, employment, and excise taxes and are carried out to the extent necessary to determine whether violations of federal tax laws have occurred. If violations took place, Special Agents must then gather sufficient evidence to prove guilt beyond a reasonable doubt. Tax fraud occurs in a variety of occupations and income groups. Examples of those who may be recommended for prosecution are attorneys, accountants, politicians, proprietors of businesses, tax protesters, corporate officers, narcotics dealers, and physicians. Tax evaders often use clever methods to avoid tax payments, and their criminal acts often take place over a period of years. As a result, investigations are made difficult by the numerous transactions taking place during those years plus the sizeable number of records requiring analysis.

The investigation process begins when the Criminal Investigation Division in a particular tax district receives reports about alleged tax violations. Typical sources of this information include IRS Agents, Tax Technicians, and Revenue Officers; IRS Special Agents working on related cases; officers of other federal, state, and local law enforcement agencies; and informants. The information is evaluated by supervisory personnel and, if criminal violations are indicated, the case is assigned to a Special Agent of the CID. Initially, Special Agents attempt to determine the true taxable income of the subject and whether a deliberate attempt was made to understate income or to avoid filing a tax return. They do this by interviewing the subject, key witnesses, and other parties to the case. Any evidence gathered is carefully recorded, evaluated, and organized. In certain instances, individuals involved in a case may be hostile or reluctant to give information, or they may give false testimony to protect the taxpayer in question. Special Agents, however, are quite skilled at spotting tax frauds and uncovering unreported income or hidden assets. In cases in which taxpayer records are withheld, lost, destroyed, or altered, Special Agents are faced with the difficult task of reconstructing these records by locating alternative sources of information. They do so by investigating the subject's personal and financial history and by examining such items as bank records and canceled checks, brokerage accounts, property transactions, and tax returns filed in past years. These activities require a sound knowledge of accounting and tax law procedures, rules of evidence, and the constitutional rights of individuals involved in the case.

In addition to gathering data, Special Agents engage in surveillance of suspects and are authorized to conduct searches and arrest individuals using physical force or firearms as necessary to protect human life. Once a case assignment is concluded, Special Agents prepare detailed reports of all information gathered during the investigation process. These reports contain a history of the investigation, evidence of additional income and intent to defraud, the subject's explanation and defense of actions, and any evidence that either proves or disproves the subject's defense. In addition, the report contains the Special Agents' conclusions about the case as well as recommendations about criminal prosecution and civil penalties.

If the subject of the investigation is brought to trial, Special Agents assist the U.S. Attorney in preparing the case and usually appear as principal witnesses for the government. An important function of IRS Special Agents involves investigations of organized crime activities. Under federal law, income from illegal sources such as bootlegging, prostitution, and narcotics sales is subject to tax. Such income is used by members of organized crime to support other illegal activities or to infiltrate legitimate businesses. As a result of IRS investigations, many crime figures have been prosecuted and convicted of tax evasion, resulting in substantial blows to the financial resources of criminal groups. As part of this effort, the Internal Revenue Service participates in the Federal Organized Crime Strike Force Program and works on a cooperating basis with other law enforcement agencies at all levels of government.

Special Agents may be assigned to work locations at the National Office of the Internal Revenue Service in Washington, D.C., or to one of the regional or district offices located throughout the United States.

Regional offices are situated in the following cities: New York, Philadelphia, Atlanta, Chicago, Cincinnati, Dallas, and San Francisco. There are fifty-eight district offices with at least one in each of the fifty states.

Special Agents may be required to travel during the course of investigations, and working hours are sometimes irregular and in excess of 40 hours a week. In addition, they often work under stress and are exposed to the risk of physical harm when participating in arrests.

- **Training and Promotion:** Special Agent candidates are required to attend a comprehensive training program at the Federal Law Enforcement Training Center. Training begins with an orientation program sponsored by the National Criminal Investigation Training Academy. Students then attend a nine-week Criminal Investigation Training Program (CITP) that covers basic federal criminal investigation techniques including federal criminal law, courtroom procedures, enforcement operations, interviewing, and firearms training common to all federal law enforcement agents. After CITP is completed, the candidates continue on to Criminal Investigation's sixteen-week specialized training which includes instruction in tax law, criminal tax fraud, money laundering, and a variety of financial fraud schemes. Candidates are also introduced to agency specific undercover operations, electronic surveillance techniques, forensic sciences, court procedures, interviewing techniques and trial preparation and testifying.

  The training emphasizes the development of both technical and behavioral skills. It incorporates a highly interactive methodology of course delivery coupled with a high expectation of trainee interaction throughout the program. It is designed to provide new Agents with the opportunity to learn and practice progressively more complex tasks required to be performed on the job.

  Prospects for advancement in this work are generally good. Individuals who demonstrate the skills needed to assume higher-level duties may eventually move into supervisory or higher managerial positions.

- **Basic Qualifications:** Applicants must be U.S. citizens and must not have reached their 37th birthday at the time of certification. Applicants must be available to work anywhere in the United States. Applicants must carry and use a firearm. They are required to possess a valid driver's license.

For specific information about working conditions, training and promotional opportunities, and application requirements, log on to the Department of the Treasury Web site at www.treas.gov.

DEPARTMENT OF VETERANS AFFAIRS

The Department of Veterans Affairs (VA) was established on March 15, 1989, succeeding the Veterans Administration. It is responsible for providing federal benefits to veterans and their families. Headed by the Secretary of Veterans Affairs, the VA is the second largest of the fifteen Cabinet departments and operates national programs for health care, financial assistance, and burial benefits.

Of the 24.8 million veterans currently alive, nearly three quarters served during a war or an official period of conflict. About a quarter of the nation's population, approximately 63 million people, are potentially eligible for VA benefits and services because they are veterans, family members, or survivors of veterans.

The responsibility to care for veterans, spouses, survivors, and dependents can last a long time. The last dependent of a Revolutionary War veteran died in 1911. Five children of Civil War veterans still draw VA benefits. About 440 children and widows of Spanish-American War veterans still receive VA compensation or pensions.

Disability compensation is a monetary benefit paid to veterans who are disabled by injury or disease incurred or aggravated during active military service. Veterans with low incomes who are permanently and totally disabled may be eligible for monetary support through the VA's pension program. In fiscal year 2004, the VA provided $27.6 billion in disability compensation, death compensation, and pension to 3.4 million people. About 2.9 million veterans received disability compensation or pensions from the VA. Also receiving VA benefits were 539,290 spouses, children, and parents of deceased veterans. Among them are 145,740 survivors of Vietnam veterans and 265,456 survivors of World War II veterans.

Since 1944, when the first GI Bill began, more than 21 million veterans, service members, and family members have received $72 billion in GI Bill benefits for education and training. The number of GI Bill recipients includes 7.8 million veterans from World War II, 2.4 million from the Korean War, and 8.2 million post–Korean War and post–Vietnam War veterans, plus active-duty personnel. Since the dependents program was enacted in 1956, the VA also has assisted in the education of more than 700,000 dependents of veterans whose deaths or total disabilities were service connected. Since the Vietnam era, there have been approximately 2 million veterans, service members, reservists, and National Guardsmen who have participated in the Veterans' Educational Assistance Program, established in 1977, and the Montgomery GI Bill, established in 1985.

Perhaps the most visible of all VA benefits and services is health care. From fifty-four hospitals in 1930, the VA's health-care system now includes 157 medical centers, with at least one in each state, Puerto Rico, and the District of Columbia. The VA operates more than 1,300 sites of care, including 862 ambulatory care and community-based outpatient clinics, 134 nursing homes, 42 residential rehabilitation treatment programs, 207 Veterans Centers, and 88 comprehensive home-care programs. VA health-care facilities provide a broad spectrum of medical, surgical, and rehabilitative care.

More than 5 million people received care in VA health-care facilities in 2004. By the end of fiscal year 2004, 78 percent of all disabled and low-income veterans had enrolled with the VA for health care; 65 percent of them were treated by the VA. In 2004, VA inpatient facilities treated 587,000 patients. The VA's outpatient clinics registered nearly 54 million visits.

From 1944, when the VA began helping veterans purchase homes under the original GI Bill, through January 2005, about 17.7 million VA home-loan guarantees have been issued, with a total value of $866 billion. The VA began fiscal year 2005 with 2.5 million active home loans reflecting amortized loans totaling $207.3 billion.

In 1973, the Army transferred eighty-two national cemeteries to the VA, which now manages them through its National Cemetery Administration. Currently, the VA maintains 120 national cemeteries in thirty-nine states and Puerto Rico.

VA Office of Security and Law Enforcement

The mission of the Office of Security and Law Enforcement is to ensure that VA facilities deliver quality police services to hospitalized veterans, their families and visitors, and to the staff who serve them.

The Office of Security and Law Enforcement is responsible for the physical security and police programs of the VA.

Police Officer

Police Officers provide direction, guidance, and support for law enforcement and physical security programs at VA medical centers and other VA facilities. Police Officers also provide consultation and liaison services to all elements of the Department and work closely with other federal law enforcement agencies.

Responsibilities include foot and vehicle patrols; enforcement of federal and state criminal laws and VA regulations; responding to calls for service, disturbances, assaults by patients and visitors, accidents, alarms, bomb threats, demonstrations, fires, crimes in progress, and emergency situations; writing detailed reports; conducting interviews and interrogations; collecting and preserving evidence; and investigating criminal incidents. Although VA Police Officers are authorized to carry chemical weapons and batons, authority to carry firearms will vary from one VA facility to another.

- **Training and Promotion:** The VA Law Enforcement Training Center provides professional training for VA Police Officers throughout the system. VA Police Officers attend a four-week Basic Police Officer Training Course that includes instruction in subjects such as criminal law, laws of arrest, use-of-force encounters, human behavior, conflict resolution, and other topics pertaining to policing in a health-care environment. Promotional opportunities depend on availability and individual performance evaluations.

- **Basic Qualifications:** Applicants must be U.S. citizens. Requirements for appointment to GS-4 include six months of general experience and six months of specialized experience, or two years of education above high school related to the occupation; for GS-5, one year of specialized experience equivalent to GS-4, or four years of undergraduate course work leading to a bachelor's degree related to law enforcement, criminal investigation or criminology; and for GS-6 through GS-9, one year of specialized experience equivalent to the next lower grade level.

  For specific information about working conditions, training and promotional opportunities, and application requirements, log on to the Department of Veterans Affairs Web site at www.va.gov.

SUMMING IT UP

- The list of departments and agencies mentioned in this chapter is by no means comprehensive. It represents the most popular law enforcement positions within the Executive Branch.

- Once you have decided on a career path, make sure to thoroughly research the job itself, including working conditions, training requirements, salary and benefits, and the details of the application process.

- Many federal law enforcement positions require extensive travel, and most require relocation at some time during one's career.

Legislative and Judicial Branches

OVERVIEW

- U.S. Capitol Police
- U.S. Supreme Court Police
- Summing it up

U.S. CAPITOL POLICE

One of the ten largest local police agencies in the United States, the Metropolitan Police District of Columbia (MPDC) is the primary law enforcement agency for the District of Columbia. Founded in 1861, the MPDC of today is on the forefront of technological crime-fighting advances—from highly developed advances in evidence analysis to state-of-the-art information technology. These modern techniques are combined with a contemporary community policing philosophy, referred to as Policing for Prevention. Community policing bonds the police and residents in a working partnership designed to organize and mobilize residents, merchants, and professionals to improve the quality of life for all who live, work, and visit the nation's Capitol.

U.S. Capitol Police Officer

U.S. Capitol Police (USCP) are responsible for protecting life and property; preventing, detecting, and investigating criminal acts; enforcing traffic regulations within the Capitol area; and provide police service and protection for government facilities, parks, and roadways within the metropolitan limits. As the agency with sole statutory responsibility for providing protective and law enforcement services for the U.S. Congress, USCP Officers monitor close-circuit television surveillance monitors, alarms, and intrusion detection devices; screen visitors and packages that enter the buildings; perform foot and vehicle patrols; respond to crimes in progress, disturbances, protests and demonstrations, bomb threats, and emergency calls for service; conduct traffic control and enforcement; assist the U.S. Secret Service with operations for the protection of the president, vice president, immediate family members of the president and vice president, and visiting dignitaries on Capitol grounds; and provide personal protection for members of Congress and their families in the Capitol complex.

chapter 3

USCP Officers may also be called upon to assist in operations to ensure that Congress is free to operate and function within a safe and secure environment by working with federal law enforcement agencies as needed.

- **Training and Promotion:** USPC Officers attend the nine-week Basic Police Training Program at the Federal Law Enforcement Training Center. After successful completion of the basic training, applicants attend a ten-week course at the Capital Police Training Academy in Washington, D.C., which focuses on the District of Columbia Criminal Code and traffic laws. This course is followed by a ten-week field training program in which new Officers perform their duties accompanied by experienced Field Training Officers. In-service training may include courses in legal issues, public relations, protective operations, firearms proficiency, defensive tactics, and other subjects. Promotions are based on availability, testing, and performance evaluations.

- **Basic Qualifications:** Applicants for USCP Officer must be U.S. citizens; possess a high school diploma or GED certificate; and be at least 21 years old but under the age of 37 at the time of appointment. Applicants must pass a written examination, oral interview, polygraph examination, background investigation, physical examination, and psychological evaluation.

For specific information about working conditions, training and promotional opportunities, and application requirements, log on to the U.S. Capitol Police Web site at www.uscapitolpolice.gov.

U.S. SUPREME COURT POLICE

U.S. Supreme Court Police Officers are responsible for the protection of personnel, visitors, and property of the U.S. Supreme Court.

U.S. Supreme Court Police Officer

These officers perform a variety of law enforcement and security functions that include foot and vehicle patrol of Court facilities, grounds, and streets; personal protection throughout the United States of the Chief Justice and Associate Justices of the Supreme Court, official guests of the Court, and officers or employees of the Court while individuals are engaged in their duties; building security and surveillance; courtroom security; responding to crimes in progress; disturbances, bomb threats, and emergency situations; policing protests and demonstrations on Supreme Court grounds; and rendering first aid and assistance to Supreme Court visitors.

- **Training and Promotion:** Supreme Court Police Officers attend the nine-week Basic Police Training Program at the Federal Law Enforcement Training Center. Basic training is followed by a six-month Orientation and Field Training Program at the Supreme Court and includes courses related to specific duties of the position under the guidance of a Field Training Officer. In-service training may include courses in security procedures, personal protective operations, legal issues and updates, firearms proficiency, defensive tactics, and first aid.

  The Supreme Court Police boasts one the highest entry-level salaries among Washington, D.C.'s myriad law-enforcement entities. A freshly minted Supreme Court Police Officer can make as much as $46,653. Promotional opportunities are limited based on availability and performance evaluations.

- **Basic Qualifications:** Applicants for this position must be U.S. citizens, possess a high school diploma, and have a valid driver's license and an excellent driving record. Two years of college education and prior law enforcement or security experience is preferred. Furthermore, applicants must be mature, reliable, and skilled in oral and written communications; have good interpersonal skills; and pass an oral interview, background investigation, and medical examination.

For specific information about working conditions, training and promotional opportunities, and application requirements, log on to the U.S. Supreme Court Web site at www.supremecourtus.gov.

SUMMING IT UP

- Though much more limited, federal law enforcement opportunities are available with the Legislative and Judicial Branches of government.

- U.S. Capitol Police Officers are responsible for protecting life and property; preventing, detecting, and investigating criminal acts; enforcing traffic regulations within the Capitol area; and providing police service and protection for government facilities, parks, and roadways within the metropolitan limits.

- U.S. Supreme Court Police Officers are responsible for the protection of personnel, visitors, and property of the U.S. Supreme Court.

Independent Agencies

OVERVIEW

- **Central Intelligence Agency**
- **Defense Nuclear Facilities Safety Board**
- **Federal Communications Commission**
- **Federal Deposit Insurance Corporation**
- **Federal Election Commission**
- **Federal Protective Service**
- **Federal Reserve Board**
- **Postal Inspection Service**
- **Summing it up**

CENTRAL INTELLIGENCE AGENCY

The Central Intelligence Agency (CIA) was created in 1947 with the signing of the National Security Act. The act also created a Director of Central Intelligence (DCI) to serve as head of the U.S. intelligence community; act as the principal adviser to the president for intelligence matters related to national security; and serve as head of the CIA.

The Director of Central Intelligence serves as the head of the CIA and reports to the Director of National Intelligence. The CIA director's responsibilities include:

- collecting intelligence through human sources and by other appropriate means, except that he or she shall have no police, subpoena, or law enforcement powers or internal security functions

- correlating and evaluating intelligence related to the national security and providing appropriate dissemination of such intelligence

- providing overall direction for and coordination of the collection of national intelligence outside the United States

- performing such other functions and duties related to intelligence affecting national security as the president or the Director of National Intelligence may direct.

The function of the Central Intelligence Agency is to assist the Director of Central Intelligence in carrying out the responsibilities outlined above. To accomplish its

chapter 4

mission, the CIA engages in research, development, and deployment of high-leverage technology for intelligence purposes. As a separate agency, the CIA serves as an independent source of analysis on topics of concern and also works closely with the other organizations in the intelligence community to ensure that the intelligence consumer—whether a national policymaker or battlefield commander—receives the best intelligence possible.

As changing global realities have reordered the national security agenda, the CIA has met these challenges by:

- creating special, multidisciplinary centers to address such high-priority issues as nonproliferation, counterterrorism, counterintelligence, international organized crime and narcotics trafficking, the environment, and arms-control intelligence
- forging stronger partnerships between the several intelligence collection disciplines and all-source analysis
- taking an active part in intelligence community analytical efforts and producing all-source analysis on the full range of topics that affect national security
- contributing to the effectiveness of the overall intelligence community by managing services of common concern in imagery analysis and open-source collection and participating in partnerships with other intelligence agencies in the areas of research and development and technical collection
- emphasizing adaptability in its approach to intelligence collection so that the CIA can tailor its support to key intelligence consumers and help them meet their needs as they face the issues of the post-Cold War world

Special Investigator

CIA Special Investigators conduct sensitive and high-profile inquiries into possible violations of laws, rules, and regulations; mismanagement; gross waste of funds; abuse of authority; or substantial and specific danger to the public health and safety within the CIA.

Special Investigators work independently and as leaders or members of investigative teams. Foreign travel opportunities are available. Special Investigators are authorized to conduct surveillance and undercover operations, carry firearms, make arrests, execute search warrants, and serve subpoenas. Investigations may be conducted jointly with other federal agencies as well as state and local agencies.

- **Training and Promotion:** Special Investigators attend an eight-week Criminal Investigator Training Program at the Federal Law Enforcement Training Center. In-service training is specific to the needs and objectives of the Agency and focuses on fraud investigations, interviewing techniques, and legal issues.

- **Basic Qualifications:** Applicants must be U.S. citizens. Other requirements include a bachelor's degree with a strong academic record and four years of investigative or equivalent experience focused on complex matters with an excellent performance record. Candidates must have considerable professional knowledge of criminal and administrative investigative techniques and procedures; be able to assemble and assimilate large quantities of data, discern key issues, and draw appropriate conclusions; have the ability to work independently or as part of an investigation team; be able to work under pressure and with short deadlines; interact effectively with people who have different values, cultures, or backgrounds; use sound judgment and elicit information in difficult and sensitive situations; prioritize multiple projects and tasks; and communicate clearly, concisely, and effectively with technical and nontechnical personnel.

  This position also requires considerable negotiation skills, employing tact, discretion, and diplomacy. All Special Investigator positions require a writing test, interviews, and preliminary reference checks. All applicants must successfully complete a thorough medical and psychological exam, a polygraph interview, and an extensive background investigation.

Protective Security Officer

It is the function of the CIA to provide timely, reliable, and useful information to the president and national policymakers. Within this mission, it is the role of the Office of Security to provide a comprehensive, worldwide security program that protects Agency personnel, programs, information, facilities, and activities. The mission of the Protective Security Officer is the protection of Agency personnel, facilities, and information through the enforcement of federal laws and agency regulations.

- **Training and Promotion:** New appointees receive intensive training at the Federal Law Enforcement Training Center and other specialized training facilities. Training includes coursework in police procedures, psychology, police/community relations, criminal law, first aid, laws of arrest, search and seizure, and physical defense techniques. Officers also attend yearly in-service training focusing on tactics, legal issues, and firearms.

- **Basic Qualifications:** Applicants must be at least 21 years old, physically fit, and possess a valid driver's license. Other requirements include a high school diploma or equivalent. Military experience (military police or Marine security guard preferred) and police or significant security experience are also needed. An associate's or bachelor's degree in criminal justice or a related field is preferred. This position requires a thirty-six–month commitment to the Agency before seeking other opportunities within the Agency.

For specific information about working conditions, training and promotional opportunities, and application requirements, log on to the Central Intelligence Agency Web site at www.cia.gov.

DEFENSE NUCLEAR FACILITIES SAFETY BOARD

For nearly half a century, the Department of Energy (DOE) and its predecessor agencies operated the nation's defense nuclear weapons complex without independent external oversight. In the late 1980s, it became increasingly clear to members of Congress that significant public health and safety issues had accumulated at many of the aging facilities in the weapons complex. As an outgrowth of these concerns, Congress created the Defense Nuclear Facilities Safety Board as an independent oversight organization within the Executive Branch. The Board is charged with providing advice and recommendations to the Secretary of Energy "to ensure adequate protection of public health and safety" at DOE's defense nuclear facilities.

Broadly speaking, the Board is responsible for independent oversight of all activities affecting nuclear safety within DOE's nuclear weapons complex. Prior to the end of the nuclear arms race, the nuclear weapons complex concentrated on the design, manufacture, test, and maintenance of the nation's nuclear arsenal. The complex is now engaged in cleanup of contaminated sites and facilities, disassembly of nuclear weapons to achieve arms-control objectives, maintenance of the smaller stockpile, and storage and disposition of excess fissionable materials. All of these hazardous activities must be carried out in strict observance of health and safety requirements.

Special Agent

Department of Energy (DOE) Office of Inspector General (OIG) Special Agents investigate fraud, waste, abuse, and mismanagement in these and other programs and operations of the Board that require large budget outlays and may be victim of fraudulent activity. Program fraud investigators will often focus on Board contractors or grantees, and include offenses such as falsification of contractor certified payrolls, overcharging for goods and services, misappropriation of funds, violation of project construction permits, and theft of government property. Special Agents also investigate Board personnel misconduct, including violations such as embezzlement, theft of government property and supplies, and fraudulent claims. Special Agents are authorized to conduct surveillance and undercover operations, carry firearms, make arrests, execute search warrants, and serve subpoenas. Investigations may be conducted jointly with other federal agencies as well as state and local governments.

- **Training and Promotion:** DOE-OIG Special Agents attend the eight-week Criminal Investigator Training Program at the Federal Law Enforcement Training Center. In-service training may include courses in DOE program investigations, legal issues and updates, DOE regulations, investigative techniques, criminal and civil law, first aid and CPR, arrest techniques, defensive tactics, and firearms proficiency. Promotional opportunities are determined by availability and performance evaluations.

- **Basic Qualifications:** Special Agent applicants must be U.S. citizens and at least 21 years old but under the age of 37. Eyesight requirements include "sufficiently good vision in each eye, with or without correction." New Agents are generally appointed at the GS-5 level while having completed a four-year course of study leading to a bachelor's degree, or three years' general experience, one year of which is equivalent to GS-4. Appointment at the GS-7 level requires one year of graduate education, or superior academic achievement during undergraduate studies.

For specific information about working conditions, training and promotional opportunities, and application requirements, log on to the Defense Nuclear Facilities Safety Board Web site at www.dnfsb.gov.

FEDERAL COMMUNICATIONS COMMISSION

The Federal Communications Commission (FCC) is an independent government agency. The FCC was established by the Communications Act of 1934 and is charged with regulating interstate and international communications by radio, television, wire, satellite, and cable. The FCC's jurisdiction covers the fifty states, the District of Columbia, and U.S. possessions.

There are six operating Bureaus and ten Staff Offices. The Bureaus' responsibilities include processing applications for licenses and other filings, analyzing complaints, conducting investigations, developing and implementing regulatory programs, and taking part in hearings. Even though the Bureaus and Offices have their individual functions, they regularly join forces and share expertise in addressing Commission issues.

The Office of Homeland Security (OHS) assists the Enforcement Bureau in its support of the Defense Commissioner, oversees rulemaking proceedings relating to the Emergency Alert System, and operates the Communication and Crisis Management Center (CCMC). It also supports the Homeland Security Policy Council and other Bureaus in achieving the objectives established in the Homeland Security portion of the agency's Strategic Plan. OHS provides intra- and interagency coordination on all matters concerning homeland security, National Security/Emergency Preparedness (NS/EP), public warning, and continuity of government.

Special Agent

Special Agents of the Enforcement Bureau conduct investigations of complaints; interview witnesses, experts, and subjects of investigation; develop sources of information; obtain and review documentary and other evidence; coordinate investigative activities with U.S. Attorneys; and testify before grand juries and in subsequent criminal proceedings. Special Agents are authorized to conduct surveillances and undercover operations, and serve subpoenas.

- **Training and Promotion:** Special Agents attend the eight-week Criminal Investigators Training Program at the Federal Law Enforcement Training Center. In-service training may include courses that focus on Commission's operations and policies, financial investigations, workers' compensation fraud, contract and procurement fraud, personnel misconduct, and investigative techniques.

- **Basic Qualifications:** Applicants must be U.S. citizens and at least 21 years old but under the age of 37.

For specific information about working conditions, training and promotional opportunities, and application requirements, log on to the Federal Communications Commission Web site at www.fcc.gov.

FEDERAL DEPOSIT INSURANCE CORPORATION

The Federal Deposit Insurance Corporation (FDIC) preserves and promotes public confidence in the U.S. financial system by insuring deposits in banks and thrift institutions for up to $100,000; by identifying, monitoring, and addressing risks to the deposit insurance funds; and by limiting the effect on the economy and the financial system when a bank or thrift institution fails.

An independent agency of the federal government, the FDIC was created in 1933 in response to the thousands of bank failures that occurred in the 1920s and early 1930s. Since the start of FDIC insurance on January 1, 1934, no depositor has lost a single cent of insured funds as a result of a failure. To protect insured depositors, the FDIC responds immediately when a bank or thrift institution fails. Institutions generally are closed by their chartering authority—the state regulator, the Office of the Comptroller of the Currency, or the Office of Thrift Supervision.

Special Agent

FDIC Special Agents investigate violations of federal statutes or regulations related to matters under FDIC jurisdiction, with particular emphasis on white-collar crime. Investigations often focus on fraud committed by FDIC contractors and include offenses such as falsification of contractor certified payrolls, billing the FDIC for work that was not performed, altering invoices from subcontractors, overcharging for goods and services, bribery, embezzlement, and kickbacks. Special Agents are authorized to conduct surveillances and undercover operations, carry firearms, make arrests, execute search warrants, and serve subpoenas.

- **Training and Promotion:** Special Agents attend the eight-week Criminal Investigator Training Program at the Federal Law Enforcement Training Center. In-service training may include courses in FDIC program investigations, legal issues and updates, FDIC regulations, investigative techniques, criminal and civil law, first aid and CPR, arrest techniques, defensive tactics, and firearms proficiency. Promotional opportunities are determined by availability and performance evaluations.

- **Basic Qualifications:** Applicants must be U.S. citizens and at least 21 years old but under the age of 37. Eyesight requirements include "sufficiently good vision in each eye, with or without correction." New Agents are generally appointed at the GS-5 level while having completed a four-year course of study leading to a bachelor's degree, or three years' general experience, one year of which is equivalent to GS-4. Appointment at the GS-7 level requires one year of graduate education, or superior academic achievement during undergraduate studies.

For specific information about working conditions, training and promotional opportunities, and application requirements, log on to the Federal Deposit Insurance Corporation Web site at www.fdic.gov.

FEDERAL ELECTION COMMISSION

In 1975 Congress created the Federal Election Commission (FEC) to administer and enforce the Federal Election Campaign Act (FECA), the statute that governs the financing of federal elections. The duties of the FEC, which is an independent regulatory agency, are to disclose campaign finance information, to enforce the provisions of the law such as the limits and prohibitions on contributions, and to oversee the public funding of presidential elections.

The FEC administers the public funding program by determining which candidates are eligible to receive the funds. Committees receiving public funds must keep detailed records of their financial activities. After the elections, the FEC audits each publicly funded committee. If an audit reveals that a committee has exceeded the spending limits or used public funds for impermissible purposes, the committee must pay back an appropriate amount to the U.S. Treasury.

The Commission has exclusive jurisdiction over the civil enforcement of the federal campaign finance law.

FEC staff may generate enforcement actions (called Matters Under Review, or MURs) in the course of reviewing the reports filed by committees. In addition, individuals and groups outside the agency may initiate MURs by filing complaints. Other government agencies may also refer enforcement matters to the FEC.

If four of the six Commissioners vote to find reason to believe that a violation of the law has occurred, the Commission may investigate the matter. If the Commission decides that the investigation by the FEC's Office of General Counsel confirms that the law has been violated, the Commission tries to resolve the matter by reaching a conciliation agreement with the respondents. The agreement may require them to pay a civil penalty and take other remedial steps. If an agreement cannot be reached, however, the Commission may file suit against the appropriate persons in a U.S. District Court.

Investigator

Investigators of the FEC plan and conduct investigations concerning violations of the Federal Election Campaign Act (FECA) relating to public funding of presidential elections, public disclosure of financial activities of political committees involved in federal elections, and limitations and prohibitions on contributions and expenditures to influence federal elections. The primary responsibilities include review of complaints of FECA violations; locating records, individuals, and entities; locating assets, and identifying personal and business affiliations; interviewing witnesses and preparation of affidavits; examining financial reports and documents; identifying money-laundering activities; analyzing and summarizing results of investigations; preparing written investigative reports; conducting follow-up investigations to obtain supplemental evidence in cases considered for litigation; assisting attorneys in disposition considerations; and participating in pretrial and trial proceedings.

- **Training and Promotion:** Initial and in-service training for FEC Investigators includes an orientation that covers the mission, policies, procedures, and rules of the agency, and periodic instruction related to specific responsibilities of the position. Promotional opportunities are limited.

- **Basic Qualifications:** FEC Investigators are generally fully trained investigators and experienced in white-collar investigations. Applicants must be U.S. citizens and at least 21 years old but under the age of 37. Eyesight requirements include "sufficiently good vision in each eye, with or without correction." New Investigators are generally appointed at the GS-5 level while having completed a four-year course of study leading to a bachelor's degree, or three years' general experience, one year of which was equivalent to GS-4. Appointment at the GS-7 level requires one year of graduate education, or superior academic achievement during undergraduate studies.

For specific information about working conditions, training and promotional opportunities, and application requirements, log on to the Federal Election Commission Web site at www.fec.gov.

FEDERAL PROTECTIVE SERVICE

The Federal Protective Service (FPS) is the law enforcement and security arm of the Public Building Service, a division of the U.S. General Service Administration (GSA). The mission of the Federal Protective Service is to provide law enforcement and security services to over one million tenants and daily visitors to all federally owned and leased facilities nationwide. The FPS focuses directly on the interior security of the nation and the reduction of crimes and potential threats to federal facilities throughout the nation.

Physical Security Specialist

FPS Physical Security Specialists are responsible for protection services to all federal facilities throughout the U.S. and its territories, which include: providing a visible uniformed police presence; management and oversight of 10,000 armed contract security guards; responding to criminal incidents and emergencies with full law enforcement authority; authority to detain and arrest individuals and seize goods or vehicles; comprehensive intelligence-sharing capability at the federal, state, and local levels; and participation in national and local Federal Antiterrorism Task Forces. Specialized response capabilities include providing Canine and Weapons of Mass Destruction Teams; providing protection during demonstrations, protests, and acts of civil unrest; investigating criminal incidents; continuous monitoring of building alarms/emergencies through four FPS mega-centers; conducting building vulnerability and security assessments; implementing appropriate security threat countermeasures; purchasing/installing/monitoring security equipment and enhancements to designated buildings; providing police emergency services in natural disasters, civil disturbances, and terrorist actions; providing protection support for special events; chairing the Interagency Security Committee to establish governmentwide security policy; presenting formal crime prevention/security awareness presentations to the federal population; conducting background suitability determinations and adjudications for contract security guards and GSA day-care workers; and providing Federal Emergency Management Agency (FEMA) support.

FPS Security Specialists are authorized to carry firearms.

- **Training and Promotion:** FPS Security Specialists normally receive training that covers agency policies and directive, intrusion detection systems and devices, security awareness, access control systems, physical security surveys, crime prevention, applicable laws and regulations, legal updates, investigative techniques, report writing, interview techniques, and agency-specific issues and instructions. Training may be presented by staff; federal, state, or local law enforcement training programs; or academies. Promotions are based on availability and performance reviews.

- **Basic Qualifications:** Applicants must be U.S. citizens and should have a bachelor's degree for appointment to GS-5 level, or three years' general experience, one year of which is equivalent to GS-4; for GS-7, applicants must have one full year of graduate education, or superior academic achievement during undergraduate studies; for GS-9, applicants must have a master's degree or two years of graduate studies, or one year of specialized experience equivalent to GS-7.

FEDERAL RESERVE BOARD

The Federal Reserve Board (FRB) was established by Congress to serve as the nation's central bank. The primary responsibility of the Board is the formulation of monetary policy. The seven Board members constitute a majority of the 12-member Federal Open Market Committee (FOMC)—the group that makes the key decisions affecting the cost and availability of money and credit in the economy.

The Board sets reserve requirements and shares the responsibility with the Reserve Banks for discount rate policy. These two functions plus open market operations constitute the monetary policy tools of the Federal Reserve System.

In addition to monetary policy responsibilities, the Federal Reserve Board has regulatory and supervisory responsibilities over banks that are members of the System, bank holding companies, international banking facilities in the United States, Edge Act and agreement corporations, foreign activities of member banks, and the U.S. activities of foreign-owned banks. The Board also sets margin requirements, which limit the use of credit for purchasing or carrying securities.

In addition, the Board plays a key role in assuring the smooth functioning and continued development of the nation's vast payments system.

Another area of Board responsibility is the development and administration of regulations that implement major federal laws governing consumer credit, such as the Truth in Lending Act, the Equal Credit Opportunity Act, the Home Mortgage Disclosure Act, and the Truth in Savings Act.

Protection Officer

FRB Protection Officers are responsible for the protection of FRB assets, property, employees, tenants, and visitors at Federal Reserve Bank facilities at the twelve bank locations in the United States as well as twenty-five branch locations. Primary responsibilities include screening visitors and controlling access to the Bank and secure areas; inspecting briefcases, packages, and other containers brought into FRB facilities; conducting static post duties and foot patrols; maintaining a control room post; monitoring alarm systems, intrusion control devices, intercoms, and closed-circuit surveillance monitors; maintaining post logs; responding to intrusion and fire alarm emergencies, disturbances, and other incidents; overseeing transfer of assets to and from armored cars; participating in building evacuation drills; and coordinating bomb searches.

- **Training and Promotion:** FRB Protection Officers attend approximately six weeks of initial training conducted by FRB staff pertaining to the mission, policies, procedure, and rules of the agency; Bank layout and design; security post and screening procedures; electronic security and surveillance systems; laws and regulations; firefighting equipment and procedures; conflict resolution; report writing; firearms proficiency; use of force; and other matters related to the dynamics of particular facilities. In-service training may include courses that focus on tactical operations, response to bomb threats, blood-borne pathogens, first aid, and firearms proficiency.

- **Basic Qualifications:** Applicants must be U.S. citizens and at least 21 years old but under the age of 37.

Special Agent

Special Agents of the Federal Reserve Board investigate allegations of wrongdoing, including administrative, civil, and criminal misconduct related to programs and operations administered or financed by the Board as well as violations of Board personnel standards of conduct.

Investigations focus on offenses involving theft or misuse of funds or Board property; false statements, documents, or claims; bribery; acceptance of gratuities; conflicts of interest; preferential treatment; disclosure of confidential information; and other unlawful acts. Special Agents are authorized to conduct surveillance and undercover operations, and serve subpoenas. Investigations may be conducted jointly with other federal agencies and state law enforcement and regulatory agencies.

- **Training and Promotion:** Federal Reserve Board Special Agents attend the eight-week Criminal Investigator Training Program at the Federal Law Enforcement Training Center. In-service training may include courses such as the three-week Inspector General Basic Training Program; instruction relating to Board program investigations, procurement fraud, and legal issues and updates; and courses presented by the Association of Certified Fraud Examiners, the Institute for Internal Auditors, or the Financial Fraud Institute.

- **Basic Qualifications:** Applicants must be U.S. citizens and at least 21 years old but under the age of 37.

For specific information about working conditions, training and promotional opportunities, and application requirements, log on to the Federal Reserve Board Web site at www.federalreserve.gov/general.htm.

POSTAL INSPECTION SERVICE

The protection of the U.S. mail and the mail system is the responsibility of the Postal Inspection Service. As the law enforcement and auditing arm of the U.S. Postal Service, the Postal Inspection Service performs investigative, law enforcement, security, and auditing functions essential to a stable and sound postal system. The Postal Inspection Service has jurisdiction in all criminal matters infringing on the integrity and security of the mail and the safety of all postal valuables, property, and personnel.

Postal Inspector

Postal Inspectors perform a variety of duties and have jurisdiction over eighty-five postal-related laws. Their responsibilities can be divided into three broad areas: criminal investigations, audit investigations, and security/administrative functions. Postal Inspectors engage in more than 250 different types of investigations pertaining to postal operations and illegal activities involving the mail. They conduct criminal investigations of mail thefts and losses caused by damage or destruction of postal property. Other responsibilities include providing security for post office personnel and recovering mail, money, or other properties lost or destroyed. In addition, Postal Inspectors determine whether postal revenues are being protected and whether the Postal Service is operating according to postal laws and regulations.

Criminal investigations deal with illegal acts committed against the U.S. Postal Service, its property, and its personnel. The following are some examples of cases in the jurisdiction of the U.S. Postal Inspection Service: post office burglaries (robberies of postal facilities, vehicles, or mail carriers); embezzlement by postal employees; and thefts from house, apartment, or U.S. Postal Service mailboxes.

Postal Inspectors also investigate cases of fraud involving use of the U.S. mail. These acts include land, charity, and advance-fee schemes; chain letters and lotteries; nonaccredited correspondence schools; and insurance, banking, and credit-card frauds. The result has been the elimination of many fraudulent or borderline operations that cheat the public.

Illegal narcotics traffic is another target of Postal Inspectors who investigate cases of suspected movement of drugs, narcotics, and other controlled substances through the U.S. mail and who work closely with other federal agents in efforts to halt such traffic. Postal Inspectors also probe incidents involving bombs or incendiary devices dispatched through the mail system or directed at properties of the U.S. Postal Service as well as investigate extortion attempts, illegal transport of concealable firearms, and obscene materials sent through the mail.

Once assigned to a case, Postal Inspectors collect, assemble, and evaluate all available data and determine a course of action. Employing professional investigative techniques, they question witnesses and victims to develop leads and identify suspects. Crime laboratory services are used to analyze certain types of evidence that may help in tracing or identifying suspects. Suspects are sometimes kept under surveillance, or stakeouts may be used to locate others involved in a case. Postal Inspectors are armed and empowered by law to apprehend, interrogate, and arrest suspects. They are also authorized to serve warrants and subpoenas to persons involved in a case. All of these powers are restricted to the enforcement of laws covering illegal use of the mail, properties of the U.S. in the custody of the U.S. Postal Service, or other postal offenses. However, these powers are valid even if the Postal Inspector is not on U.S. Postal Service property. Postal Inspectors make comprehensive oral and written reports of data and evidence gathered in a case and submit them to supervisory personnel for evaluation. They work closely with U.S. Attorneys in preparing and prosecuting cases and are often called upon to give testimony during court proceedings.

The next area of responsibility dealt with by Postal Inspectors involves *audits,* which are investigations aimed at evaluating postal operations and identifying problems within the system itself. Using thorough investigative methods, Postal Inspectors determine whether the Postal Service is operating according to postal laws and regulations and in the best interests of the public. They also determine whether postal revenues are adequately protected and used economically. The results of these audits are often beneficial. They lead to reductions in operating costs and increases in management effectiveness in such areas as customer service, mail handling, financial operations, data systems, and work methods and procedures.

Security and administrative functions make up the last area dealt with by Postal Inspectors. Background and security investigations of designated personnel make certain that Postal Service standards are met. Effectiveness of fire, safety, and security systems used in postal facilities are evaluated, and surveys are conducted to determine whether improvements can be introduced. In cases of disaster such as floods, fires, and air or train wrecks, Postal Inspectors direct activities of mobile response units composed of postal security personnel responsible for recovering mail and providing security against theft or looting.

- **Training and Promotion:** Postal Inspectors attend a sixteen-week Basic Training Program at the Postal Inspector Training Academy in Potomac, Maryland. Basic Inspector Training at the Career Development Division (CDD) covers academics, firearms, physical fitness and defensive tactics, and practical exercises. In-service training may include courses that focus on subjects such as criminal law, search and seizure, postal regulations and operations, investigative techniques, defensive tactics, and firearms proficiency. Each candidate must participate fully in all program areas and achieve specific minimum academic and performance levels to graduate. Graduation from basic training is a condition of employment. Failure to meet the minimum academic and performance levels will result in the termination of the appointment.

  Postal Inspectors are appointed at EAS-17 with nearly automatic promotion to EAS-21 within $2\frac{1}{2}$ years. Further promotion is possible to Specialist at EAS-23 and Team Leader at EAS-24. In addition, Postal Inspectors receive a cost-of-living allowance and are eligible for merit increases.

  The advancement potential for Postal Inspectors is excellent, and those who qualify can compete for promotions to supervisory or administrative positions.

- **Basic Qualifications:** Applicants must be U.S. citizens at least 21 years old but under the age of 37; in good physical condition; and possess a bachelor's degree. Applicants must have experience in at least one of the following areas: Postal Service Systems, including two years of Postal Service experience in a supervisory or specialized capacity; internal auditor, including that of Certified Public Accountant, Certified Management Accountant, Certified Internal Auditor, or Certified Information Systems Auditor, and two years' experience conducting internal audits; law enforcement, including two years' experience as a criminal investigator with statutory authority to make arrests; military officers, including active-duty and former commissioned military officers who apply within two years from their date of separation, served at least two years on active duty as an officer, and received an honorable discharge; or foreign language expertise. Applicants must pass a written test, polygraph, drug screen, medical examination, and detailed background investigation.

Postal Police Officer

A Postal Police Officer provides a full range of security services at major post offices and at other postal installations and facilities. The Postal Police Officer may work inside postal buildings or outdoors at loading docks and in parking lots. A Postal Police Officer may be armed.

Postal Police Officers perform all the functions of municipal police officers but within the limited jurisdiction of postal property. Their assignments tend to be concentrated in and near population centers where postal buildings are large and heavily trafficked and where many postal vehicles are garaged and dispatched.

Within postal buildings, Postal Police Officers maintain security against ordinary hazards and sabotage. They assist postal patrons and employees in giving simple directions and when called upon in cases of accident or emergency. While security against fraud within the postal community is the province of Postal Inspectors, Postal Police Officers protect the mails and postal resources against theft.

In other postal facilities—garages, warehouses, equipment repair shops—Postal Police Officers provide the full range of security services, guarding against burglary, hijacking, and other illegal acts. As the nature of criminals and their crimes has become more sophisticated, the work of the Postal Police Officer has become more complex, more challenging, and more dangerous.

- **Training and Promotion:** Advancement opportunities are available for most postal workers because there is a management commitment to provide career development. Also, employees can get preferred assignments, such as the day shift, as their seniority increases. When an opening occurs, employees may submit written requests, called "bids," for assignment to the vacancy. The bidder who meets the qualifications and has the most seniority gets the job.

  Postal Police Officers can advance through police ranks—Sergeant, Lieutenant, Captain—in a manner similar to Municipal, County, or State Police Officers. They may also advance into the ranks of the Postal Inspection Service and become Postal Inspectors.

- **Basic Qualifications:** Applicants must be U.S. citizens at least 21 years old but under the age of 37; possess a conferred, four-year degree from an accredited college or university; pass a comprehensive visual exam; pass a hearing acuity test; be in good physical condition, with weight in proportion to height, and possess emotional and mental stability; have no felony convictions (felony charges may render candidates ineligible); have no misdemeanor conviction of domestic violence (other misdemeanor charges or convictions may render candidates ineligible); and have a current, valid state driver's license, held for at least two years.

For specific information about working conditions, training and promotional opportunities, and application requirements, log on to the U.S. Postal Inspection Service Web site at www.usps.com/postalinspectors.

SUMMING IT UP

- In addition to career opportunities available with the three main branches of government, there are myriad independent agencies that also offer federal law enforcement employment opportunities. These agencies include, but are not limited, to the CIA, Defense Nuclear Facilities Safety Board, FDIC, Federal Election Commission, FCC, Federal Protective Services, Federal Reserve Board, and Postal Inspection Service.

- Always contact the particular agency in which you are interested for information about working conditions, training and promotional opportunities, and application requirements.

Department of Homeland Security

OVERVIEW

- Protecting against a new enemy
- Federal Emergency Management Agency
- Transportation Security Administration
- U.S. Citizenship and Immigration Services
- U.S. Coast Guard
- U.S. Customs and Border Protection
- U.S. Immigration and Customs Enforcement
- U.S. Secret Service
- Summing it up

PROTECTING AGAINST A NEW ENEMY

Since the terrorist attacks of September 11, 2001, the issue of national security has been elevated to the top priority of federal government. Initially, much of the discussion concerning national security focused on the failures of federal law enforcement and intelligence agencies as well as the lack of communication channels between agencies. Add to these problems the traditional protective and competitive nature of government bureaucracies and organizational rivalries; it was very easy to understand the challenges that faced those responsible for the safety and security of this nation. Not an easy task by any measure. Although homeland security is a process of evolution, the effort has been focused on mobilizing the resources of the federal government, state and local governments, the private sector, and the American people to prevent terrorist attacks within the borders of the United States; reduce our nation's vulnerability to terrorist activities; and, should attacks take place, reduce the potential for damage as well as aid in the recovery process.

NOTE

With the creation of the Department of Homeland Security, a single federal agency has been given the authority to directly command existing and yet-to-be established agencies responsible for federal law enforcement and security duties.

The Department, headquartered in Washington, D.C., has its own staff of senior executives and may have its own special agents at some future date. Currently, certain federal civilian law enforcement and security agencies are under the Department's chain of command with certain specific military agencies providing levels of intelligence. The review that follows will focus on the law enforcement and security careers that currently fall under the umbrella of the Department.

FEDERAL EMERGENCY MANAGEMENT AGENCY

The Federal Emergency Management Agency (FEMA), a former independent agency that became part of the Department of Homeland Security in 2003, is tasked with responding to, planning for, recovering from, and mitigating against disasters.

The terrorist attacks of September 11, 2001, and the tragedy resulting from Hurricane Katrina in 2005 focused the Agency on issues of national preparedness and homeland security, and tested the Agency in unprecedented ways. The Agency coordinated its activities with the newly formed Office of Homeland Security, and FEMA's Office of National Preparedness was given responsibility for helping to ensure that the nation's first responders were trained and equipped to deal with Weapons of Mass Destruction.

NOTE

FEMA's mission is to lead America to prepare, prevent, respond, and recover from disasters.

Billions of dollars of new funding were directed to FEMA to help communities face the threat of terrorism. Just a few years past its twentieth anniversary, FEMA was actively directing its "all-hazards" approach to disasters toward homeland security issues. In 2003 FEMA joined twenty-two other federal agencies, programs, and offices in becoming the Department of Homeland Security. The new department was designed to bring a coordinated approach to national security from emergencies and disasters—both natural and manmade. Today FEMA is one of four major branches of DHS. More than 5,000 standby disaster reservists supplement about 2,500 full-time employees in the Emergency Preparedness and Response Directorate.

Special Agent

Special Agents conduct investigations to detect fraud, waste, abuse, and corruption in FEMA programs and operations. Investigations often focus on fraud committed by contractors in FEMA programs and operations. Typical allocations involve false claims by disaster assistant applicants who use fictitious names and addresses, disaster assistant recipients victimized by contractors who inflate repair fees, unlawful filing of applications for disaster relief for losses that were not incurred, embezzlement of funds by Emergency Food and Shelter Program grantees, and various forms of insurance fraud and theft of government property. Investigations also focus on official misconduct by Agency personnel, including offenses such as bribery, collusion, conflict of interest, kickbacks, and embezzlement of federal funds. Specialists such as engineers, auditors, and personnel with expertise in other disciplines are sometimes asked to assist Special Agents with investigations as needed. Special Agents are authorized to conduct surveillance and undercover operations, carry firearms, make arrests, execute search warrants, and serve subpoenas. Investigations may be conducted jointly with other federal agencies as well as with state and local governments.

- **Training and Promotion:** Special Agents attend the eight-week Criminal Investigator Training Program at the Federal Law Enforcement Training Center. In-service training may include courses in FEMA program investigations, legal issues and updates, FEMA regulations, investigative techniques, criminal and civil law, first aid and CPR, arrest techniques, defensive tactics, and firearms proficiency. Promotional opportunities are determined by availability and performance evaluations.

- **Basic Qualifications:** Applicants must meet the minimum qualification requirements as contained in the Office of Personnel Management's Qualification Operating Manual. These are available online at www.opm.gov. The manual states that one year of specialized experience equivalent to the next lower grade in the federal service is required. Specialized experience is experience that is in or directly related to the line of work of the position to be filled and that has equipped the applicant with the particular knowledge, skills, and abilities (KSA) to successfully perform the duties of that position.

Personal Security Specialist

Personal Security Specialists conduct investigations into the suitability, integrity, and loyalty of FEMA employees, applicants for employment, contractors, and other designated personnel.

Responsibilities include preparation, review, and evaluation of investigative reports to determine whether current or prospective employees meet security standards; processing requests concerning Special Access Program and Sensitive Compartmented Information, including access to restricted data pertaining to the North Atlantic Treaty Organization and Department of Energy Operations; processing clearance applications for national security and public trust positions; conducting pre-employment interviews, subject interviews, record checks, and other investigative functions; preparing recommendations for interim suspension of security clearances of cleared personnel on whom significant derogatory information becomes known; and conducting security briefings involving Special Access Program information, foreign contacts, and counterintelligence.

- **Training and Promotion:** Training of Personal Security Specialists consists of instruction that focuses on Agency personnel standards, security clearance eligibility requirements, position sensitivity and security determinations, adverse personnel action and derogatory information, interview techniques, report writing, applicable laws and regulations, legal updates, agency policies and procedures, and other agency-specific training.

- **Basic Qualifications:** Applicants must meet the minimum qualification requirements as contained in the Office of Personnel Management's Qualification Operating Manual. These are available on line at www.opm.gov. The manual states that one year of specialized experience equivalent to the next lower grade in the federal service is required. Specialized experience is experience that is in or directly related to the line of work of the position to be filled and that has equipped the applicant with the particular knowledge, skills, and abilities (KSA) to successfully perform the duties of that position.

U.S. Fire Administration Special Agent

The mission of the U.S. Fire Administration (USFA) is to reduce life and economic losses due to fire and related emergencies, through leadership, advocacy, coordination, and support.

America's fire death rate is one of the highest per capita in the industrialized world. Fire kills 3,700 and injures more than 20,000 people each year. Ironically, America's fire losses today represent a dramatic improvement from more than twenty years ago. In 1971 the United States lost more than 12,000 citizens and 250 firefighters to fire. Acting to halt these tragic losses, Congress passed the Federal Fire Prevention and Control Act in 1974. It established the U.S. Fire Administration and its National Fire Academy (NFA). Since that time, through data collection, public education, research and training efforts, the USFA has helped reduce fire deaths by at least half.

Investigations often focus on fraud committed by contractors in USFA programs and operations. Typical allocations involve false claims by disaster assistant applicants that use fictitious names and addresses; disaster assistant recipients victimized by contractors who inflate repair fees; unlawful filing of applications for disaster relief for losses that were not incurred; embezzlement of funds by grantees; and various forms of insurance fraud and theft of government property. Investigations also focus on official misconduct by USFA personnel, including offenses such as bribery, collusion, conflict of interest, kickbacks, and embezzlement of federal funds. Specialists such as arson investigators, engineers, auditors, and personnel with expertise in other disciplines are sometimes asked to assist Special Agents with investigations as needed. Special Agents are authorized to conduct surveillance and undercover operations, carry firearms, make arrests, execute search warrants, and serve subpoenas. Investigations may be conducted jointly with other federal agencies as well as state and local governments.

- **Training and Promotion:** Special Agents attend the eight-week Criminal Investigator Training Program at the Federal Law Enforcement Training Center. In-service training may include courses in FEMA program investigations, legal issues and updates, FEMA regulations, investigative techniques, criminal and civil law, first aid and CPR, arrest techniques, defensive tactics, and firearms proficiency. Promotional opportunities are determined by availability and performance evaluations.

- **Basic Qualifications:** Applicants must meet the minimum qualification requirements as contained in the Office of Personnel Management's Qualification Operating Manual. These are available on line at www.opm.gov. The manual states that one year of specialized experience equivalent to the next lower grade in the federal service is required. Specialized experience is experience that is in or directly related to the line of work of the position to be filled and that has equipped the applicant with the particular knowledge, skills, and abilities (KSA) to successfully perform the duties of that position.

For specific information about working conditions, training and promotional opportunities, and application requirements, log on to the Federal Emergency Management Web site at www.fema.gov/career/index.jsp.

TRANSPORTATION SECURITY ADMINISTRATION

The Transportation Security Administration (TSA) was created in response to the terrorist attacks of September 11, 2001, as part of the Aviation and Transportation Security Act signed into law by President George W. Bush on November 19, 2001. The TSA was originally part of the Department of Transportation but was moved to the Department of Homeland Security in 2003.

TSA's mission is to protect the nation's transportation systems by ensuring the freedom of movement for people and commerce. In 2002 the TSA assumed responsibility for security at the nation's airports and by the end of the year had deployed a federal workforce to meet challenging congressional deadlines for screening all passengers and baggage.

Transportation Security Screener

Transportation Security Screeners (TSS) perform a variety of duties related to providing security and protection of air travelers, airports, and aircraft. They are responsible for identifying dangerous objects in baggage, cargo, and on passengers and preventing those objects from being transported onto the aircraft. TSS are required to perform various tasks such as wanding, pat-down searches, operation of X-ray machines, lifting of baggage (weighing at least 70 pounds), and screening and ticket review using electronic and imaging equipment.

- **Training and Promotion:** Candidates must successfully complete required training, including 56 to 72 hours of classroom training, 112 to 128 hours of on-the-job training, and a certification examination. Continued employment is contingent upon passing recurrent training and certification exams on a periodic basis.

- **Basic Qualifications:** Applicants must be U.S. citizens; have a high school diploma, GED, or equivalent or at least one year of full-time work experience in security work, aviation screener work, or X-ray technician work; pass a drug and alcohol screening and a background investigation, including a criminal check and a credit check.

For specific information about working conditions, training and promotional opportunities, and application requirements, log on to the Transportation Security Administration Web site at www.tsa.gov/public/display?theme=2.

U.S. CITIZENSHIP AND IMMIGRATION SERVICES

In 2003 service and benefit functions of the U.S. Immigration and Naturalization Service (INS) transitioned to the Department of Homeland Security (DHS) as the U.S. Citizenship and Immigration Services (USCIS). The USCIS is responsible for the administration and naturalization adjudication functions and for establishing immigration services policies and priorities. These functions include adjudication of immigration visa petitions, adjudication of naturalization petitions, adjudication of asylum and refugee applications, adjudications performed at the service centers, and all other adjudications previously performed by INS.

Adjudications Officer

Each year hundreds of thousands of people apply for various types of immigration benefits from the U.S. government. The benefits they seek include permission to import foreign workers, permission for relatives to immigrate, and permission to become American citizens. Adjudications Officers determine eligibility for this wide variety of benefits. They review applications and often conduct interviews of the applicants. Adjudications Officers have the dual responsibility of providing courteous service to the public while being alert to the possibility of fraud and misrepresentation. They usually perform their duties in an office environment.

- **Training and Promotion:** The Adjudications Officer basic training course is approximately a one-month residential program and includes instruction in the following subject areas: Immigration Law, USCIS Adjudication Process and Procedures, Naturalization Process and Procedures, Fraudulent Document Detection, Equal Employment Opportunity (EEO), Sexual Harassment, and Utilization of Immigration Data Base Systems. In order to successfully complete basic training, all Adjudications Officers must obtain a score of 70 percent or better in each of the major areas of study satisfactorily complete all required Practical Exercises.

   Individuals are hired at the GS-5 or GS-7 level; progression is to the GS-12 level after successful completion of the preceding grade(s). Competition is required to move above the GS-12 level.

- **Basic Qualifications:** Applicants must be U.S. citizens; have three years of progressively responsible experience or possess a bachelor's degree in any field from an accredited college or university; pass a written exam; possess a valid driver's license; and pass a background investigation. In addition, candidates must have, for three of the last five years immediately before applying for the position:
   - resided in the United States;
   - worked in the U.S. government as an employee overseas in a federal or military capacity; or
   - been a dependent of a U.S. federal or military employee serving overseas.

Asylum Officer

Asylum Officers determine if an applicant for asylum satisfies the requirements of the Immigration and Nationality Act while they are outside the United States, while they are in the United States or its borders, or while awaiting deportation. Asylum Officers must be knowledgeable of human rights conditions around the world and possess a keen insight into human behavior in order to determine the credibility and consistency of information elicited through interviews they conduct.

- **Training and Promotion:** The Asylum Officer basic training course is approximately a three-month residential program. Part 1 of the Asylum Officer basic training course is $5\frac{1}{2}$ weeks and includes instruction in the following subject areas: Immigration Law, U.S. Citizenship and Immigration Services Adjudication Process and Procedures, Naturalization Process and Procedures, Fraudulent Document Detection, EEO, Sexual Harassment, and Utilization of Immigration Data Base Systems. Part 2 of the Asylum Officer basic training course is a five-week Asylum-specific training program. Topics include U.S. Asylum and Refugee Law, International Human Rights Law, Interviewing Techniques, Decision-Making and Decision-Writing Skills, Effective Country Conditions Research Using Computer Data Bases and Other Reference Materials, and Utilization of Immigration Asylum Data Base System. In order to successfully complete basic training, all Asylum Officers must attain a score of 70 percent or better on each of the major areas of study as well as satisfactorily complete all required Practical Exercises.

  Individuals are hired at the GS-5 level; progression is to the GS-12 level after successful completion of the preceding grade(s). Competition is required to move to grade levels above GS-12.

- **Basic Qualifications:** Applicants must be U.S. citizens; have three years of progressively responsible experience or possess a bachelor's degree in any field from an accredited college or university; pass a written exam; possess a valid driver's license; and pass a background investigation. In addition, candidates must have, for three of the last five years immediately before applying for the position:

  - resided in the United States;
  - worked in the U.S. government as an employee overseas in a federal or military capacity; or
  - been a dependent of a U.S. federal or military employee serving overseas.

Immigration Information Officer

Immigration Information Officers (IIO) provide information about immigration and nationality law and regulations. They assist with information necessary to complete required forms and explain the administrative procedures and normal processing times for each application.

- **Training and Promotion:** The Immigration Information Officer basic training course is approximately a one-month residential program and includes instruction in the following subject areas: Immigration Law, Immigration Officer Duties and Responsibilities, Fraudulent Document Detection, Customer Service, EEO, Sexual Harassment, and Utilization of Immigration Data Base Systems. In order to successfully complete basic training, all Immigration Information Officers must obtain a score of 70 percent or better in each of the major areas of study.

Individuals may be hired at the GS-5 level; progression is to the GS-8 level after successful completion of the preceding grade(s). Competition is required to move to grade levels above GS-8.

- **Basic Qualifications:** Applicants must be U.S. citizens; have three years of progressively responsible experience or possess a bachelor's degree in any field from an accredited college or university; pass a written exam; possess a valid driver's license; and pass a background investigation. In addition, candidates must have, for three of the last five years immediately before applying for the position:
  - ○ resided in the United States;
  - ○ worked in the U.S. government as an employee overseas in a federal or military capacity; or
  - ○ been a dependent of a U.S. federal or military employee serving overseas.

For specific information about working conditions, training and promotional opportunities, and application requirements, log on to the U.S. Citizenship and Immigration Services Web site at http://uscis.gov/graphics/workfor/index.htm.

U.S. COAST GUARD

The U.S. Coast Guard is one of five branches of the U.S. Armed Forces and falls under the jurisdiction of the U.S. Department of Homeland Security. The Coast Guard is the country's oldest continuous seagoing service with responsibilities including Search and Rescue (SAR), Maritime Law Enforcement (MLE), Aids to Navigation (ATON), Icebreaking, Environmental Protection, and Port Security and Military Readiness. In order to accomplish these missions, the Coast Guard's 38,000 active-duty men and women, 8,000 Reservists, and 35,000 Auxiliarists serve in a variety of job fields ranging from operation specialists and small-boat operators and maintenance specialists to electronic technicians and aviation mechanics.

Boarding Officer

The basic element of the Coast Guard's Operational Law Enforcement effort is the boarding team. This team is made up of members of a station's or cutter's crew that is specially trained and qualified to conduct boardings of vessels at sea.

The boarding team is led by a Boarding Officer (BO). A BO is the individual in charge of the team with law enforcement authority. Some teams may also have an Assistant Boarding Officer (ABO). The remaining members make up the Boarding Team Members (BTM). All Coast Guard boarding teams are armed, uniformed, federal law enforcement officers. The assignments of BOs, ABOs, and BTMs are based on competence, experience, and ability. It is possible to have an ABO or BTM who out ranks the BO, but during the course of the boarding will be subordinate to the BO.

Units that routinely conduct law enforcement (Stations, White Hulled Cutters) have boarding teams composed of members of their crew. When a crew member has met the qualifications and completed the training, he or she can join the unit's boarding team. Boarding teams can be made up of various combinations of personnel, including Deck Watch Officers, mechanics, cooks, and so on. When the boarding team is not conducting a law enforcement boarding (or patrol for station boats), it returns to its normal duties at the unit.

- **Training and Promotion:** The Coast Guard's Maritime Law Enforcement Academy was established in 2004 at the Federal Law Enforcement Training Center in Charleston, South Carolina, to provide Coast Guard personnel the necessary skills to conduct their jobs as federal law enforcement officers. The academy currently offers three courses: the Boarding Officer Course (BOC), the Boarding Team Member Course (BTM), and the Marine Patrol Officer Course (MPOC).

- **Basic Qualifications:** Landing a position on a boarding team takes place after several major steps take place—the first being enlistment or commissioning in the Coast Guard. Then the applicant must be assigned to a unit that conducts law enforcement.

  Boarding teams and Boarding Officer positions are usually open to Officers and Petty Officers at units that conduct law enforcement. All members of a boarding team must do the following:

  ○ Successfully qualify in firing the 9mm pistol and pass tests judging the individual's ability to make judgments concerning the use of force.

  ○ Meet certain physical fitness qualifications.

  ○ Complete all the training objectives for BTM or BO.

  ○ Be qualified by the unit's Commanding Officer to be on the team.

  For specific information about working conditions, training and promotional opportunities, and application requirements, log on to the U.S. Coast Guard Web site at www.uscg.mil/jobs.

U.S. CUSTOMS AND BORDER PROTECTION

U.S. Customs and Border Protection (CBP) assesses and collects duties and taxes on imported merchandise and controls carriers and goods imported into, or exported from, the United States.

Import Specialist

Import Specialists enforce regulations of the U.S. Customs Service through the precise examination, classification, and appraisal of imported merchandise. Guided by federal revenue laws, they translate the language of trade into the legal terms of Customs regulations. As required by import regulations, Import Specialists examine and ap-

NOTE

The Coast Guard does have Tactical Law Enforcement Teams whose job is to conduct boardings while embarked on U.S. Navy ships.

praise merchandise and accompanying documentation based on such factors as legal restrictions, country of origin, import quotas, and current market values. Next, Import Specialists perform the critical task of determining the unit value of the merchandise—often a difficult task—when calculating the amount of money due the government. They interview importers or their representatives and, after a thorough check of import entry documents, make certain that the imports match the descriptions contained in itemized lists. They classify merchandise according to U.S. tariff schedules and determine the exact duties and taxes payable to U.S. Customs.

Import Specialists may be called upon to provide technical assistance to the Department of Justice in defending the U.S. government's position in Customs cases. They assist federal attorneys in the preparation of cases for Customs Court by supplying technical information and advice and by securing qualified witnesses and evidence. They give testimony in court and may be called upon to defend merchandise appraisals during appeals proceedings requested by importers.

- **Training and Promotion:** Training is designed to keep employees abreast of new techniques and improve particular skills and knowledge. Training is provided at the U.S. Citizenship and Immigration Services Academy. Seven weeks of specialized training is provided to develop an expert knowledge of import and export trends and commodities and industries as well as complex international trade agreements. Entry-level appointments to the position of Import Specialist are made at grades GS-5 and GS-7. After a one-year probationary period, employees may achieve permanent status. Import Specialists have excellent advancement potential, with opportunities to apply for supervisory and management slots at grades GS-13 and above.

- **Basic Qualifications:** Applicants must be U.S. citizens and pass a background security investigation and drug screening. In addition, CBP requires that for the three years prior to filing an application for employment, individuals must meet one or more of the following primary residence criteria:

  ○ Applicant resided in the United States or its protectorates or territories (short trips abroad, such as vacations, will not necessarily disqualify an applicant); or

  ○ Applicant worked for the U.S. government as an employee overseas in a federal or military capacity; or

  ○ Applicant was a dependent of a U.S. federal or military employee serving overseas.

Agriculture Specialist

Agriculture Specialists with the CBP serve as experts and technical consultants in the areas of inspection, intelligence, analysis, examination, and law enforcement activities related to the importation of agricultural/commercial commodities and conveyances at the various ports of entry. The mission is critical and the duties varied. Agriculture Specialists apply a wide range of federal, state, and local laws and agency regulations when determining the admissibility of agriculture commodities while preventing the introduction of harmful pests, diseases, and potential agro-terrorism into the United States.

- **Training and Promotion:** New hires must successfully complete eight to twelve weeks of paid training at the Professional Development Center.

- **Basic Qualifications:** Applicants must be U.S. citizens, possess a valid state driver's license at the time of appointment, and pass a drug test. In addition, CBP requires that for the three years prior to filing an application for employment, individuals must meet one or more of the following primary residence criteria:

  ○ Applicant resided in the United States or its protectorates or territories (short trips abroad, such as vacations, will not necessarily disqualify an applicant); or

  ○ Applicant worked for the U.S. government as an employee overseas in a federal or military capacity; or

  ○ Applicant was a dependent of a U.S. federal or military employee serving overseas.

  To qualify for a GS-5 level position, applicants must have earned a bachelor's degree in biological sciences, agriculture, natural resource management, chemistry, or a closely related field such as botany or entomology, or have a combination of experience and education that includes 24 semester hours in the disciplines listed above and job experience in areas such as pest control, pesticide application, inspecting aircraft or passengers, X-ray or environmental monitoring, or farm management related to disease control, insect detection/eradication, or pest control.

CBP Pilot

CBP Pilots are responsible for detecting intruders into U.S. airspace. Pilots play a critical role in stopping drugs from entering the United States. A wide variety of single-engine, multi-engine, and rotary aircraft make up the CBP fleet, including: C-550 Citations, Piper Cheyennes, AS350s, UH-60 Blackhawks, C206/210s and B-200/C-12s. CBP Pilots are assigned to a variety of challenges— from patrolling the border and assisting in the pursuit of suspects to providing critical support services required by fellow law enforcement agencies.

- **Training and Promotion:** Applicants are required to undergo sixteen weeks of specialized training at the Federal Law Enforcement Training Center. Also, all pilots must earn and maintain firearms qualifications during their careers.

- **Basic Qualifications:** Applicants must be U.S. citizens at the time of application and must present proof of citizenship upon selection. In addition, CBP requires that for the three years prior to filing an application for employment, individuals must meet one or more of the following primary residence criteria:

  - ❍ Applicant resided in the United States or its protectorates or territories (short trips abroad, such as vacations, will not necessarily disqualify an applicant); or

  - ❍ Applicant worked for the U.S. government as an employee overseas in a federal or military capacity; or

  - ❍ Applicant was a dependent of a U.S. federal or military employee serving overseas.

  To qualify, airplane pilot applicants must possess a valid FAA commercial pilot certificate with a(n):

  - ❍ single-engine land airplane class rating.

  - ❍ multi-engine land airplane class rating.

  - ❍ instrument-airplane rating.

  - ❍ helicopter rotorcraft class rating.

  - ❍ instrument-helicopter rating.

Aviation Enforcement Officer

Aviation Enforcement Officers (AEOs) serve as primary law enforcement officers on CBP interdiction aircraft and must be able to perform arrests, surveillance, intelligence, and communications duties.

- **Training and Promotion:** Prior military aviation surveillance experience is a good starting point. Sixteen weeks of specialized training at the Federal Law Enforcement Training Center is required, and all AEOs must earn and maintain firearms qualifications during their careers.

- **Basic Qualifications:** Applicants must be U.S. citizens at the time of application, present proof of citizenship upon selection, and have three years of general experience or a bachelor's degree. A physical examination is required, as are a background investigation and drug test. In addition, CBP requires that for the three years prior to filing an application for employment, individuals must meet one or more of the following primary residence criteria:

  - ❍ Applicant resided in the United States or its protectorates or territories (short trips abroad, such as vacations, will not necessarily disqualify an applicant); or

  - ❍ Applicant worked for the U.S. government as an employee overseas in a federal or military capacity; or

  - ❍ Applicant was a dependent of a U.S. federal or military employee serving overseas.

P-3 Pilot

P-3 Pilots are primarily responsible for detecting intruders into U.S. airspace. They are routinely involved in active drug interdiction as part of a combined operations team.

- **Training and Promotion:** Prior military aviation surveillance experience is a good starting point. Sixteen weeks of specialized training at the Federal Law Enforcement Training Center is required, and all P-3 Pilots must earn and maintain firearms qualifications during their careers.

- **Basic Qualifications:** Candidates must be U.S.citizens at the time of application and must present proof of citizenship upon selection. In addition, CBP requires that for the three years prior to filing an application for employment, individuals must meet one or more of the following primary residence criteria:
  - ❍ Applicant resided in the United States or its protectorates or territories (short trips abroad, such as vacations, will not necessarily disqualify an applicant); or
  - ❍ Applicant worked for the U.S. government as an employee overseas in a federal or military capacity; or
  - ❍ Applicant was a dependent of a U.S. federal or military employee serving overseas.

  To qualify, P-3 Pilot applicants must possess a valid FAA Commercial Pilot Certificate with a(n):
  - ❍ multi-engine land airplane class rating.
  - ❍ instrument airplane rating.

  P-3 Pilot applicants must also possess Pilot in Command/Aircraft Commander experience in any P-3 or its civilian counterpart, the L-188 Electra. Applicants applying based on civilian experience must possess an Air Transport Pilot certificate with an L-188 type rating. Successful completion of the Navy P-3 Naval Air Training and Operating Procedures Standardization Program (NATOPS) and designation as Aircraft Commander fully meets this requirement.

Marine Enforcement Officer

Marine Enforcement Officers (MEOs) protect the United States from terrorists, apprehend smugglers of illegal narcotics by interdicting suspect vessels entering U.S. waters, and coordinating interdiction efforts with the support of CBP aviation units and other agencies within Homeland Security. The MEO also works with other federal, state, and local law enforcement agencies and foreign governments. MEO duties primarily involve patrolling the seas along the U.S. coastlines and the Caribbean to detect, intercept, and search suspect vessels. They confiscate contraband and arrest violators of customs and related laws as well as prepare documentation to be used as a basis for prosecution. MEOs also perform port patrols in support of the U.S. Coast Guard.

- **Training and Promotion:** The MEO is trained to operate a variety of high-performance vessels, utility vessels, and platform-style vessels. MEOs must attend and successfully complete vigorous training at the Federal Law Enforcement

Training Center. They also must successfully complete Marine Law Enforcement Training and Advanced Marine Law Enforcement Training before operating a high-speed interceptor vessel.

- **Basic Qualifications:** Candidates must be U.S. citizens at the time of application and must present proof of citizenship upon selection. In addition, CBP requires that for the three years prior to filing an application for employment, individuals must meet one or more of the following primary residence criteria:

  ○ Applicant resided in the United States or its protectorates or territories (short trips abroad, such as vacations, will not necessarily disqualify an applicant); or

  ○ Applicant worked for the U.S. government as an employee overseas in a federal or military capacity; or

  ○ Applicant was a dependent of a U.S. federal or military employee serving overseas.

It is helpful for candidates to have a U.S. Coast Guard Captain's license and prior marine law enforcement experience, but not required.

CBP Officer

CBP Officers protect and safeguard the nation's ports of entry (air, land, and sea), preventing terrorists and terrorist weapons from entering the United States. CBP Officers conduct comprehensive customs, immigration, and agriculture inspections; stem the flow of illegal drugs and other contraband; protect agricultural and economic interests from harmful pests and diseases; protect American business from intellectual property theft; regulate and facilitate international trade; collect import duties; and enforce U.S. immigration and trade laws.

- **Training and Promotion:** Every recruit must successfully complete twelve weeks of rigorous physical, educational, and firearms training at the U.S. Customs and Border Protection Academy, located at the Federal Law Enforcement Training Center. Some locations require Spanish language skills, so demonstrated language proficiency or an additional period of language training may be required. Beyond the basic courses, training continues throughout the CBP Officer's career.

- **Basic Qualifications:** Applicants must be U.S. citizens; have a valid U.S. driver's license; and successfully complete a thorough background investigation, medical and fitness examinations, and a drug test. In addition, CBP requires that for the three years prior to filing an application for employment, individuals must meet one or more of the following primary residence criteria:

  ○ Applicant resided in the United States or its protectorates or territories (short trips abroad, such as vacations, will not necessarily disqualify an applicant); or

  ○ Applicant worked for the U.S. government as an employee overseas in a federal or military capacity; or

  ○ Applicant was a dependent of a U.S. federal or military employee serving overseas.

Border Patrol Agent

A job with the Border Patrol will place an Agent on the front line of efforts to strengthen homeland security. Border Patrol Agents are responsible for the prevention, detection, and apprehension of those illegally entering the United States as well as intercepting drug smugglers. Border Patrol Agents must be willing to work overtime and shift work under arduous conditions and be proficient in the use of and carry firearms. They may also be sent on temporary assignments on short notice and on permanent reassignments to any duty.

- **Training and Promotion:** New hires must successfully complete approximately five months of paid training at the CBP Border Patrol Academy in Artesia, New Mexico, on topics such as immigration and nationality laws, Spanish language, physical training, and marksmanship. Border Patrol Agents are subject to random drug testing. Promotional opportunities depend on availability and performance evaluations.

- **Basic Qualifications:** Applicants must U.S. citizens, possess a valid state driver's license at the time of appointment, and be under the age of 37. In addition, CBP requires that for the three years prior to filing an application for employment, individuals must meet one or more of the following primary residence criteria:

  ○ Applicant resided in the United States or its protectorates or territories (short trips abroad, such as vacations, will not necessarily disqualify an applicant); or

  ○ Applicant worked for the U.S. government as an employee overseas in a federal or military capacity; or

  ○ Applicant was a dependent of a U.S. federal or military employee serving overseas.

For specific information about working conditions, training and promotional opportunities, and application requirements, log on to the U.S. Customs and Border Protection Web site at www.cbp.gov/xp/cgov/careers.

U.S. IMMIGRATION AND CUSTOMS ENFORCEMENT

U.S. Immigration and Customs Enforcement (ICE) is a component of Border and Transportation Security within the Department of Homeland Security. ICE's enforcement mission is carried out by a wide variety of law enforcement, security, and intelligence professionals.

Immigration Enforcement Agent

Immigration Enforcement Agents (IEAs) are responsible for processing and deporting or escorting aliens who have been ordered removed from the United States to their country of citizenship. IEAs work in the detention program where they ensure the care of aliens in ICE's custody. IEAs also handle intake and outtake processing; counseling regarding personal and family matters; and supervision and transportation of detained aliens.

- **Training and Promotion:** IEAs receive a fourteen- to eighteen-week Immigration Officer's Basic Training Course at one of the Service's training centers and must pass a course of study in immigration law, nationality law, Spanish language, police training, and branch-specific operational training.

  Initial appointments are at grade GS-5. Career progression to grades GS-7, GS-9, and journeyman GS-11 generally follows at one-year intervals. Thereafter, promotions to higher grades and to supervisory levels are made through the competitive procedures of the Federal Merit Promotion System.

- **Basic Qualifications:** Applicants must be U.S. citizens; be under 37 years of age; have three years of progressively responsible experience or possess a bachelor's degree in any field from an accredited college or university, or possess a combination of qualifying education and experience; pass a written exam; possess a valid driver's license; and pass a physical exam and background investigation. In addition, candidates must have, for three of the last five years immediately before applying for the position:

  ○ resided in the United States;

  ○ worked in the U.S. government as an employee overseas in a federal or military capacity; or

  ○ been a dependent of a U.S. federal or military employee serving overseas.

Deportation Officer

The mission of Deportation Officers is to provide for the control and removal of persons who have been ordered for deportation or otherwise required to depart from the United States. Officers must closely monitor deportation proceedings from initiation to conclusion. Close liaison with foreign consulates and embassies is necessary to facilitate the timely issuance of passports and travel documents required for deportation. Deportation Officers may also be required to respond to congressional inquiries.

- **Training and Promotion:** Deportation Officers receive a fourteen- to eighteen-week Immigration Officer's Basic Training Course at one of the Service's training centers and must pass a course of study in immigration law, nationality law, Spanish language, police training, and branch-specific operational training.

  Initial appointments are at grade GS-5. Career progression to grades GS-7, GS-9, and journeyman GS-11 generally follows at one-year intervals. Thereafter, promotions to higher grades and to supervisory levels are made through the competitive procedures of the Federal Merit Promotion System.

- **Basic Qualifications:** Applicants must be U.S. citizens; be under 37 years of age; have three years of progressively responsible experience or possess a bachelor's degree in any field from an accredited college or university, or possess a combination of qualifying education and experience; pass a written exam; possess a valid driver's license; and pass a physical exam and background investigation. In addition, candidates must have, for three of the last five years immediately before applying for the position:

○   resided in the United States;

○   worked in the U.S. government as an employee overseas in a federal or military capacity; or

○   been a dependent of a U.S. federal or military employee serving overseas.

Federal Protective Service Officer

The mission of the Federal Protective Service (FPS) is to provide law enforcement and security services to over one million tenants and daily visitors to all federally owned and leased facilities nationwide. The FPS focuses directly on the interior security of the nation and the reduction of crimes and potential threats to federal facilities throughout the nation.

Federal Protective Service Officers perform the following duties as uniformed, armed law enforcement officers:

•   Provide crime response and make arrests.

•   Conduct preliminary criminal investigations, protect life and property on federally controlled property, and capture and detain suspects.

•   Respond to counterterrorist operations, demonstrations, threats, or natural disasters.

FPS Officers may patrol on foot, by automobile, motorcycle, or bicycle. Officers also apprehend wanted persons on federal property, work with other law enforcement agencies to provide special protection during federal court trials, process criminal arrests by FPS, and present educational programs on workplace violence and crime prevention to customers.

•   **Training and Promotion:** The Federal Law Enforcement Training Center serves as the national training center for the FPS. It offers a diversified spectrum of dynamic educational programming. The Federal Law Enforcement Training Center facility offers state-of-the-art training in criminal investigations, professional development, Weapons of Mass Destruction and physical security. The FPS actively employs the Federal Law Enforcement Training Center to keep its protection workforce abreast of the latest field expertise.

•   **Basic Qualifications:** Applicants must be U.S. citizens and pass a background security investigation and drug screening.

    A degree and/or work experience is required. Some of the degrees FPS Officers have are in criminal justice, international trade and finance, foreign languages, and computer science. Prior law enforcement experience is beneficial.

Criminal Investigator

FPS Criminal Investigators serve in plainclothes, as armed Special Agents. They investigate felonies; make arrests; gather criminal intelligence; perform criminal and noncriminal investigations; and network with other federal, state, and local law enforcement agencies. In addition to these duties, Criminal Investigators analyze criminal statistics and recommend action; search crime scenes; collect and preserve evidence; participate in Federal Task Forces; conduct surveillance and interviews; present investigative results to U.S. Attorneys; testify at grand juries, courts, and administrative hearings; and gather and evaluate threat assessment data.

- **Training and Promotion:** The Federal Law Enforcement Training Center serves as the national training center for the FPS. It offers a diversified spectrum of dynamic educational programming. The Federal Law Enforcement Training Center facility offers state-of-the-art training in criminal investigations, professional development, Weapons of Mass Destruction and physical security. The FPS actively employs the Federal Law Enforcement Training Center to keep its protection workforce abreast of the latest field expertise.

- **Basic Qualifications:** Applicants must be U.S. citizens and pass a background security investigation and drug screening.

  A degree and/or work experience is required. Some of the degrees Criminal Investigators have are in criminal justice, international trade and finance, foreign languages, and computer science. Prior law enforcement experience is beneficial.

Inspector

Inspectors perform as uniformed, armed law enforcement officers who respond to crimes and make arrests; conduct Building Security Assessments; and develop action plans to reduce vulnerabilities. Inspectors are responsible for determining security systems or services for client agencies; promoting positive working relationships serving as a liaison with top management officials; and serving as a Contracting Officer Representative, ensuring contract compliance.

- **Training and Promotion:** The Federal Law Enforcement Training Center serves as the national training center for the FPS. It offers a diversified spectrum of dynamic educational programming. The Federal Law Enforcement Training Center facility offers state-of-the-art training in criminal investigations, professional development, Weapons of Mass Destruction and physical security. The FPS actively employs the Federal Law Enforcement Training Center to keep its protection workforce abreast of the latest field expertise.

- **Basic Qualifications:** Applicants must be U.S. citizens and pass a background security investigation and drug screening.

  A degree and/or work experience is required. Some of the degrees Inspectors have are in criminal justice, international trade and finance, foreign languages, and computer science. Prior law enforcement experience is beneficial.

Criminal Investigator (Special Agent)

The ICE law enforcement mission has matured and expanded to cover everything from trade fraud and money laundering, to drug and illegal weapons interdiction, to child pornography, to use of the Internet for cyber smuggling or alien smuggling activity.

In all these areas, the ICE Special Agent plays a critical role. The position is both a challenging investigative role and an enforcement role. Every day is different. Unlike other federal investigative careers, being an ICE Special Agent requires the individual to investigate multiple types of criminal activity. Agents do not work in just one area. One day it may be international narcotics smuggling, the next it could be a complex money laundering or fraud scheme or violation of immigration law. With over 400 laws to enforce, broad powers of search and seizure at the border and transnational authority, there are many challenges every day in the complex series of missions.

ICE enforces laws for each of these critical areas of national security:

Narcotics: Use unified intelligence, interdiction, and investigative efforts to penetrate and dismantle drug-smuggling organizations and reduce the flow of narcotics across U.S. borders.

Money Laundering: Identify, track, disrupt, and dismantle the systems and criminal organizations that launder money generated from smuggling, trade fraud, and/or export violations.

Trade Fraud: Identify and target illicit trade practices that negatively affect the United States.

Strategic Investigations: Investigate traffic of a host of illegal commodities and components, including arms; controlled substances; and the building blocks for nuclear, chemical, and biological Weapons of Mass Destruction. Also to enforce international embargoes and sanctions imposed by other government agencies.

Cyber Investigations: Initiate online investigations to facilitate enforcement of any of the more than 400 laws within ICE's scope of authority where perpetrators use the Internet as a tool for criminal activities.

Immigration and Nationality Act Violations: Plan and conduct investigations, often undercover, concerning possible violations of criminal and administrative provisions of the act and other related statutes.

Every one of these areas is a frontline defense against terrorism. Each area is also a barrier to drug trafficking, and a deterrent against domestic and international fraud. ICE Special Agents are tasked to protect America's streets from drugs and illegal guns; children from pornographers; businesses and government from fraud; consumers from tainted food and medicines; and the people of America from terrorism.

- **Training and Promotion:** After twenty weeks of specialized training at the ICE Law Enforcement Academy, the successful candidate will take on the job of an ICE Special Agent. From that point on, the agent will be called upon to take part in investigations in any area under ICE's jurisdiction.

- **Basic Qualifications:** Applicants must be a U.S. citizen and pass a background security investigation and drug screening.

  A degree and/or work experience is required. Some of the degrees Special Agents have are in criminal justice, international trade and finance, foreign languages, and computer science. Prior law enforcement experience is beneficial.

Federal Air Marshal

The mission of the Federal Air Marshal (FAM) is to protect air security and promote public confidence in the nation's civil aviation system.

On September 11, 2001, the Federal Air Marshal Service consisted of 33 FAMs. President George W. Bush quickly authorized an increase in the number of Federal Air Marshals, and almost overnight the Service received more than 200,000 applications. A classified number of these applicants were screened, hired, trained, certified, and deployed on flights around the world. Today these FAMs serve as a key component of ICE in the war against terrorism.

As one of the six divisions of ICE, the Federal Air Marshal Service continues its mission to promote confidence in the nation's civil aviation system through the effective deployment of Federal Air Marshals to detect, deter, and defeat hostile acts targeting U.S. air carriers, airports, passengers, and crews.

- **Training and Promotion:** Every Federal Air Marshal candidate must successfully complete a two-phase training program to fulfill the requirements necessary to become a Federal Air Marshal. The initial phase consists of a seven-week basic law enforcement officer training program conducted at the Federal Law Enforcement Training Center. The basic training, Phase I, has been specifically tailored to prepare recruits for the unique and critical mission of the Federal Air Marshal Service. The core curriculum taught during basic training is drawn from the following disciplines: constitutional law, basic marksmanship, physical fitness, defensive tactics, emergency medical care, and fundamental law enforcement investigative/administrative practices. Candidates who successfully complete the basic training curriculum continue to Phase II training, conducted at the Federal Air Marshal Training Center in Atlantic City, New Jersey.

  Phase II training is dedicated to providing candidates with the knowledge, skills, and abilities specifically applicable to the environment in which they will perform their duties. Emphasis is placed on developing advanced firearms and defensive techniques proficiency, advanced operational tactics, strength conditioning and aerobic training, aircraft systems emergency procedures, and legal and adminis-trative protocols. Upon graduation from Phase II, newly appointed Federal Air Marshals are assigned to one of twenty-one field offices to begin flying missions.

- **Basic Qualifications:** Applicants must be U.S. citizens, be under 40 years of age at appointment, and meet strict FAA medical standards.

For specific information about working conditions, training and promotional opportunities, and application requirements, log on to the U.S. Immigration and Customs Enforcement Web site at www.ice.gov/graphics/careers.

U.S. SECRET SERVICE

The U.S. Secret Service is mandated by statute and executive order to carry out two significant missions: protection and criminal investigations. The Secret Service protects the president and vice president, their families, heads of state, and other designated individuals; investigates threats against the protected; protects the White House, vice president's residence, foreign missions, and other buildings within Washington, D.C.; and plans and implements security designs for designated National Special Security Events. The Secret Service also investigates violations of laws relating to counterfeiting of obligations and securities of the U.S.; financial crimes that include, but are not limited to, access device fraud, financial institution fraud, identity theft, computer fraud; and computer-based attacks on our nation's financial, banking, and telecommunications infrastructure.

Special Agent

Special Agents are charged with two missions: protection and investigation. During the course of their careers, Special Agents carry out assignments in both of these areas and must be available to be assigned to duty stations anywhere in the world.

Newly appointed special agents may be assigned to duty stations anywhere in the United States. Throughout their careers, Agents may experience frequent travel and reassignments to Secret Service offices located throughout the United States or liaison assignments in foreign countries.

Special Agents are required to work long hours in undesirable conditions on short notice; travel away from home for periods of time; carry a firearm while performing duties; carry out assignments in the areas of protection and investigations; relocate to duty stations throughout the United States and abroad as organizational needs dictate; and work undercover assignments.

- **Training and Promotion:** Newly appointed Special Agents receive approximately eleven weeks of intensive training at the Federal Law Enforcement Training Center. Upon successful completion of training, they receive approximately eleven weeks of specialized instruction at the James J. Rowley Training Center in Laurel, Maryland. Special Agents are required to maintain firearms proficiency throughout their careers.

- **Basic Qualifications:** Applicants must be U.S. citizens; be at least 21 years old but under the age of 37 at time of appointment; be registered with selective service, if required to do so; hold a bachelor's degree from an accredited college or university or have three years' work experience in the criminal investigative or law enforcement fields that require knowledge and application of laws relating to criminal violations or equivalent combination of education and related experience; pass the Treasury Enforcement Agent Exam; and pass a background, drug screening, medical, and polygraph examinations.

Uniformed Division Officer

Uniformed Division Officers provide protection for the president, vice president, president-elect, vice president–elect, their immediate families, former presidents, their spouses and minor children until the age of 16, visiting foreign heads of states/governments, their accompanying spouses, major presidential and vice presidential candidates, their spouses, and others designated by law. In addition, Uniformed Division Officers provide protection for the White House Complex, the vice president's residence, the main Treasury Building and Annex, and foreign diplomatic missions and embassies in Washington, D.C.

Uniformed Division Officers are required to work long hours in undesirable conditions on short notice, travel frequently, and carry a firearm while performing duties.

- **Training and Promotion:** Newly appointed Uniformed Division Officers receive approximately eight weeks of intensive training at the Federal Law Enforcement Training Center. Upon successful completion of training, they receive approximately eleven weeks of specialized instruction at the James J. Rowley Training Center in Laurel, Maryland. Uniformed Division Officers are required to maintain firearms proficiency throughout their careers.

- **Basic Qualifications:** Applicants must be U.S. citizens; be at least 21 years old but under the age of 37 at time of appointment; be registered with selective service, if required to do so; have a high school diploma or equivalent; complete interviews and pass a written exam; and complete background investigation to include driving record check, drug screening, and medical, and polygraph examinations.

For specific information about working conditions, training and promotional opportunities, and application requirements, log on to the U.S. Secret Service Web site at www.secretservice.gov/opportunities.shtml.

SUMMING IT UP

- The establishment of the Department of Homeland Security has created many new opportunities for people interested in a career in federal law enforcement.

- Applying for positions with the Department of Homeland Security requires a thorough understanding of the complex application process.

- The requirements for each Department of Homeland Security position can be extensive. To get the most accurate and up-to-date information, contact the agency for which you wish to apply.

PART III

PRACTICE TEST

ANSWER SHEET PRACTICE TEST

Reading Comprehension and Verbal Ability

1. Ⓐ Ⓑ Ⓒ Ⓓ Ⓔ   24. Ⓐ Ⓑ Ⓒ Ⓓ Ⓔ   47. Ⓐ Ⓑ Ⓒ Ⓓ Ⓔ   70. Ⓐ Ⓑ Ⓒ Ⓓ Ⓔ
2. Ⓐ Ⓑ Ⓒ Ⓓ Ⓔ   25. Ⓐ Ⓑ Ⓒ Ⓓ Ⓔ   48. Ⓐ Ⓑ Ⓒ Ⓓ Ⓔ   71. Ⓐ Ⓑ Ⓒ Ⓓ Ⓔ
3. Ⓐ Ⓑ Ⓒ Ⓓ Ⓔ   26. Ⓐ Ⓑ Ⓒ Ⓓ Ⓔ   49. Ⓐ Ⓑ Ⓒ Ⓓ Ⓔ   72. Ⓐ Ⓑ Ⓒ Ⓓ Ⓔ
4. Ⓐ Ⓑ Ⓒ Ⓓ Ⓔ   27. Ⓐ Ⓑ Ⓒ Ⓓ Ⓔ   50. Ⓐ Ⓑ Ⓒ Ⓓ Ⓔ   73. Ⓐ Ⓑ Ⓒ Ⓓ Ⓔ
5. Ⓐ Ⓑ Ⓒ Ⓓ Ⓔ   28. Ⓐ Ⓑ Ⓒ Ⓓ Ⓔ   51. Ⓐ Ⓑ Ⓒ Ⓓ Ⓔ   74. Ⓐ Ⓑ Ⓒ Ⓓ Ⓔ
6. Ⓐ Ⓑ Ⓒ Ⓓ Ⓔ   29. Ⓐ Ⓑ Ⓒ Ⓓ Ⓔ   52. Ⓐ Ⓑ Ⓒ Ⓓ Ⓔ   75. Ⓐ Ⓑ Ⓒ Ⓓ Ⓔ
7. Ⓐ Ⓑ Ⓒ Ⓓ Ⓔ   30. Ⓐ Ⓑ Ⓒ Ⓓ Ⓔ   53. Ⓐ Ⓑ Ⓒ Ⓓ Ⓔ   76. Ⓐ Ⓑ Ⓒ Ⓓ Ⓔ
8. Ⓐ Ⓑ Ⓒ Ⓓ Ⓔ   31. Ⓐ Ⓑ Ⓒ Ⓓ Ⓔ   54. Ⓐ Ⓑ Ⓒ Ⓓ Ⓔ   77. Ⓐ Ⓑ Ⓒ Ⓓ Ⓔ
9. Ⓐ Ⓑ Ⓒ Ⓓ Ⓔ   32. Ⓐ Ⓑ Ⓒ Ⓓ Ⓔ   55. Ⓐ Ⓑ Ⓒ Ⓓ Ⓔ   78. Ⓐ Ⓑ Ⓒ Ⓓ Ⓔ
10. Ⓐ Ⓑ Ⓒ Ⓓ Ⓔ   33. Ⓐ Ⓑ Ⓒ Ⓓ Ⓔ   56. Ⓐ Ⓑ Ⓒ Ⓓ Ⓔ   79. Ⓐ Ⓑ Ⓒ Ⓓ Ⓔ
11. Ⓐ Ⓑ Ⓒ Ⓓ Ⓔ   34. Ⓐ Ⓑ Ⓒ Ⓓ Ⓔ   57. Ⓐ Ⓑ Ⓒ Ⓓ Ⓔ   80. Ⓐ Ⓑ Ⓒ Ⓓ Ⓔ
12. Ⓐ Ⓑ Ⓒ Ⓓ Ⓔ   35. Ⓐ Ⓑ Ⓒ Ⓓ Ⓔ   58. Ⓐ Ⓑ Ⓒ Ⓓ Ⓔ   81. Ⓐ Ⓑ Ⓒ Ⓓ Ⓔ
13. Ⓐ Ⓑ Ⓒ Ⓓ Ⓔ   36. Ⓐ Ⓑ Ⓒ Ⓓ Ⓔ   59. Ⓐ Ⓑ Ⓒ Ⓓ Ⓔ   82. Ⓐ Ⓑ Ⓒ Ⓓ Ⓔ
14. Ⓐ Ⓑ Ⓒ Ⓓ Ⓔ   37. Ⓐ Ⓑ Ⓒ Ⓓ Ⓔ   60. Ⓐ Ⓑ Ⓒ Ⓓ Ⓔ   83. Ⓐ Ⓑ Ⓒ Ⓓ Ⓔ
15. Ⓐ Ⓑ Ⓒ Ⓓ Ⓔ   38. Ⓐ Ⓑ Ⓒ Ⓓ Ⓔ   61. Ⓐ Ⓑ Ⓒ Ⓓ Ⓔ   84. Ⓐ Ⓑ Ⓒ Ⓓ Ⓔ
16. Ⓐ Ⓑ Ⓒ Ⓓ Ⓔ   39. Ⓐ Ⓑ Ⓒ Ⓓ Ⓔ   62. Ⓐ Ⓑ Ⓒ Ⓓ Ⓔ   85. Ⓐ Ⓑ Ⓒ Ⓓ Ⓔ
17. Ⓐ Ⓑ Ⓒ Ⓓ Ⓔ   40. Ⓐ Ⓑ Ⓒ Ⓓ Ⓔ   63. Ⓐ Ⓑ Ⓒ Ⓓ Ⓔ   86. Ⓐ Ⓑ Ⓒ Ⓓ Ⓔ
18. Ⓐ Ⓑ Ⓒ Ⓓ Ⓔ   41. Ⓐ Ⓑ Ⓒ Ⓓ Ⓔ   64. Ⓐ Ⓑ Ⓒ Ⓓ Ⓔ   87. Ⓐ Ⓑ Ⓒ Ⓓ Ⓔ
19. Ⓐ Ⓑ Ⓒ Ⓓ Ⓔ   42. Ⓐ Ⓑ Ⓒ Ⓓ Ⓔ   65. Ⓐ Ⓑ Ⓒ Ⓓ Ⓔ   88. Ⓐ Ⓑ Ⓒ Ⓓ Ⓔ
20. Ⓐ Ⓑ Ⓒ Ⓓ Ⓔ   43. Ⓐ Ⓑ Ⓒ Ⓓ Ⓔ   66. Ⓐ Ⓑ Ⓒ Ⓓ Ⓔ   89. Ⓐ Ⓑ Ⓒ Ⓓ Ⓔ
21. Ⓐ Ⓑ Ⓒ Ⓓ Ⓔ   44. Ⓐ Ⓑ Ⓒ Ⓓ Ⓔ   67. Ⓐ Ⓑ Ⓒ Ⓓ Ⓔ   90. Ⓐ Ⓑ Ⓒ Ⓓ Ⓔ
22. Ⓐ Ⓑ Ⓒ Ⓓ Ⓔ   45. Ⓐ Ⓑ Ⓒ Ⓓ Ⓔ   68. Ⓐ Ⓑ Ⓒ Ⓓ Ⓔ
23. Ⓐ Ⓑ Ⓒ Ⓓ Ⓔ   46. Ⓐ Ⓑ Ⓒ Ⓓ Ⓔ   69. Ⓐ Ⓑ Ⓒ Ⓓ Ⓔ

Arithmetic Reasoning

1. Ⓐ Ⓑ Ⓒ Ⓓ Ⓔ   8. Ⓐ Ⓑ Ⓒ Ⓓ Ⓔ   15. Ⓐ Ⓑ Ⓒ Ⓓ Ⓔ   22. Ⓐ Ⓑ Ⓒ Ⓓ Ⓔ
2. Ⓐ Ⓑ Ⓒ Ⓓ Ⓔ   9. Ⓐ Ⓑ Ⓒ Ⓓ Ⓔ   16. Ⓐ Ⓑ Ⓒ Ⓓ Ⓔ   23. Ⓐ Ⓑ Ⓒ Ⓓ Ⓔ
3. Ⓐ Ⓑ Ⓒ Ⓓ Ⓔ   10. Ⓐ Ⓑ Ⓒ Ⓓ Ⓔ   17. Ⓐ Ⓑ Ⓒ Ⓓ Ⓔ   24. Ⓐ Ⓑ Ⓒ Ⓓ Ⓔ
4. Ⓐ Ⓑ Ⓒ Ⓓ Ⓔ   11. Ⓐ Ⓑ Ⓒ Ⓓ Ⓔ   18. Ⓐ Ⓑ Ⓒ Ⓓ Ⓔ   25. Ⓐ Ⓑ Ⓒ Ⓓ Ⓔ
5. Ⓐ Ⓑ Ⓒ Ⓓ Ⓔ   12. Ⓐ Ⓑ Ⓒ Ⓓ Ⓔ   19. Ⓐ Ⓑ Ⓒ Ⓓ Ⓔ
6. Ⓐ Ⓑ Ⓒ Ⓓ Ⓔ   13. Ⓐ Ⓑ Ⓒ Ⓓ Ⓔ   20. Ⓐ Ⓑ Ⓒ Ⓓ Ⓔ
7. Ⓐ Ⓑ Ⓒ Ⓓ Ⓔ   14. Ⓐ Ⓑ Ⓒ Ⓓ Ⓔ   21. Ⓐ Ⓑ Ⓒ Ⓓ Ⓔ

Comparisons and Sequence

1. Ⓐ Ⓑ Ⓒ Ⓓ Ⓔ   11. Ⓐ Ⓑ Ⓒ Ⓓ Ⓔ   21. Ⓐ Ⓑ Ⓒ Ⓓ Ⓔ   31. Ⓐ Ⓑ Ⓒ Ⓓ Ⓔ
2. Ⓐ Ⓑ Ⓒ Ⓓ Ⓔ   12. Ⓐ Ⓑ Ⓒ Ⓓ Ⓔ   22. Ⓐ Ⓑ Ⓒ Ⓓ Ⓔ   32. Ⓐ Ⓑ Ⓒ Ⓓ Ⓔ
3. Ⓐ Ⓑ Ⓒ Ⓓ Ⓔ   13. Ⓐ Ⓑ Ⓒ Ⓓ Ⓔ   23. Ⓐ Ⓑ Ⓒ Ⓓ Ⓔ   33. Ⓐ Ⓑ Ⓒ Ⓓ Ⓔ
4. Ⓐ Ⓑ Ⓒ Ⓓ Ⓔ   14. Ⓐ Ⓑ Ⓒ Ⓓ Ⓔ   24. Ⓐ Ⓑ Ⓒ Ⓓ Ⓔ   34. Ⓐ Ⓑ Ⓒ Ⓓ Ⓔ
5. Ⓐ Ⓑ Ⓒ Ⓓ Ⓔ   15. Ⓐ Ⓑ Ⓒ Ⓓ Ⓔ   25. Ⓐ Ⓑ Ⓒ Ⓓ Ⓔ   35. Ⓐ Ⓑ Ⓒ Ⓓ Ⓔ
6. Ⓐ Ⓑ Ⓒ Ⓓ Ⓔ   16. Ⓐ Ⓑ Ⓒ Ⓓ Ⓔ   26. Ⓐ Ⓑ Ⓒ Ⓓ Ⓔ   36. Ⓐ Ⓑ Ⓒ Ⓓ Ⓔ
7. Ⓐ Ⓑ Ⓒ Ⓓ Ⓔ   17. Ⓐ Ⓑ Ⓒ Ⓓ Ⓔ   27. Ⓐ Ⓑ Ⓒ Ⓓ Ⓔ   37. Ⓐ Ⓑ Ⓒ Ⓓ Ⓔ
8. Ⓐ Ⓑ Ⓒ Ⓓ Ⓔ   18. Ⓐ Ⓑ Ⓒ Ⓓ Ⓔ   28. Ⓐ Ⓑ Ⓒ Ⓓ Ⓔ   38. Ⓐ Ⓑ Ⓒ Ⓓ Ⓔ
9. Ⓐ Ⓑ Ⓒ Ⓓ Ⓔ   19. Ⓐ Ⓑ Ⓒ Ⓓ Ⓔ   29. Ⓐ Ⓑ Ⓒ Ⓓ Ⓔ   39. Ⓐ Ⓑ Ⓒ Ⓓ Ⓔ
10. Ⓐ Ⓑ Ⓒ Ⓓ Ⓔ   20. Ⓐ Ⓑ Ⓒ Ⓓ Ⓔ   30. Ⓐ Ⓑ Ⓒ Ⓓ Ⓔ   40. Ⓐ Ⓑ Ⓒ Ⓓ Ⓔ

answer sheet

Problems for Investigation

1. Ⓐ Ⓑ Ⓒ Ⓓ Ⓔ   3. Ⓐ Ⓑ Ⓒ Ⓓ Ⓔ   5. Ⓐ Ⓑ Ⓒ Ⓓ Ⓔ
2. Ⓐ Ⓑ Ⓒ Ⓓ Ⓔ   4. Ⓐ Ⓑ Ⓒ Ⓓ Ⓔ

Judgment

1. Ⓐ Ⓑ Ⓒ Ⓓ Ⓔ   4. Ⓐ Ⓑ Ⓒ Ⓓ Ⓔ   7. Ⓐ Ⓑ Ⓒ Ⓓ Ⓔ   10. Ⓐ Ⓑ Ⓒ Ⓓ Ⓔ
2. Ⓐ Ⓑ Ⓒ Ⓓ Ⓔ   5. Ⓐ Ⓑ Ⓒ Ⓓ Ⓔ   8. Ⓐ Ⓑ Ⓒ Ⓓ Ⓔ
3. Ⓐ Ⓑ Ⓒ Ⓓ Ⓔ   6. Ⓐ Ⓑ Ⓒ Ⓓ Ⓔ   9. Ⓐ Ⓑ Ⓒ Ⓓ Ⓔ

Logical Reasoning

1. Ⓐ Ⓑ Ⓒ Ⓓ Ⓔ   2. Ⓐ Ⓑ Ⓒ Ⓓ Ⓔ   3. Ⓐ Ⓑ Ⓒ Ⓓ Ⓔ

Tabular Completion

1. Ⓐ Ⓑ Ⓒ Ⓓ Ⓔ   3. Ⓐ Ⓑ Ⓒ Ⓓ Ⓔ   5. Ⓐ Ⓑ Ⓒ Ⓓ Ⓔ
2. Ⓐ Ⓑ Ⓒ Ⓓ Ⓔ   4. Ⓐ Ⓑ Ⓒ Ⓓ Ⓔ

Self-Rating Questions

1. Ⓐ Ⓑ Ⓒ Ⓓ Ⓔ   11. Ⓐ Ⓑ Ⓒ Ⓓ Ⓔ   21. Ⓐ Ⓑ Ⓒ Ⓓ Ⓔ   31. Ⓐ Ⓑ Ⓒ Ⓓ Ⓔ
2. Ⓐ Ⓑ Ⓒ Ⓓ Ⓔ   12. Ⓐ Ⓑ Ⓒ Ⓓ Ⓔ   22. Ⓐ Ⓑ Ⓒ Ⓓ Ⓔ   32. Ⓐ Ⓑ Ⓒ Ⓓ Ⓔ
3. Ⓐ Ⓑ Ⓒ Ⓓ Ⓔ   13. Ⓐ Ⓑ Ⓒ Ⓓ Ⓔ   23. Ⓐ Ⓑ Ⓒ Ⓓ Ⓔ   33. Ⓐ Ⓑ Ⓒ Ⓓ Ⓔ
4. Ⓐ Ⓑ Ⓒ Ⓓ Ⓔ   14. Ⓐ Ⓑ Ⓒ Ⓓ Ⓔ   24. Ⓐ Ⓑ Ⓒ Ⓓ Ⓔ   34. Ⓐ Ⓑ Ⓒ Ⓓ Ⓔ
5. Ⓐ Ⓑ Ⓒ Ⓓ Ⓔ   15. Ⓐ Ⓑ Ⓒ Ⓓ Ⓔ   25. Ⓐ Ⓑ Ⓒ Ⓓ Ⓔ   35. Ⓐ Ⓑ Ⓒ Ⓓ Ⓔ
6. Ⓐ Ⓑ Ⓒ Ⓓ Ⓔ   16. Ⓐ Ⓑ Ⓒ Ⓓ Ⓔ   26. Ⓐ Ⓑ Ⓒ Ⓓ Ⓔ   36. Ⓐ Ⓑ Ⓒ Ⓓ Ⓔ
7. Ⓐ Ⓑ Ⓒ Ⓓ Ⓔ   17. Ⓐ Ⓑ Ⓒ Ⓓ Ⓔ   27. Ⓐ Ⓑ Ⓒ Ⓓ Ⓔ   37. Ⓐ Ⓑ Ⓒ Ⓓ Ⓔ
8. Ⓐ Ⓑ Ⓒ Ⓓ Ⓔ   18. Ⓐ Ⓑ Ⓒ Ⓓ Ⓔ   28. Ⓐ Ⓑ Ⓒ Ⓓ Ⓔ   38. Ⓐ Ⓑ Ⓒ Ⓓ Ⓔ
9. Ⓐ Ⓑ Ⓒ Ⓓ Ⓔ   19. Ⓐ Ⓑ Ⓒ Ⓓ Ⓔ   29. Ⓐ Ⓑ Ⓒ Ⓓ Ⓔ   39. Ⓐ Ⓑ Ⓒ Ⓓ Ⓔ
10. Ⓐ Ⓑ Ⓒ Ⓓ Ⓔ   20. Ⓐ Ⓑ Ⓒ Ⓓ Ⓔ   30. Ⓐ Ⓑ Ⓒ Ⓓ Ⓔ   40. Ⓐ Ⓑ Ⓒ Ⓓ Ⓔ

Practice Test

Federal law enforcement positions are filled through a number of different examinations. Most of these have been developed over the years by the Office of Personnel Management (OPM). Some exams are administered by the OPM for the agencies at their request. Others are administered directly by the agencies. Some of these exams are known by their distinctive names such as the Treasury Enforcement Agent (TEA) Exam, given to Special Agent candidates in a number of agencies and departments. Other OPM exams are simply known by the job titles for which they test, as in the Border Patrol Agent and Postal Police Officer Exams. Still other exams are tailor-made for specific positions. These exams tend to draw questions from the whole gamut of OPM exams. If you find yourself taking one of these tailor-made exams, you will surely recognize elements of exams described in these pages. Your best preparation for any unspecified exam is familiarity and competence with all exam question types found in the following pages.

READING COMPREHENSION AND VERBAL ABILITY

90 Questions • 75 Minutes

Directions: Read each passage carefully and choose the correct answer based on the material in the passage.

1. Impressions made by the ridges on the ends of the fingers and thumbs are useful means of identification since no two persons have the same pattern of ridges. If finger patterns from fingerprints are not decipherable, then they cannot be classified by general shape and contour or by pattern type. If they cannot be classified by these characteristics, then it is impossible to identify the person to whom the fingerprints belong.

The paragraph best supports the statement that if

(A) it is impossible to identify the person to whom fingerprints belong, then the fingerprints are not decipherable.

(B) finger patterns from fingerprints are not decipherable, then it is impossible to identify the person to whom the fingerprints belong.

(C) fingerprints are decipherable, then it is impossible to identify the person to whom they belong.

(D) fingerprints can be classified by general shape and contour or by pattern type, then they are not decipherable.

(E) it is possible to identify the person to whom fingerprints belong, then the fingerprints cannot be classified by general shape and contour or pattern.

2. Law enforcement agencies use scientific techniques to identify suspects or to establish guilt. One obvious application of such techniques is the examination of a crime scene. Some substances found at a crime scene yield valuable clues under microscopic examination. Clothing fibers, dirt particles, and even pollen grains may reveal important information to the careful investigator. Nothing can be overlooked because all substances found at a crime scene are potential sources of evidence.

The paragraph best supports the statement that

(A) all substances that yield valuable clues under microscopic examination are substances found at a crime scene.

(B) some potential sources of evidence are substances that yield valuable clues under microscopic examination.

(C) some substances found at a crime scene are not potential sources of evidence.

(D) no potential sources of evidence are substances found at a crime scene.

(E) some substances that yield valuable clues under microscopic examination are not substances found at a crime scene.

3. A trucking company may act as a "common carrier" for hire to the general public at published rates. As a common carrier, a company is liable for any cargo damage, unless the company can show that it was not negligent. If the company can demonstrate that it is not negligent, then the company is not liable for cargo damage. In contrast, a "contract carrier" (a company hired by a shipper under a specific contract) is only responsible for cargo damage as specifically defined in the contract. Company, Inc., acting under common carrier authority, was in a five-vehicle accident that damaged its cargo. Ajax, Inc., acting under contract carrier authority, was involved in the same accident, and its cargo was also damaged.

    From the above information, it can be validly concluded that, in reference to the accident, if

    (A) Company, Inc. is liable, then it can show that it was not negligent.

    (B) Company, Inc. cannot show that it was not negligent, then it is liable.

    (C) Company, Inc. can show that it was not negligent, then it is not liable.

    (D) Ajax, Inc. is liable, then it cannot show that it is negligent.

    (E) Ajax, Inc. can show that it is not negligent, then it is not liable.

4. John is a former Federal employee who was entitled to benefits under the Federal Employee Compensation Act because of job-related, disabling injury. When an eligible Federal employee has such an injury, the benefit is determined by this test: If the beneficiary is married or has dependents, the benefits are $\frac{3}{4}$ of the person's salary at the time of the injury; otherwise, benefits are set at $\frac{2}{3}$ of the salary. John's benefits were $\frac{2}{3}$ of his salary when he was injured.

    From the above information, it can be validly concluded that, when John was injured, he

    (A) was married but without dependents.

    (B) was not married and had no dependents.

    (C) was not married but had dependents.

    (D) was married and had dependents.

    (E) had never been married.

5. A rapidly changing technical environment in government is promoting greater reliance on electronic mail (e-mail) systems. As this usage grows, there are increasing chances of conflict between electronic user's expectations of privacy and public access rights. In some investigations, access to all e-mail, including those messages stored in archival files and messages outside the scope of the investigation, has been sought and granted. In spite of this, some people send messages through e-mail that would never be said face-to-face or formally written.

From the above information, it cannot be validly concluded that

(A) some e-mail messages that have been requested as part of the investigations have contained messages that never would be said face-to-face.

(B) some messages that people would never say face-to-face are sent in e-mail messages.

(C) some e-mail messages have been requested as part of investigations.

(D) e-mail messages have not been exempted from investigations.

(E) some e-mail messages contain information that would be omitted from formal writing.

6. Some 500,000 immigrants were living in a certain country in 2004. Most of these immigrants were to be employed in professional occupations. Many of them were engineers and many of them were nurses. Very few of these immigrants were librarians, another professional occupation.

From the above information, it can be validly concluded that, in 2004, in the country described above,

(A) most immigrants were either engineers or nurses.

(B) it is not the case that some of the nurses were immigrants.

(C) none of the engineers were immigrants.

(D) most of those not employed in professional occupations were immigrants.

(E) some of the engineers were immigrants.

7. ATF Special Agents were led to believe that many weapons sold at a certain gun store were sold illegally. On investigating a lead, the agents learned that all the weapons sold by the store that were made by Pride Firearms were sold legally. Also, none of the illegally sold weapons were .45 caliber.

From the above information, it can be validly concluded that, concerning the weapons sold at the store,

(A) all of the .45 caliber weapons were made by Pride Firearms.

(B) none of the .45 caliber weapons were made by Pride Firearms.

(C) some of the weapons made by Pride Firearms were .45 caliber weapons.

(D) all of the .45 caliber weapons were sold legally.

(E) some of the weapons made by Pride Firearms were sold illegally.

8. Explosives are substances or devices capable of producing a volume of rapidly expanding gases that exert a sudden pressure on their surroundings. Chemical explosives are the most commonly used, although there are mechanical and nuclear explosives. All mechanical explosives are devices in which a physical reaction is produced, such as that caused by overloading a container with compressed air. While nuclear explosives are by far the most powerful, all nuclear explosives have been restricted to military weapons.

From the above information, it can be validly concluded that

(A) all explosives that have been restricted to military weapons are nuclear explosives.

(B) no mechanical explosives are devices in which a physical reaction is produced, such as that caused by overloading a container with compressed air.

(C) some nuclear explosives have not been restricted to military weapons.

(D) all mechanical explosives have been restricted to military weapons.

(E) some devices in which a physical reaction is produced, such as that caused by overloading a container with compressed air, are mechanical devices.

9. The Supreme Court's power to invalidate legislation that violates the Constitution is a strong restriction on the powers of Congress. If an Act of Congress is deemed unconstitutional by the Supreme Court, then the Act is voided. Unlike a presidential veto, which can be overridden by a two-thirds vote of the House and Senate, a constitutional ruling by the Supreme Court must be accepted by the Congress.

From the above information, it can be validly concluded that if an act of Congress

(A) is voided, then it has been deemed unconstitutional by the Supreme Court.

(B) has not been voided, then it has not been deemed unconstitutional by the Supreme Court.

(C) has not been deemed unconstitutional by the Supreme Court, then it is voided.

(D) is deemed unconstitutional by the Supreme Court, then it is not voided.

(E) has not been voided, then it has been deemed unconstitutional by the Supreme Court.

10. The alphanumeric coding of a fingerprint is a systematic description of the main patterns on the print. Within a certain metropolitan district, 90 percent of the population has fingerprints that can be alphanumerically coded.

From the above information, it can be validly concluded that the fingerprints of a person from this district, selected at random,

(A) can be alphanumerically coded, with a probability of 10%.

(B) can be alphanumerically coded, with a probability of less than 90%.

(C) cannot be alphanumerically coded, with a probability of 10%.

(D) cannot be alphanumerically coded, with a probability of up to 90%.

(E) may be coded alphanumerically, but the probability is unknown.

11. Just as the procedure of a collection department must be clear-cut and definite, the steps being taken with the sureness of a skilled chess player, so too must the various paragraphs of a collection letter show clear organization, giving evidence of a mind that, from the beginning, has had a specific end in view.

The paragraph best supports the statement that a collection letter should always

(A) show a spirit of sportsmanship.

(B) be divided into several paragraphs.

(C) be brief but courteous.

(D) be carefully planned.

(E) be written by the head of the collection department.

12. To prevent industrial accidents, it is not only necessary that safety devices be used to guard exposed machinery, but also that mechanics be instructed in the safety rules they must follow for their own protection and that the lighting in the plant be adequate.

The paragraph best supports the statement that industrial accidents

(A) may be due to ignorance.

(B) are always avoidable.

(C) usually result from unsafe machinery.

(D) cannot be entirely overcome.

(E) usually result from inadequate lighting.

13. Through advertising, manufacturers exercise a high degree of control over consumers' desires. However, the manufacturer assumes enormous risks in attempting to predict what consumers will want and in producing goods in quantity and distributing them in advance of final selection by the consumers.

The paragraph best supports the statement that manufacturers

(A) can eliminate the risk of overproduction by advertising.

(B) distribute goods directly to the consumers.

(C) must depend on the final consumers for the success of their undertakings.

(D) can predict with great accuracy the success of any product they put on the market.

(E) are more concerned with advertising than with the production of goods.

14. "Some fire-resistant buildings, although wholly constructed of materials that will not burn, may be completely gutted by the spread of fire through their contents by way of hallways and other openings. They may even suffer serious structural damage by the collapse of metal beams and columns."

The quotation best supports the statement that some fire-resistant buildings

(A) can be damaged seriously by fire.

(B) have specially constructed halls and doors.

(C) afford less protection to their contents than would ordinary buildings.

(D) will burn readily.

15. Civilization started to move ahead more rapidly when people freed themselves of the shackles that restricted their search for the truth.

The paragraph best supports the statement that the progress of civilization

(A) came as a result of people's dislike for obstacles.

(B) did not begin until restrictions on learning were removed.

(C) has been aided by people's efforts to find the truth.

(D) is based on continually increasing efforts.

16. The likelihood of America's exhausting its natural resources seems to be growing less. All kinds of waste are being reworked and new uses are constantly being found for almost everything. We are getting more use out of our goods and are making many new byproducts out of what was formerly thrown away.

The paragraph best supports the statement that we seem to be in less danger of exhausting our resources because

(A) economy is found to lie in the use of substitutes.

(B) more service is obtained from a given amount of material.

(C) we are allowing time for nature to restore them.

(D) supply and demand are better controlled.

17. Telegrams should be clear, concise, and brief. Omit all unnecessary words. The parts of speech most often used in telegrams are nouns, verbs, adjectives, and adverbs. If possible, do without pronouns, articles, and copulative verbs. Use simple sentences rather than complex or compound ones.

The paragraph best supports the statement that in writing telegrams one should always use

(A) common and simple words.

(B) only nouns, verbs, adjectives, and adverbs.

(C) incomplete sentences.

(D) only the words essential to the meaning.

18. The prevention of accidents makes it necessary not only that safety devices be used to guard exposed machinery but also that mechanics be instructed in safety rules to follow for their own protection, and that the lighting in the plant be adequate.

The paragraph best supports the statement that industrial accidents

(A) may be caused by lack of knowledge.

(B) are always avoidable.

(C) usually result from inadequate machinery.

(D) cannot be entirely prevented.

19. The English language is peculiarly rich in synonyms, and there is scarcely a language spoken that has not some representative in English speech. The spirit of the Anglo-Saxon race has subjugated these various elements to one idiom, making not a patchwork, but a composite language.

The paragraph best supports the statement that the English language

(A) has few idiomatic expressions.

(B) is difficult to translate.

(C) is used universally.

(D) has absorbed words from other languages.

20. Through advertising, manufacturers exercise a high degree of control over consumers' desires. However, the manufacturer assumes enormous risks in attempting to predict what consumers will want and in producing goods in quantity and distributing them in advance of final selection by the consumers.

The paragraph best supports the statement that manufacturers

(A) can eliminate the risk of overproduction by advertising.

(B) distribute goods directly to the consumer.

(C) must depend upon the final consumer for the success of their undertakings.

(D) can predict with great accuracy the success of any product they put on the market.

21. In the relationship between humans and nature, the procuring of food and shelter is fundamental. With the migration of humans to various climates, new adjustments to the food supply and to the climate became necessary.

The paragraph best supports the statement that the means by which humans gather their material needs are

(A) accidental.

(B) varied.

(C) limited.

(D) inadequate.

22. What constitutes skill in any line of work is not always easy to determine. Economy of time must be carefully distinguished from economy of energy, as the quickest method may require the greatest expenditure of muscular effort and may not be essential or desirable.

The paragraph best supports the statement that

(A) the most efficiently executed task is not always the one done in the shortest time.

(B) energy and time cannot both be conserved in performing a single task.

(C) a task is well done when it is performed in the shortest time.

(D) skill in performing a task should not be acquired at the expense of time.

23. It is difficult to distinguish between bookkeeping and accounting. In an attempt to so, we can say that bookkeeping is the art and accounting the science of recording business transactions. Bookkeeping gives the history of the business systematically; accounting classifies, analyzes, and interprets the facts recorded.

The paragraph best supports the statement that

(A) accounting is less systematic than bookkeeping.

(B) accounting and bookkeeping are closely related.

(C) bookkeeping and accounting cannot be distinguished from one another.

(D) bookkeeping has been superseded by accounting.

FOR QUESTIONS 24–51, CHOOSE THE WORD THAT MEANS MOST NEARLY THE SAME AS THE WORD IN ITALICS.

24. *FRAUDULENT*
   (A) suspicious
   (B) unproven
   (C) deceptive
   (D) unfair

25. *ALLEGATION*
   (A) response
   (B) inquiry
   (C) assertion
   (D) revelation

26. *PREVIOUS*
   (A) abandoned
   (B) former
   (C) unused
   (D) recent

27. *VERIFY*
   (A) examine
   (B) explain
   (C) confirm
   (D) believe

28. *OPTION*
   (A) use
   (B) direction
   (C) hope
   (D) choice

29. *FLEXIBLE*
   (A) breakable
   (B) flammable
   (C) pliable
   (D) weak

30. *RESPIRATION*
   (A) recovery
   (B) breathing
   (C) pulsation
   (D) sweating

31. *INDOLENT*
   (A) moderate
   (B) hopeless
   (C) selfish
   (D) lazy

32. *VIGILANT*
   (A) sensible
   (B) watchful
   (C) suspicious
   (D) restless

33. *INCIDENTAL*
   (A) independent
   (B) needless
   (C) infrequent
   (D) accompanying

34. *CONCILIATORY*
   (A) pacific
   (B) contentious
   (C) obligatory
   (D) offensive

35. *ALTERCATION*
   (A) defeat
   (B) concurrence
   (C) controversy
   (D) vexation

36. *IRRESOLUTE*
   (A) wavering
   (B) insubordinate
   (C) impudent
   (D) unobservant

37. *COUNTERACT*
    (A) undermine
    (B) censure
    (C) preserve
    (D) neutralize

38. *DEFERRED*
    (A) reversed
    (B) delayed
    (C) considered
    (D) forbidden

39. *FEASIBLE*
    (A) capable
    (B) justifiable
    (C) practicable
    (D) beneficial

40. *ENCOUNTER*
    (A) meet
    (B) recall
    (C) overcome
    (D) retreat

41. *INNATE*
    (A) eternal
    (B) well-developed
    (C) native
    (D) prospective

42. *ACQUIESCE*
    (A) assent
    (B) acquire
    (C) complete
    (D) participate

43. *UNANIMITY*
    (A) emphasis
    (B) namelessness
    (C) harmony
    (D) impartiality

44. *PRECEDENT*
    (A) example
    (B) theory
    (C) law
    (D) conformity

45. *VERSATILE*
    (A) broad-minded
    (B) well-known
    (C) up-to-date
    (D) many-sided

46. *AUTHENTIC*
    (A) detailed
    (B) reliable
    (C) valuable
    (D) practical

47. *STRIDENT*
    (A) swaggering
    (B) domineering
    (C) angry
    (D) harsh

48. *CONFINE*
    (A) hide
    (B) restrict
    (C) eliminate
    (D) punish

49. *ACCENTUATE*
    (A) modify
    (B) hasten
    (C) sustain
    (D) intensify

50. *BANAL*
    (A) commonplace
    (B) forceful
    (C) tranquil
    (D) indifferent

practice test

51. *INCORRIGIBLE*

    (A) intolerable

    (B) retarded

    (C) irreformable

    (D) brazen

FOR QUESTIONS 52–71, CHOOSE THE WORD THAT BEST COMPLETES THE ANALOGY.

52. PLUMBER : WRENCH :: PAINTER :

    (A) brush

    (B) pipe

    (C) shop

    (D) hammer

53. LETTER : MESSAGE :: PACKAGE :

    (A) sender

    (B) merchandise

    (C) insurance

    (D) business

54. FOOD : HUNGER :: SLEEP :

    (A) night

    (B) dream

    (C) weariness

    (D) rest

55. KEY : COMPUTER :: DIAL :

    (A) sun

    (B) number

    (C) circle

    (D) telephone

56. DARKNESS : SUNLIGHT :: STILLNESS :

    (A) quiet

    (B) moonlight

    (C) sound

    (D) dark

57. DESIGNED : INTENTION :: ACCIDENTAL :

    (A) purpose

    (B) caution

    (C) damage

    (D) chance

58. ERROR : PRACTICE :: SOUND :

    (A) deafness

    (B) noise

    (C) muffler

    (D) horn

59. RESEARCH : FINDINGS :: TRAINING :

    (A) skill

    (B) tests

    (C) supervision

    (D) teaching

60. STUDENT : TEACHER :: DISCIPLE :

    (A) follower

    (B) master

    (C) principal

    (D) pupil

61. LECTURE : AUDITORIUM :: EXPERIMENT :

    (A) scientist

    (B) chemistry

    (C) laboratory

    (D) discovery

62. BODY : FOOD :: ENGINE :

    (A) wheels

    (B) fuel

    (C) motion

    (D) smoke

63. SCHOOL : EDUCATION :: THEATER :

    (A) management

    (B) stage

    (C) recreation

    (D) preparation

64. BIOGRAPHY : FACT :: NOVEL :

    (A) fiction

    (B) literature

    (C) narration

    (D) book

65. COPY : CARBON PAPER :: MOTION PICTURE :
   (A) theater
   (B) film
   (C) duplicate
   (D) television

66. EFFICIENCY : REWARD :: CARELESSNESS :
   (A) improvement
   (B) disobedience
   (C) reprimand
   (D) repetition

67. ABUNDANT : CHEAP :: SCARCE :
   (A) ample
   (B) costly
   (C) inexpensive
   (D) unobtainable

68. POLICE OFFICER : ORDER :: DOCTOR :
   (A) physician
   (B) hospital
   (C) sickness
   (D) health

69. ARTIST : EASEL :: WEAVER :
   (A) loom
   (B) cloth
   (C) threads
   (D) spinner

70. CROWD : PERSONS :: FLEET :
   (A) expedition
   (B) officers
   (C) navy
   (D) ships

71. CALENDAR : DATE :: MAP :
   (A) drive
   (B) trip
   (C) location
   (D) vacation

FOR QUESTIONS 72–90, CHOOSE THE SENTENCE THAT IS BEST WITH RESPECT TO GRAMMAR AND USAGE.

72. (A) The officer should of answered courteously the questions asked by the callers.
   (B) The officer must answer courteously the questions of all them callers.
   (C) The officer must answer courteously the questions what are asked by the callers.
   (D) There would have been no trouble if the officer had have always answered courteously.

73. (A) There are less mistakes in his work since he took the training course.
   (B) The training course being completed, he makes very few mistakes in his work.
   (C) Since he completed the training course, he has made few mistakes in his work.
   (D) After taking the training course, his work was found to contain hardly any mistakes.

74. (A) I think that they will promote whoever has the best record.
   (B) The firm would have liked to have promoted all employees with good records.
   (C) Such of them that have the best records have excellent prospects of promotion.
   (D) I feel sure they will give the promotion to whomever has the best record.

75. (A) The receptionist must answer courteously the questions of all them callers.

   (B) The receptionist must answer courteously the questions what are asked by the callers.

   (C) There would have been no trouble if the receptionist had have always answered courteously.

   (D) The receptionist should answer courteously the questions of the callers.

76. (A) If properly addressed, the letter will reach my mother and I.

   (B) The letter had been addressed to myself and my mother.

   (C) I believe the letter was addressed to either my mother or I.

   (D) My mother's name, as well as mine, was on the letter.

77. (A) The supervisors reprimanded the typists, whom she believed had made careless errors

   (B) The typists would have corrected the errors had they of known that the supervisor would see the report.

   (C) The errors in the typed reports were so numerous that they could hardly be overlooked.

   (D) Many errors were found in the reports which they typed and could not disregard them.

78. (A) Most all these statements have been supported by persons who are reliable and can be depended upon.

   (B) The persons which have guaranteed these statements are reliable.

   (C) Reliable persons guarantee the facts with regards to the truth of these statements.

   (D) These statements can be depended on, for their truth has been guaranteed by reliable persons.

79. (A) The success of the book pleased both the publishers and the authors.

   (B) Both the publisher and they was pleased with the success of the book.

   (C) Neither they or their publisher was disappointed with their success of the book.

   (D) Their publisher was as pleased as them with the success of the book.

80. (A) Brown's & Company employees have recently received increases in salary.

   (B) Brown & Company recently increased the salaries of all its employees.

   (C) Recently Brown & Company has increased their employees' salaries.

   (D) Brown & Company have recently increased the salaries of all its employees.

81. (A) In reviewing the typists' work reports, the job analyst found records of unusual typing speeds.

   (B) It says in the job analyst's report that some employees type with great speed.

   (C) The job analyst found that, in reviewing the typists' work reports, that some unusual typing speeds had been made.

   (D) In the reports of typists' speeds, the job analyst found some records that are kind of unusual.

82. (A) Since the report lacked the needed information, it was of no use to them.

   (B) This report was useless to them because there were no needed information in it.

   (C) Since the report did not contain the needed information, it was not real useful to them.

   (D) Being that the report lacked the needed information, they could not use it.

83. **(A)** The company had hardly declared the dividend till the notices were prepared for mailing.

    (B) They had no sooner declared the dividend when they sent the notices to stockholders.

    (C) No sooner had the dividend been declared than the notices were prepared for mailing.

    (D) Scarcely had the dividend been declared than the notices were sent out.

84. **(A)** Double parking is when you park your car alongside one that is already having been parked.

    (B) When one double parks, you park your car alongside one that is already parked.

    (C) Double parking is parking alongside a car already parked.

    (D) To double park is alongside a car already parked.

85. **(A)** This is entirely among you and him.

    (B) This is completely among him and you.

    (C) This is between you and him.

    (D) This is between he and you.

86. **(A)** As I said, "neither of them are guilty."

    (B) As I said, "neither of them are guilty".

    (C) As I said, "neither of them is guilty."

    (D) As I said, neither of them is guilty.

87. **(A)** "Are you absolutely certain, she asked, that you are right?"

    (B) "Are you absolutely certain," she asked, "that you are right?"

    (C) "Are you absolutely certain," she asked, "That you are right""

    (D) "Are you absolutely certain", she asked, "That you are right?"

88. **(A)** He goes only to church on Christmas and Easter.

    (B) He only goes to church on Christmas and Easter.

    (C) He goes to only church on Christmas and Easter.

    (D) He goes to church only on Christmas and Easter.

89. **(A)** You have to get rid of some of these people if you expect to have the quality of the work improve.

    (B) The quality of the work should improve if they would leave fewer people do it.

    (C) I believe it would be desirable to have fewer persons doing this work.

    (D) If you had planned on employing fewer people than this to do the work, this situation would not have arose.

90. **(A)** The paper we use for this purpose must be light, glossy, and stand hard usage as well.

    (B) Only a light and a glossy, but durable, paper must be used for this purpose.

    (C) For this purpose, we want a paper that is light, glossy, but that will stand hard wear.

    (D) For this purpose, paper that is light, glossy, and durable is essential.

ARITHMETIC REASONING

25 Questions • 50 Minutes

> **Directions:** In this part, you will have to solve problems formulated in both verbal and numeric form. You will have to analyze a paragraph to set up the problem and then solve it. If the exact answer is not given as one of the response choices, you should select choice (E).

1. A police department purchases badges at $16 each for all the graduates of the police training academy. The last training class graduated 10 new officers. What is the total amount of money the department will spend for badges for these new officers?

   (A) $70

   (B) $116

   (C) $160

   (D) $180

   (E) None of these

2. Assume that your unit ordered 14 staplers at a total cost of $30.20, and each stapler costs the same amount. The cost of one stapler was most nearly

   (A) $1.02

   (B) $1.61

   (C) $2.16

   (D) $2.26

   (E) None of the above

3. If 314 clerks filed 6,594 papers in 10 minutes, what is the number filed per minute by the average clerk?

   (A) 2

   (B) 2.4

   (C) 2.1

   (D) 2.5

   (E) None of these

4. Four men working together can dig a ditch in 42 days. They begin, but one man works only half-days. How long will it take to complete the job?

   (A) 48 days

   (B) 45 days

   (C) 43 days

   (D) 44 days

   (E) None of the above

5. Assume that you are responsible for counting and recording licensing fees collected by your department. On a particular day, your department collected 40 checks in the amount of $6.00 each; 80 checks in the amount of $4.00 each; 45 $20 bills; 30 $10 bills; 42 $5 bills; and 186 $1 bills. The total amount in fees collected on that day was

   (A) $1,406

   (B) $1,706

   (C) $2,156

   (D) $2,356

   (E) None of the above

6. A clerk is requested to file 800 cards. If he can file cards at a rate of 80 cards per hour, the number of cards remaining to be filed after seven hours of work is

   (A) 140

   (B) 240

   (C) 260

   (D) 560

   (E) None of the above

7. If it takes four days for three machines to do a certain job, it will take two machines

    (A) 6 days

    (B) $5\frac{1}{2}$ days

    (C) 5 days

    (D) $4\frac{1}{2}$ days

    (E) None of the above

8. A stenographer has been assigned to place entries on 500 forms. She places entries on 25 forms by the end of half an hour when she is joined by another stenographer. The second stenographer places entries at the rate of 45 per hour. Assuming that both stenographers continue to work at their respective rates of speed, the total number of hours required to carry out the entire assignment is

    (A) 5

    (B) $5\frac{1}{2}$

    (C) $6\frac{1}{2}$

    (D) 7

    (E) None of the above

9. Assume that you are responsible for your agency's petty cash fund. During the month of February, you pay out seven subway fares at $1.25 each and one taxi fare for $7.30. You pay out nothing else from the fund. At the end of February, you count the money left in the fund and find three $1 bills, four quarters, five dimes, and four nickels. The amount of money you had available in the petty cash fund at the beginning of February was

    (A) $4.70

    (B) $11.35

    (C) $16.05

    (D) $20.75

    (E) None of the above

10. If in five days a clerk can copy 125 pages, 36 lines each, 11 words to the line, how many pages of 30 lines each and 12 words per line can he copy in six days?

    (A) 145

    (B) 155

    (C) 160

    (D) 165

    (E) None of the above

11. A and B do a job together in 2 hours. Working alone, A does the job in 5 hours. How long will it take B to do the job alone?

    (A) $3\frac{1}{3}$ hours

    (B) $2\frac{1}{4}$ hours

    (C) 3 hours

    (D) 2 hours

    (E) None of the above

12. If a certain job can be performed by 18 workers in 26 days, the number of workers needed to perform the job in 12 days is

    (A) 24

    (B) 30

    (C) 39

    (D) 52

    (E) None of the above

13. A stenographer transcribes her notes at the rate of one line typed in 10 seconds. At this rate, how long (in minutes and seconds) will it take her to transcribe notes that require seven pages of typing, 25 lines per page?

    (A) 29 min. and 10 sec.

    (B) 17 min. and 50 sec.

    (C) 40 min. and 10 sec.

    (D) 20 min. and 30 sec.

    (E) None of the above

14. Assume you are assigned to sell tickets at a city-owned ice skating rink. An adult's ticket costs $3.75, and a children's ticket costs $2. At the end of the day, you have sold 36 adult tickets and 80 children's tickets. The total amount of money you collected for the day was

    (A) $285.50

    (B) $295.00

    (C) $298.75

    (D) $301.00

15. If each office worker files 487 index cards in one hour, how many cards can 26 office workers file in one hour?

    (A) 10,662

    (B) 12,175

    (C) 12,662

    (D) 14,266

16. An investigator rented a car for six days and was charged $450. The car rental company charged $35 per day plus $.30 per mile driven. How many miles did the investigator drive the car?

    (A) 800

    (B) 900

    (C) 1,290

    (D) 1,500

    (E) None of these

17. In one federal office, $\frac{1}{6}$ of the employees favored abandoning a flexible work schedule system. In a second office that had the same number of employees, $\frac{1}{4}$ of the workers favored abandoning it. What is the average of the fractions of the workers in the two offices who favored abandoning the system?

    (A) $\dfrac{1}{10}$

    (B) $\dfrac{1}{5}$

    (C) $\dfrac{5}{24}$

    (D) $\dfrac{5}{12}$

    (E) None of the above

18. A federal agency had a personal computer repaired at a cost of $49.20. This amount included a charge of $22 per hour for labor and a charge for a new switch that cost $18 before a 10% government discount was applied. How long did the repair job take?

    (A) 1 hour and 6 min.

    (B) 1 hour and 11 min.

    (C) 1 hour and 22 min.

    (D) 1 hour and 30 min.

    (E) None of the above

19. In a large agency where mail is delivered in motorized carts, two tires were replaced on a cart at a cost of $34 per tire. If the agency had expected to pay $80 for a pair of tires, what percent of its expected cost did it leave?

    (A) 7.5%

    (B) 17.6%

    (C) 57.5%

    (D) 75.0%

    (E) None of the above

20. An interagency task force has representatives from three different agencies. Half of the task force members represent Agency A, one third represent Agency B, and three represent Agency C. How many people are on the task force?

(A) 12

(B) 15

(C) 18

(D) 24

(E) None of the above

21. It has been established in recent productivity studies that, on the average, it takes a filing clerk 2 hours and 12 minutes to fill four drawers of a filing cabinet. At this rate, how long would it take two clerks to fill 16 drawers?

(A) 4 hours

(B) 4 hours and 20 min.

(C) 8 hours

(D) 8 hours and 40 min.

(E) None of the above

22. It costs $60,000 per month to maintain a small medical facility. The basic charge per person for treatment is $40, but 50% of those seeking treatment require laboratory work at an additional average charge of $20 per person. How many patients per month would the facility have to serve in order to cover its costs?

(A) 1,000

(B) 1,200

(C) 1,500

(D) 2,000

(E) None of the above

23. An experimental anti-pollution vehicle powered by electricity traveled 33 kilometers (km) at a constant speed of 110 kilometers per hour (km/h). How many minutes did it take this vehicle to complete its experimental run?

(A) 3

(B) 10

(C) 18

(D) 20

(E) None of the above

24. It takes two typists three eight-hour workdays to type a report on a word processor. How many typists would be needed to type two reports of the same length in one eight-hour workday?

(A) 4

(B) 6

(C) 8

(D) 12

(E) None of the above

25. A clerk is able to process 40 unemployment compensation claims in one hour. After deductions of 18% for benefits and taxes, the clerk's net pay is $6.97 per hour. If the clerk processed 1,200 claims, how much would the government have to pay for the work based on the clerk's hourly wage before deductions?

(A) $278.80

(B) $255.00

(C) $246.74

(D) $209.10

(E) None of the above

COMPARISONS AND SEQUENCE

40 Questions • 15 Minutes

Directions: Each line includes three names or numbers that are very similar. Compare the three names or numbers and decide which ones are exactly alike. Choose:

(A) if ALL THREE names or numbers are exactly ALIKE
(B) if only the FIRST and SECOND names or numbers are exactly ALIKE
(C) if only the FIRST and THIRD names or numbers are exactly ALIKE
(D) if only the SECOND and THIRD names or numbers are exactly ALIKE
(E) if ALL THREE names or numbers are DIFFERENT

1.	Davis Hazen	David Hozen	David Hazen
2.	Lois Appel	Lois Appel	Lois Apfel
3.	June Allan	Jane Allan	Jane Allan
4.	Emily Neal Rouse	Emily Neal Rowse	Emily Neal Rowse
5.	H. Merritt Audubon	H. Merriott Audubon	H. Merritt Audubon
6.	6219354	6219354	6219354
7.	2312793	2312793	2312793
8.	1065407	1065407	1065047
9.	3457988	3457986	3457986
10.	4695682	4695862	4695682
11.	Francis Ransdell	Frances Ramsdell	Francis Ramsdell
12.	Cornelius Detwiler	Cornelius Detwiler	Cornelius Detwiler
13.	Stricklund Kanedy	Stricklund Kanedy	Stricklund Kanedy
14.	Joy Harlor Witner	Joy Harloe Witner	Joy Harloe Witner
15.	R.M.O. Uberroth	R.M.O. Uberroth	R.N.O. Uberroth
16.	2395890	2395890	2395890
17.	1926341	1926347	1926314
18.	5261383	5261383	5261338
19.	8125690	8126690	8125609

20. 6177396	6177936	6177396
21. W. E. Johnston	W.E. Johnson	W.E. Johnson
22. Vergil L. Muller	Vergil L. Muller	Vergil L. Muller
23. Atherton R. Warde	Asheton R. Warde	Atherton P. Warde
24. 6452054	6452654	6452054
25. E. Owens McVey	E. Owen McVey	E. Owen McVay
26. 8501268	8501268	8501286
27. Ella Burk Newham	Ella Burk Newnham	Elena Burk Newnham
28. Jno. K. Ravencroft	Jno. H. Ravencroft	Jno. H. Ravencroft
29. 1592514	1592574	1592574
30. Martin Wills Pullen	Martin Wills Pulen	Martin Wills Pullen

FOR QUESTIONS 31–40, SELECT THE PAIR OF NUMBERS THAT CORRECTLY COMPLETES THE SERIES.

31. 1 2 3 4 5 6 7
  - (A) 1 2
  - (B) 5 6
  - (C) 8 9
  - (D) 4 5
  - (E) 7 8

32. 15 14 13 12 11 10 9
  - (A) 2 1
  - (B) 17 16
  - (C) 8 9
  - (D) 8 7
  - (E) 9 8

33. 20 20 21 21 22 22 23
  - (A) 23 23
  - (B) 23 24
  - (C) 19 19
  - (D) 22 23
  - (E) 21 22

34. 17 3 17 4 17 5 17
  - (A) 6 17
  - (B) 6 7
  - (C) 17 6
  - (D) 5 6
  - (E) 17 7

35. 1 2 4 5 7 8 10
  - (A) 11 12
  - (B) 12 14
  - (C) 10 13
  - (D) 12 13
  - (E) 11 13

36. 21 21 20 20 19 19 18
  - (A) 18 18
  - (B) 18 17
  - (C) 17 18
  - (D) 17 17
  - (E) 18 19

37. 1 20 3 19 5 18 7
  - (A) 8 9
  - (B) 8 17
  - (C) 17 10
  - (D) 17 9
  - (E) 9 18

38. 30 2 28 4 26 6 24
  - (A) 23 9
  - (B) 26 8
  - (C) 8 9
  - (D) 26 22
  - (E) 8 22

39. 5 6 20 7 8 19 9
  - (A) 10 18
  - (B) 18 17
  - (C) 10 17
  - (D) 18 19
  - (E) 10 11

40. 1 11 12 2 13
  - (A) 2 14
  - (B) 3 14
  - (C) 14 3
  - (D) 14 15
  - (E) 14 1

PROBLEMS FOR INVESTIGATION

5 Questions • 15 Minutes

Directions: Read each passage carefully and choose the correct answer based on the material in the passage.

On October 30, the Belton First National Bank discovered that the $3,000 it had received that morning from the Greenville First National Bank was in counterfeit $10, $20, and $50 bills. The genuine $3,000 had been counted by Greenville First National bank clerk Iris Stewart the preceding afternoon. They were packed in eight black leather satchels and were stored in the bank vault overnight. Greenville First National clerk Brian Caruthers accompanied carriers James Clark and Howard O'Keefe to Belton in an armored truck. Belton First National clerk Cynthia Randall discovered the counterfeit bills when she examined the serial numbers of the bills.

During the course of the investigation, the following statements were made:

(1) Gerald Hathaway, clerk of the Greenville bank, told investigators that he had found the bank office open when he arrived to work on the morning of October 30. The only articles that appeared to be missing were eight black leather satchels of the type used to transport large sums of money.

(2) Jon Perkins, head teller of the Greenville bank, told investigators that he did not check the contents of the black leather satchels after locking them in the vault around 4:30 p.m. on October 29.

(3) Henry Green, janitor of the Greenville bank, said that he noticed Jon Perkins leaving the bank office around 5:30 p.m., one-half hour after the bank closed on October 29. He said that Perkins locked the door.

(4) A scrap of cloth, identical to the material of the carriers' uniforms, was found caught in the seal of one of the black leather satchels delivered to Belton.

(5) Brian Caruthers, clerk, said he saw James Clark and Howard O'Keefe talking in a secretive manner in the armored truck.

(6) Thomas Stillman, Greenville bank executive, identified the eight black leather satchels containing the counterfeit money that arrived at the Belton First National Bank as the eight satchels that had disappeared from the bank office. He had noticed a slight difference in the linings of the satchels.

(7) Virginia Fowler, bank accountant, noticed two $10 bills with the same serial numbers as the lost bills in a bank deposit from Ferdinand's Restaurant of Greenville.

(8) Vincent Johnson, manager of Ferdinand's Restaurant, told police that Iris Stewart frequently dined there with her boyfriend.

1. Which one of the following statements best indicates that satchels containing the counterfeit bills were substituted for satchels containing genuine bills while they were being transported from Greenville to Belton?

   (A) Statement (1)
   (B) Statement (3)
   (C) Statement (4)
   (D) Statement (5)
   (E) Statement (7)

2. Which one of the following statements best links the information given in statement (1) with the substitution of the counterfeit bills?

   (A) Statement (2)
   (B) Statement (3)
   (C) Statement (4)
   (D) Statement (5)
   (E) Statement (6)

3. Which one of the following statements, along with statement (7), best indicates that the substitution of the counterfeit bills casts suspicion on at least one employee of the Greenville bank?

   (A) Statement (1)
   (B) Statement (2)
   (C) Statement (3)
   (D) Statement (5)
   (E) Statement (8)

4. Which one of the following statements would least likely be used in proving a case?

   (A) Statement (1)
   (B) Statement (3)
   (C) Statement (4)
   (D) Statement (5)
   (E) Statement (7)

5. Which one of the following statements best indicates that the substitution of the counterfeit bills could have taken place before the satchels left the Greenville bank?

   (A) Statement (1)
   (B) Statement (2)
   (C) Statement (3)
   (D) Statement (4)
   (E) Statement (7)

JUDGMENT

10 Questions • 10 Minutes

> **Directions:** Use your judgment and general knowledge to select the best or most important answer.

1. Decisions about handcuffing or restraining inmates are often up to the corrections officers involved. An officer is legally responsible for exercising good judgment and for taking necessary precautions to prevent harm both to the inmate involved and to others. In which one of the following situations is handcuffing or other physical restraint likely to be needed?

   (A) An inmate seems to have lost control of his senses and is banging his fists repeatedly against the bars of his cell.

   (B) During the past two weeks, an inmate has deliberately tried to start three fights with other inmates.

   (C) An inmate claims to be sick and refuses to leave his cell for a scheduled meal.

   (D) During the night, an inmate begins to shout and sing, disturbing the sleep of other inmates.

2. While you are working on a routine assignment, a coworker asks you to help her for a few minutes so that she can complete an assignment that has top priority and must be completed immediately. Of the following, the best action for you to take should be to

   (A) Tell her to find somebody else who does not look busy and ask that person for help.

   (B) Tell her you will help her as soon as you complete your own work.

   (C) Help her to complete her assignment and then go back to your work.

   (D) Tell her that your work is as important to you as her work is to her, and continue to work on your own assignment.

3. A police officer stationed along the route of a parade has been ordered not to allow cars to cross the route while the parade is in progress. An ambulance driver on an emergency run attempts to drive across the parade route. Under these circumstances, the officer should

   (A) ask the driver to wait while the officer calls headquarters and obtains a decision.

   (B) stop the parade long enough to permit the ambulance to cross the street.

   (C) direct the ambulance driver to the shortest detour available, which will add at least ten minutes to the run.

   (D) hold up the ambulance in accordance with the order.

4. An office worker frequently complains to the building custodian that her office is poorly lit. The best action for the building custodian to follow is to

   (A) ignore the complaints because they come from a habitual crank.

   (B) inform the worker that illumination is a fixed item built into the building originally and evidently is the result of faulty planning by the architect.

   (C) request a licensed electrician to install additional ceiling lights.

   (D) investigate for faulty illumination features in the room, such as dirty lamp globes and incorrect lamp wattage.

5. Suppose one of your neighbors walks into the police precinct where you are an administrative aide and asks you to make 100 photocopies of a flyer he intends to distribute in the neighborhood. Of the following, what action should you take in this situation?

   (A) Pretend that you do not know the person and order him to leave the building.

   (B) Call a police officer and report the person for attempting to make illegal use of police equipment.

   (C) Tell the person that you will make copies when you are off duty.

   (D) Explain that you cannot use police equipment for non-police work.

6. A police officer, walking a beat at 3 a.m., notices heavy smoke coming from the top floor of a large apartment building. From the following choices, the officer should first

   (A) make certain there is really a fire.

   (B) enter the building and warn all the occupants.

   (C) attempt to extinguish the fire before it spreads.

   (D) call the fire department.

7. An elevator inspector on routine inspection for the Building Department notices a number of dangerous situations in the basement of the building she is in. Of the following conditions, which is the most dangerous and should be reported immediately?

   (A) Gas is leaking from a broken pipe.

   (B) The sewer pipe is broken.

   (C) Water is seeping into the basement.

   (D) The basement is unlit.

8. There are times when an employee of one city department should notify and seek assistance from employees of another department. A parking enforcement agent is checking meters on a busy one-way street. Of the following situations, which should he report immediately?

   (A) A rat runs out of a building and into the storm sewer across the street.

   (B) A wire is dangling over the sidewalk, giving off sparks.

   (C) A car is parked directly in front of a hydrant.

   (D) Two men are sitting on the front steps of a building smoking marijuana.

9. Acquaintance with all types of ammunition commonly in use is extremely valuable to the worker in crime detection chiefly because

(A) all criminals possess this knowledge.

(B) a broad background is desirable for success in investigative work.

(C) the worker's safety is thus ensured in time of danger.

(D) the worker can thus eventually become a specialist in this line.

(E) such knowledge often simplifies the problem of investigation.

10. From the standpoint of the prisoners, the chief advantage to be derived from a properly administered parole system is the

(A) freedom from fear of being returned to prison.

(B) opportunity to adjust themselves to release from imprisonment.

(C) removal of the temptation to commit crime.

(D) reduced cost of supervising prisoners.

(E) opportunity to save whatever they are able to earn.

LOGICAL REASONING

3 Questions • 5 Minutes

Directions: Each of these questions consists of five related events followed by five suggested orders in which the events could have occurred. Each suggested order represents the sequence in which the five sentences should be read. For example, 3-5-1-2-4 indicates that the third sentence should be read first, the fifth sentence second, the first sentence third, and so on. Select the one of the five suggested orders, lettered (A), (B), (C), (D), and (E), in which the events most probably happened.

1.
1. The maid discovered the body and called the police.
2. The police found Mary at the home of her sister.
3. A man was shot while swimming in his private pool.
4. A gun was found in Mary's purse and was identified as the murder weapon.
5. The police questioned the maid and discovered that the victim had had a heated argument with his wife, Mary, the night before.

(A) 1-3-5-4-2
(B) 3-5-1-4-2
(C) 3-1-5-2-4
(D) 1-5-2-4-3
(E) 3-1-2-4-5

2.
1. The inspector realized that Ms. Smith was wearing a wig and had her searched.
2. The inspector decided to search Ms. Smith's luggage.
3. Although the inspector could not place the face, he knew that Ms. Smith looked familiar.
4. Narcotics were found sewn to the crown of Ms. Smith's wig.
5. The inspector found nothing in Ms. Smith's luggage, but her passport photograph revealed her identity as a suspected smuggler.

(A) 2-5-3-1-4
(B) 3-1-4-2-5
(C) 1-4-2-5-3
(D) 3-2-5-1-4
(E) 2-1-3-5-4

3. 1. In addition to the paper, a printing press and a stack of freshly printed $10 bills were found in Mr. Hayes's basement.

2. A detective saw Mr. Hayes leave a printing shop with a large package.

3. Mr. Hayes was arrested for counterfeiting and taken to the station.

4. The owner of the shop said Mr. Hayes had bought very high-quality paper.

5. Mr. Hayes was under surveillance as a suspect in a counterfeiting case.

(A) 2-4-1-5-3

(B) 5-2-4-1-3

(C) 3-2-4-1-5

(D) 2-5-1.4-3

(E) 5-2-3-4-1

TABULAR COMPLETION

5 Questions • 10 Minutes

> **Directions:** These questions are based on information presented in tables. Calculate these unknown values by using the known values given in the table. In some questions, the exact answer will not be given as one of the response choices. In such cases, you should select choice (E).

REVENUE (IN MILLIONS OF DOLLARS) OF ALL GOVERNMENTS BY SOURCE AND LEVEL OF GOVERNMENT

Source	Total	Federal	State	Local
Total revenue	1,259,421	660,759	310,828	V
Intergovernmental	184,033	1,804	70,786	111,443
From federal government	90,295	—	III	22,427
From state or local government	93,738	1,804	2,918	89,016
Revenue from own sources	1,075,388	II	240,042	176,391
General	820,814	487,706	187,373	145,735
Taxes	I	405,714	149,738	94,776
Property	74,969	—	2,949	72,020
Individual and corporate income	407,257	346,688	55,039	5,530
Sales and gross receipts	134,532	48,561	72,751	13,220
Other	33,470	10,465	18,999	4,006
Charges and miscellaneous	170,586	81,992	37,635	50,959
Utility and liquor stores	29,896	—	4,628	25,268
Insurance trust	224,678	171,249	48,041	5,388
Employee and railroad retirement	36,962	6,580	IV	5,260
Unemployment compensation	18,733	162	18,443	128
Old age, disability, and health insurance	168,983	164,507	4,476	—

1. What is the value of I in millions of dollars?
   - (A) 695,097
   - (B) 616,758
   - (C) 555,452
   - (D) 254,574
   - (E) None of these

2. What is the value of II in millions of dollars?
   - (A) 835,346
   - (B) 662,563
   - (C) 658,955
   - (D) 417,433
   - (E) None of these

3. What is the value of III in millions of dollars?

(A) 73,704

(B) 68,868

(C) 67,868

(D) 67,978

(E) None of these

4. What is the value of IV in millions of dollars?

(A) 43,565

(B) 29,598

(C) 25,122

(D) 22,919

(E) None of these

5. What is the value of V in millions of dollars?

(A) 821,567

(B) 464,175

(C) 318,490

(D) 287,834

(E) None of these

SELF-RATING QUESTIONS

40 Questions • 15 Minutes

Directions: The self-rating sections of federal examinations are set up to look like multiple-choice tests and are timed like tests, but they are not really tests at all. There are no right or wrong answers. You cannot study for the self-rating questions; your preparation consists only of gathering statistical records from your school years and thinking about what you achieved and when. On a typical self-rating section, you will find questions about your best and worst grades in school and about your favorite and least favorite subjects, questions about your extracurricular activities in school and college (if you went to college) and about your participation in sports, and questions about attendance, part-time jobs, and leadership positions. Other questions refer to your working life or school relationships. These questions ask what you think your peers think of you; others ask similar questions with respect to your supervisors or teachers. The questions ask how you think your teachers or employers might rate you on specific traits. Similar questions ask you to suggest what your friends might say about you. Still other questions ask how you rate yourself against others.

Some of these questions offer hard choices, but you do not have time to dwell on the answers. The self-rating sections are timed in the same manner as test questions. Just answer honestly and to the best of your ability. Do not try to second-guess and give the answers you think the examiners want. Some exams include two separate self-rating sections to check for honesty. Even where there is only one such section, it has built-in measures of general consistency.

Note: There are no official self-rating sample questions. The following questions are representative.

1. My favorite subject in high school was
   (A) math.
   (B) English.
   (C) physical education.
   (D) social studies.
   (E) science.

2. My GPA upon graduation from high school (on a 4.0 scale) was
   (A) lower than 2.51.
   (B) 2.51 to 2.80.
   (C) 2.81 to 3.25.
   (D) 3.26 to 3.60.
   (E) higher than 3.60.

3. In my second year of high school, I was absent
   (A) never.
   (B) not more than 3 days.
   (C) 4 to 10 days.
   (D) more often than 10 days.
   (E) an amount that I do not recall.

4. My best grades in high school were in
   (A) art.
   (B) math.
   (C) English.
   (D) social studies.
   (E) music.

5. While in high school, I participated in
   (A) one sport.
   (B) two sports and one other extracurricular activity.
   (C) three non-athletic extracurricular activities.
   (D) no extracurricular activities.
   (E) something other than the above.

6. During my senior year in high school, I held a paying job
   (A) 0 hours a week.
   (B) 1 to 5 hours a week.
   (C) 6 to 10 hours a week.
   (D) 11 to 16 hours a week.
   (E) more than 16 hours a week.

7. The number of semesters in which I failed a course in high school was
   (A) none.
   (B) one.
   (C) two or three.
   (D) four or five.
   (E) more than five.

8. In high school, I did volunteer work
   (A) more than 10 hours a week.
   (B) 5 to 10 hours a week on a regular basis.
   (C) sporadically.
   (D) seldom.
   (E) not at all.

IF YOU DID NOT GO TO COLLEGE, GO TO QUESTION 25.

9. My general area of concentration in college was
   (A) performing arts.
   (B) humanities.
   (C) social sciences.
   (D) business.
   (E) none of the above.

10. At college graduation, my age was
    (A) under 20.
    (B) 20.
    (C) 21 to 24.
    (D) 25 to 29.
    (E) 30 or over.

11. My standing in my graduating class was in the
    (A) bottom third.
    (B) middle third.
    (C) top third.
    (D) top quarter.
    (E) top 10 percent.

12. In college, I was elected to a major office in a class or in a club or organization
    (A) more than six times.
    (B) four or five times.
    (C) two or three times.
    (D) once.
    (E) never.

13. In comparison to my peers, I cut classes
    (A) much less often than most.
    (B) somewhat less often than most.
    (C) just about the same as most.
    (D) somewhat more often than most.
    (E) much more often than most.

14. The campus activities in which I participated most were
    (A) social service.
    (B) political.
    (C) literary.
    (D) I did not participate in campus activities.
    (E) I did not participate in any of these activities.

15. My name appeared on the dean's list
    (A) never.
    (B) once or twice.
    (C) in three or more terms.
    (D) in more terms than it did not appear.
    (E) I do not remember.

16. The volunteer work I did while in college was predominantly
    (A) health-care related.
    (B) religious.
    (C) political.
    (D) educational.
    (E) I did not volunteer.

17. While a college student, I spent most of my summers
    (A) in summer school.
    (B) earning money.
    (C) traveling.
    (D) in service activities.
    (E) resting.

18. My college education was financed
    (A) entirely by my parents.
    (B) by my parents and my own earnings.
    (C) by scholarships, loans, and my own earnings.
    (D) by my parents and loans.
    (E) by a combination of sources not listed above.

19. In the college classroom, I was considered a(n)
    (A) listener.
    (B) occasional contributor.
    (C) average participant.
    (D) frequent contributor.
    (E) leader.

20. The person on campus whom I most admired was
    (A) another student.
    (B) an athletic coach.
    (C) a teacher.
    (D) an administrator.
    (E) a journalist.

21. Of the skills I developed at college, the one I value most is
    (A) foreign language ability.
    (B) oral expression.
    (C) writing skills.
    (D) facility with computers.
    (E) analytical skills.

22. I made my greatest mark in college through my
    (A) athletic prowess.
    (B) success in performing arts.
    (C) academic success.
    (D) partying reputation.
    (E) conciliatory skill with my peers.

23. My cumulative GPA (on a 4.0 scale) in courses in my major was
    (A) lower than 3.00.
    (B) 3.00 to 3.25.
    (C) 3.26 to 3.50.
    (D) 3.51 to 3.75.
    (E) higher than 3.75.

24. While in college I
    (A) worked full-time and was a part-time student.
    (B) worked 20 hours a week and was a full-time student.
    (C) worked 20 hours a week and was a part-time student.
    (D) was a full-time student working more than 10 but less than 20 hours a week.
    (E) was a full-time student.

25. In the past six months, I have been late to work (or school)

    (A) never.

    (B) only one time.

    (C) very seldom.

    (D) more than five times.

    (E) I don't recall.

26. My supervisors (or teachers) would be most likely to describe me as

    (A) competent.

    (B) gifted.

    (C) intelligent.

    (D) fast-working.

    (E) detail oriented.

27. My peers would probably describe me as

    (A) analytical.

    (B) glib.

    (C) organized.

    (D) funny.

    (E) helpful.

28. According to my supervisors (or teachers), my greatest asset is my

    (A) ability to communicate orally.

    (B) written expression.

    (C) ability to motivate others.

    (D) organization of time.

    (E) friendly personality.

29. In the past two years, I have applied for

    (A) no jobs other than this one.

    (B) one other job.

    (C) two to four other jobs.

    (D) five to eight other jobs.

    (E) more than eight jobs.

30. In the past year, I read strictly for pleasure

    (A) no books.

    (B) one book.

    (C) two books.

    (D) three to six books.

    (E) more than six books.

31. When I read for pleasure, I read mostly

    (A) history.

    (B) fiction.

    (C) poetry.

    (D) biography.

    (E) current events.

32. My peers would say of me that, when they ask me a question, I am

    (A) helpful.

    (B) brusque.

    (C) condescending.

    (D) generous.

    (E) patient.

33. My supervisors (or teachers) would say that my area of least competence is

    (A) analytical ability.

    (B) written communication.

    (C) attention to detail.

    (D) public speaking.

    (E) self-control.

34. In the past two years, the number of full-time (35 hours or more) jobs I have held is

    (A) none.

    (B) one.

    (C) two or three.

    (D) four.

    (E) five or more.

35. Compared to my peers, my supervisors (or teachers) would rank my dependability

    (A) much better than average.

    (B) somewhat better than average.

    (C) about average.

    (D) somewhat less than average.

    (E) much less than average.

36. In my opinion, the most important of the following attributes in an employee is

    (A) discretion.

    (B) loyalty.

    (C) open-mindedness.

    (D) courtesy.

    (E) competence.

37. My peers would say that the word that describes me least is

    (A) sociable.

    (B) reserved.

    (C) impatient.

    (D) judgmental.

    (E) independent.

38. My supervisors (or teachers) would say that I react to criticism with

    (A) a defensive attitude.

    (B) quick capitulation.

    (C) anger.

    (D) interest.

    (E) shame.

39. My attendance record over the past year has been

    (A) not as good as I would like it to be.

    (B) not as good as my supervisors (or teachers) would like it to be.

    (C) a source of embarrassment.

    (D) satisfactory.

    (E) a source of pride.

40. My peers would say that, when I feel challenged, my reaction is one of

    (A) determination.

    (B) energy.

    (C) defiance.

    (D) caution.

    (E) compromise.

ANSWER KEY AND EXPLANATIONS

Reading Comprehension and Verbal Ability

1.	B	20.	C	39.	C	58.	C	77.	C
2.	B	21.	B	40.	A	59.	A	78.	D
3.	C	22.	A	41.	C	60.	B	79.	A
4.	B	23.	B	42.	A	61.	C	80.	B
5.	A	24.	C	43.	C	62.	B	81.	A
6.	E	25.	D	44.	A	63.	C	82.	A
7.	D	26.	B	45.	D	64.	A	83.	C
8.	E	27.	C	46.	B	65.	B	84.	C
9.	B	28.	D	47.	D	66.	C	85.	C
10.	C	29.	C	48.	B	67.	B	86.	D
11.	D	30.	B	49.	D	68.	D	87.	B
12.	A	31.	D	50.	A	69.	A	88.	D
13.	C	32.	B	51.	C	70.	D	89.	C
14.	A	33.	D	52.	A	71.	C	90.	D
15.	C	34.	A	53.	B	72.	E		
16.	B	35.	C	54.	C	73.	C		
17.	D	36.	A	55.	D	74.	A		
18.	A	37.	D	56.	C	75.	D		
19.	D	38.	B	57.	D	76.	D		

1. **The correct answer is (B).** The essential information from which the answer can be inferred is contained in the second and third sentences. These sentences state that "if finger patterns from fingerprints are not decipherable, then they cannot be classified by general shape and contour or by pattern type. If they cannot be classified by these characteristics, then it is impossible to identify the person to whom they belong."

2. **The correct answer is (B).** The essential information from which the answer can be inferred is contained in the third and fifth sentences. The third sentence tells us that "some substances found at a crime scene yield valuable clues under microscopic examination." The fifth sentence explains that " . . . all substances found at a crime scene are potential sources of evidence." Therefore, we can conclude that "some potential sources of evidence are substances that yield valuable clues under microscopic examination."

3. **The correct answer is (C).** The second sentence states the liability rule for common carriers: all common carriers are liable for cargo damage unless they can show that they are not negligent; if they can show that they are not negligent, then they are not liable for the cargo damage. Ajax, Inc. is a common carrier, and accordingly this rule applies to it. From this rule it follows that if Ajax, Inc. can show it is not negligent, then it is not liable.

4. **The correct answer is (B).** This question concerns an either/or situation. The

paragraph states that benefits under the Federal Employees Compensation Act are awarded at one level ($\frac{3}{4}$ of salary) if a beneficiary is married or has dependents when injured and at another level ($\frac{2}{3}$ of salary) if this is not true. John is eligible for benefits under the Act. The paragraph states that John's benefit level was $\frac{2}{3}$ of his salary. Given this benefit level, it is clear that John did not meet either of the conditions for the $\frac{3}{4}$ level. Therefore, choices (A), (C), and (D) cannot be correct. Choice (A) states that he was married; (C) states that he had dependents; (D) states that he was married and had dependents. Choice (E) goes beyond the facts given because prior marriages are not listed as a factor relating to this benefit. The one correct conclusion is that John did not meet either requirement to qualify for the higher benefit level, so choice (B) is correct.

5. **The correct answer is (A).** This is an example of a test question with a negative lead-in statement. It asks for the conclusion that is not supported by the paragraph. That means that four of the statements are valid conclusions from the paragraph while one is not. Choice (B) is a valid conclusion because it restates a fact given in the last sentence of the paragraph. Choice (E) is valid because it restates the other fact in the last sentence of the paragraph. The next-to-last sentence in the paragraph is the source of both choices (C) and (D). Both of these choices restate information in that sentence, based on the fact that access to e-mail messages was sought and granted. This leaves only choice (A), which is the only choice that does not represent a valid conclusion. Even though it is known from the paragraph that there is a group of e-mail messages that are requested in investigations and also that there is a group of messages that contain information that people would not say face-to-

face, there is nothing that says that these groups overlap. It is simply not known.

6. **The correct answer is (E).** Choice (E) is correct because it restates the third sentence in terms of the overlap between immigrants and engineers in the country described in the paragraph. Choice (A) states that most immigrants are engineers or nurses, which are professional occupations. However, the second sentence states that most immigrants are not employees in professional occupations, so choice (A) is false. Choice (B) is false because it denies that there is any overlap between immigrants and nurses, even though this overlap is clear from the third sentence of the paragraph. Choice (C) is false because it denies the overlap between immigrants and engineers. Because the paragraph does not give complete information about the nonprofessionals in the country described in the paragraph, choice (D) is invalid.

7. **The correct answer is (D).** The second and last sentences provide the main premises of the paragraph. These two sentences give information about the three categories of weapons. The last sentence states that none of the illegally sold weapons were .45 caliber weapons. This means that none of the .45 caliber weapons were sold illegally. Notice that this new statement is a double negative. In affirmative form, the statement means that all of the .45 caliber weapons were sold legally, choice (D).

8. **The correct answer is (E).** The third sentence states the overlap between all mechanical explosives and devices in which a physical reaction is produced, such as that caused by overloading a container with compressed air. From this, it can be concluded that some devices in which a physical reaction is produced, such as that caused by overloading a container with compressed air, are me-

chanical explosives. Choice (A) is not correct because the paragraph does not provide sufficient information to validly conclude that all explosives that have been restricted to military weapons are nuclear weapons. It may be that some types of explosives other than nuclear weapons also have been restricted to military weapons. Choices (B) and (C) are incorrect because they contradict the paragraph information. Choice (B) contradicts the third sentence, and choice (C) contradicts the last sentence. Choice (D) is incorrect because the paragraph provides no information about whether or not mechanical explosives are restricted to military weapons.

9. **The correct answer is (B).** The essential information in the paragraph is contained in the second sentence, which states that if an Act of Congress has been deemed unconstitutional, then it is void. In choice (B), it is stated that an Act of Congress is not voided; therefore, it can be concluded that it has not been deemed unconstitutional by the Supreme Court. Choice (A) is not supported by the paragraph because the paragraph does not indicate whether an Act of Congress is voided only when it has been deemed unconstitutional or if it could be voided for other reasons. Choice (C) cannot be inferred from the paragraph because the paragraph does not indicate whether or not an Act of Congress would be voided if the Supreme Court did not declare it to be unconstitutional. Choices (D) and (E) are incorrect because they both contradict the paragraph.

10. **The correct answer is (C).** It is known from the second sentence that 90 percent of the people in this district have fingerprints that can be coded. Therefore, it is known that 10 percent of the population has fingerprints that cannot be coded. Given this information, the chance of selecting a person from this district with

fingerprints that can be coded is 90 percent and the chance of selecting a person from this district with fingerprints that cannot be coded is 10 percent. Choice (A) is incorrect because a probability of 10 percent is an understatement of the probability that the fingerprints of a person from this district can be coded. Choice (B) is incorrect because it too is an underestimate. Choice (D) is incorrect because it is an overestimate of the probability that the fingerprints of a person from the district cannot be coded. Choice (E) is incorrect because the probability that the fingerprints can be coded is known to be 90 percent.

11. **The correct answer is (D).** Choice (D) is supported by the paragraph's statement that a collection letter should show clear organization and should be written with a specific end in view. There is nothing in the paragraph to support choices (A) and (E). Although the paragraph does imply that collection letters may contain several paragraphs, it does not state that they should always be so divided. Also, the paragraph says nothing about the length or tone of a collection letter. It only refers to the letter's clarity of thought and organization.

12. **The correct answer is (A).** Choice (A) is supported by the paragraph's statement that instructing mechanics in safety rules can help prevent industrial accidents, which implies that in some cases accidents may be caused by ignorance of these rules. The paragraph does not support the statements that, in actual practice, industrial accidents are either always avoidable or cannot be entirely overcome. It merely states the requirements of successful accident prevention. Although the paragraph does imply that industrial accidents can be caused by unsafe machinery and inadequate lighting, it does not support the statements that such accidents are usually the result of these causes.

13. The correct answer is (C). Choice (C) is supported by the paragraph's statement that, although advertising gives manufacturers considerable control over consumers' demands for their products, there are still big risks involved in producing and distributing their goods in advance of consumers' final selections. This implies that manufacturers' ultimate success depends on consumers. The paragraph's statement that there are such risks, in spite of advertising, contradicts choices (A) and (D). There also is no support for the statements that manufacturers distribute goods directly to consumers, choice (B), or that they are more concerned with advertising than production, choice (E).

14. The correct answer is (A). The paragraph presents the problems of fire in fire-resistant buildings. It suggests that the contents of the buildings may burn even though the structural materials themselves do not, and the ensuing fire may even cause the collapse of the buildings. The paragraph does not compare the problem of fire in fire-resistant buildings with that of fire in ordinary buildings, as stated in choice (C).

15. The correct answer is (C). The search for truth has speeded the process of civilization. Choice (B) is incorrect in its statement that "civilization did not begin until . . . "; rather, civilization moved ahead slowly even before restrictions on learning were removed.

16. The correct answer is (B). In a word, we are preserving our natural resources through recycling.

17. The correct answer is (D). If you omit all unnecessary words, you only use the words essential to the meaning.

18. The correct answer is (A). If instruction in safety rules will help to prevent accidents, some accidents must occur because of a lack of knowledge.

19. The correct answer is (D). The language that has some representative in English speech has had some of its words absorbed into English.

20. The correct answer is (C). Since manufacturers are assuming risks in attempting to predict what consumers will want, their success depends on the purchases made by consumers.

21. The correct answer is (B). Humans migrate to various climates and adjust the food supply in each climate. The means by which they supply their needs are varied.

22. The correct answer is (A). Time and effort cannot be equated. Efficiency must be measured in terms of results.

23. The correct answer is (B). The first sentence of the paragraph makes this statement.

24. The correct answer is (C). The word *fraudulent* is characterized by deceit or trickery, especially deliberate misrepresentation.

25. The correct answer is (D). An *allegation* is a declaration that something is true, sometimes with little or no proof.

26. The correct answer is (B). *Previous* means *former*. If you did not know the meaning of the word, but remembered that the prefix "pre" usually means "before," you could use that clue to choose the correct answer.

27. The correct answer is (C). To *verify* is "to check the accuracy" of or *confirm*.

28. The correct answer is (D). An *option* is a *choice*.

29. The correct answer is (C). *Flexible*, the opposite of "rigid" or "stiff," means "easily bent," "adjustable," or *pliable*.

30. The correct answer is (B). *Respiration* is *breathing*.

31. **The correct answer is (D).** *Indolent* means "idle" or *lazy.*

32. **The correct answer is (B).** *Vigilant* means "alert" or *watchful.*

33. **The correct answer is (D).** *Incidental* means "likely to ensue as a chance or minor consequence" or *accompanying.*

34. **The correct answer is (A).** *Conciliatory* means "tending to reconcile" or "to make peace."

35. **The correct answer is (C).** An *altercation* is a "quarrel" or a *controversy.*

36. **The correct answer is (A).** *Irresolute* means "indecisive" or *wavering.*

37. **The correct answer is (D).** To *counteract* means "to act directly against" or to *neutralize.*

38. **The correct answer is (B).** *Deferred* means "postponed" or *delayed.*

39. **The correct answer is (C).** *Feasible* means "possible" or *practicable.*

40. **The correct answer is (A).** To *encounter* is "to come upon" or to *meet.*

41. **The correct answer is (C).** *Innate* means "existing naturally" or *native.*

42. **The correct answer is (A).** To *acquiesce* is "to give in" or to *assent.*

43. **The correct answer is (C).** *Unanimity* is "complete agreement" or *harmony.*

44. **The correct answer is (A).** A *precedent* is an *example* that sets a standard.

45. **The correct answer is (D).** *Versatile* means "adaptable" or *many-sided.*

46. **The correct answer is (B).** *Authentic* means "genuine" or *reliable.*

47. **The correct answer is (D).** *Strident* means "grating" or *harsh.*

48. **The correct answer is (B).** To *confine* is "to limit" or to *restrict.*

49. **The correct answer is (D).** To *accentuate* is to "stress," "emphasize," or *intensify.*

50. **The correct answer is (A).** *Banal* means "insipid" or *commonplace.*

51. **The correct answer is (C).** One who is *incorrigible* cannot be changed or corrected; the person is *irreformable.*

52. **The correct answer is (A).** A *brush* is a tool of the PAINTER's trade just as a WRENCH is a tool of the PLUMBER's trade.

53. **The correct answer is (B).** A PACKAGE transports *merchandise* just as a LETTER transports a MESSAGE.

54. **The correct answer is (C).** SLEEP alleviates *weariness* just as FOOD alleviates HUNGER.

55. **The correct answer is (D).** The DIAL is an input device of a *telephone* just as a KEY is an input device of a COMPUTER.

56. **The correct answer is (C).** STILLNESS and *sound* are opposites, as are DARKNESS and SUNLIGHT.

57. **The correct answer is (D).** That which is ACCIDENTAL happens by *chance* as that which is DESIGNED is INTENTIONAL.

58. **The correct answer is (C).** A *muffler* reduces SOUND as PRACTICE reduces ERRORS.

59. **The correct answer is (A).** The desired result of TRAINING is the development of a *skill* as the described result of RESEARCH is scientific FINDINGS.

60. **The correct answer is (B).** The DISCIPLE learns from a *master* just as a STUDENT learns from a TEACHER.

61. **The correct answer is (C).** An EXPERIMENT occurs in a *laboratory* just as a LECTURE occurs in an AUDITORIUM.

62. **The correct answer is (B).** *Fuel* powers the ENGINE just as FOOD powers the BODY.

63. **The correct answer is (C).** *Recreation* occurs in the THEATER just as EDUCATION occurs in a SCHOOL.

64. **The correct answer is (A).** The information and substance of a NOVEL is *fiction,* while the information and substance of BIOGRAPHY is FACT.

65. **The correct answer is (B).** *Film* is the medium through which the action of a MOTION PICTURE is projected onto a screen; CARBON PAPER is the medium through which a COPY of words or drawings is transmitted from one piece of paper to another.

66. **The correct answer is (C).** CARELESSNESS earns a *reprimand* as EFFICIENCY earns a REWARD.

67. **The correct answer is (B).** That which is SCARCE is likely to be *costly,* while that which is ABUNDANT is likely to be CHEAP.

68. **The correct answer is (D).** A DOCTOR promotes *health* just as a POLICE OFFICER promotes ORDER.

69. **The correct answer is (A).** A WEAVER creates on a *loom* just as an ARTIST creates on an EASEL.

70. **The correct answer is (D).** Many *ships* make up a FLEET just as many PERSONS make up a CROWD.

71. **The correct answer is (C).** A CALENDAR visually represents DATES just as a MAP visually represents a *location.*

72. **The correct answer is (E).** Choice (A) is incorrect because the word "have" should have been used instead of the word "of." Choice (B) is incorrect because the word "those" should have been used instead of the word "them." Choice (C) is incorrect because the word "that" should have been used instead of the word "what." Choice (C) is incorrect because the phrase "had have" is incorrect grammar; only the word "had" should have been used.

73. **The correct answer is (C).** Choice (A) is incorrect because the word "fewer" should have been used instead of the word "less." Choice (B) is incorrect because poor word usage makes it seem as if "he" refers to the "training course." Choice (D) is incorrect because the word "few" should have been used instead of the phrase "hardly any." Choice (E) is incorrect because the word "ever" should not follow the word "seldom."

74. **The correct answer is (A).** "Whoever" is the subject of the phrase "whoever has the best record" and is used incorrectly in choice (D). Choices (B) and (C) are wordy and awkward.

75. **The correct answer is (D).** All the other choices contain obvious errors.

76. **The correct answer is (D).** Choices (A) and (C) are incorrect in use of the subject form "I" instead of the object of the preposition "me." Choice (B) incorrectly uses the reflexive "myself."

77. **The correct answer is (C).** All the other choices contain obvious errors.

78. **The correct answer is (D).** Choice (A) might state either "most" or "all" but not both; choice (B) should read "persons who"; choice (C) should read "with regard to . . . ."

79. **The correct answer is (A).** Choice (B) is incorrect because it requires the plural verb "were"; choice (C) requires the correlative construction "neither . . . nor"; choice (D) requires the nominative "they."

80. **The correct answer is (B).** In choice (A), the placement of the apostrophe is inappropriate; choices (C) and (D) use the plural, but there is only one company.

81. **The correct answer is (A).** Choices (C) and (D) are glaringly poor. Choice (B) is not incorrect, but choice (A) is better.

82. **The correct answer is (A).** The other choices are quite clearly incorrect.

83. **The correct answer is (C).** Choices (A) and (B) use adverbs incorrectly; choice (D) is awkward and not part of everyday speech.

84. **The correct answer is (C).** Choice (A) has two grammatical errors: "when" to introduce a definition and the unacceptable verb form "is already having been parked." Choice (B) incorrectly shifts subjects from "one" to "you." Choice (D) does not make sense.

85. **The correct answer is (C).** Choices (A) and (B) are incorrect because only two persons are involved in the statement; "between" is used when there are only two, and "among" is reserved for three or more. Choices (A) and (D) use the pronoun "he"; the object of a preposition, in this case "between" must be in the objective case, "him."

86. **The correct answer is (D).** Punctuation aside, both choices (A) and (B) incorrectly place the verb in the plural. "Neither" is a singular indefinite pronoun and requires a singular verb. The choice between (C) and (D) is more difficult, but this is a simple statement and not a direct quote.

87. **The correct answer is (B).** Only the quoted material should be enclosed by quotation marks, so choice (A) is correct. Only the first word of a sentence should begin with a capital letter, so choices (C) and (D) are wrong. In addition, only the quoted material itself is a question; the entire sentence is a statement. Therefore, the question mark must be placed inside the quotes.

88. **The correct answer is (D).** Choices (A), (B), and (C) imply that he stays in church all day on Christmas and Easter and goes nowhere else. In addition, choice (C) splits the infinitive awkwardly. In choice (D), the modifier "only" is correctly placed to tell us that the only times he goes to church are on Christmas and Easter.

89. **The correct answer is (C).** Choice (A) is wordy. In choice (B), the correct verb should be "have" in place of "leave." In choice (D), the word "arose" should be "arisen."

90. **The correct answer is (D).** The first three sentences lack parallel construction. All of the words that modify "paper" must be in the same form.

Arithmetic Reasoning

1.	C	6.	B	11.	A	16.	A	21.	E
2.	C	7.	A	12.	C	17.	C	22.	B
3.	C	8.	B	13.	A	18.	D	23.	C
4.	A	9.	D	14.	B	19	E	24.	D
5.	C	10.	D	15.	C	20.	C	25.	B

1. **The correct answer is (C).** It can be obtained by computing $16 \times 10 = 160$.

2. **The correct answer is (C).** $\$30.20 \div 14 = \$2.157$; round up to $\$2.16$.

3. **The correct answer is (C).** 6,594 papers ÷ 314 clerks = 21 papers filed by each clerk in 10 minutes; 21 papers ÷ 10 minutes = 2.1 papers per minute filed by the average clerk.

4. **The correct answer is (A).** It takes one man $42 \times 4 = 168$ days to complete the job, working alone. If $3\frac{1}{2}$ men are working (one works half-days, the other full days), the job takes $168 \div 3\frac{1}{2} = 48$ days.

5. **The correct answer is (C).** 40 checks × $\$6 = \$240$; 80 checks × $\$4 = \$320$; 45 bills × $\$20 = \$900$; 30 bills × $\$10 = \$300$; 42 bills × $\$5 = \$210$; 186 bills × $\$1 = \$186$; $\$240 + \$320 + \$900 + \$300 + \$210 + \$186 = \$2,156$.

6. **The correct answer is (B).** In seven hours the clerk files $7 \times 80 = 560$ cards. Because 800 cards must be filed, there are $800 - 560 = 240$ remaining.

7. **The correct answer is (A).** It takes one machine $3 \times 4 = 12$ days to complete the job. Two machines can do the job in $12 \div 2 = 6$ days.

8. **The correct answer is (B).** At the end of the first half-hour, there are $500 - 25 = 475$ forms remaining. If the first stenographer completed 25 forms in half an hour, her rate is $25 \times 2 = 50$ forms per hour. The combined rate of the two stenographers is $50 + 45 = 95$ forms per hour. The remaining forms can be completed in $475 \div 95 = 5$ hours. Adding the first half-hour, the entire job requires $5\frac{1}{2}$ hours.

9. **The correct answer is (D).** 7 Subway fares × $\$1.25 = \$8.75$; 1 taxi fare × $\$7.30 = \$7.30$; $\$8.75 + \$7.30 = \$16.05$, the total amount spent during the month. 3 dollar bills = $\$3$; 4 quarters = $\$1$; 5 dimes = $\$.50$; 4 nickels = $\$.20$; $\$3 + \$1 + \$.50 + \$.20 = \$4.70$, the total amount left at the end of the month. $\$16.05 + \$4.70 = \$20.75$, the total amount at the beginning of the month.

10. **The correct answer is (D).** 36 lines × 11 words = 396 words per page; 125 pages × 396 words = 49,500 words copied in five days; $49,500 \div 5 = 9,900$ words copied in one day. 12 words × 30 lines = 360 words on each page; $9,900 \div 360 = 27\frac{1}{2}$ pages copied in one day; $27\frac{1}{2} \times 6 = 165$ pages copied in six days.

11. **The correct answer is (A).** If A can finish the job alone in 5 hours, A can do $\frac{1}{5}$ of the job in one hour. Working together, A and B can complete the job in 2 hours; therefore, in one hour, they finish half the job. In one hour, B alone completes $\frac{1}{2} - \frac{1}{5} = \frac{3}{10}$ of the job. It would take B $\frac{10}{3}$ hours, or $3\frac{1}{3}$ hours, to finish the whole job alone.

12. **The correct answer is (C).** The job could be completed by one worker in $18 \times 26 = 468$ days. Completing the job in 12 days requires $468 \div 12 = 39$ workers.

13. **The correct answer is (A).** She must type $7 \times 25 = 175$ lines. At the rate of one line per 10 seconds, the job takes $175 \times 10 = 1{,}750$ seconds. $1{,}750$ seconds $\div 60 = 29\frac{1}{6}$ minutes, or 29 minutes and 10 seconds.

14. **The correct answer is (B).** 36 adults $\times$ \$3.75 = \$135; 80 children $\times$ \$2 = \$160; \$135 + \$160 = \$295.

15. **The correct answer is (C).** 487 cards $\times$ 26 workers = 12,662.

16. **The correct answer is (A).** The investigator rented the car for 6 days at \$35 per day; $6 \times 35 = \$210$; \$210 subtracted from the total charge of \$450 equals \$240, the portion of the total charge that was expended for the miles driven; \$450 − \$210 = \$240. This amount is divided by the charge per mile, which equals the number of miles driven by the investigator; \$240 ÷ .30 = 800.

17. **The correct answer is (C).** The average of the two fractions is $\left(\frac{1}{6} + \frac{1}{4}\right) \div 2 = \frac{5}{24}$.

18. **The correct answer is (D).** The government discount is \$18 × 10% = \$1.80. The cost of the switch is \$18.00 − \$1.80 = \$16.20. The charge for labor is \$49.20 − \$16.20 = \$33.00. The number of hours worked is \$33 ÷ \$22 = 1.5 hours, or 1 hour and 30 min.

19. **The correct answer is (E).** The correct answer is not given. The difference between the actual cost of \$34 per tire and the expected cost of \$40 per tire (\$80 ÷ 2) is \$6; \$6 ÷ \$40 = .15, or 15% of the expected cost.

20. **The correct answer is (C).** Obtain the correct answer by computing $\frac{1}{2}x + \frac{1}{3}x + 3 = x$, where x is the total number of task force members; $\frac{1}{2}x$ is the number from Agency A; $\frac{1}{3}x$ is the number from Agency B; and 3 is the number from Agency C. Add the two fractions: $\frac{1}{2}x + \frac{1}{3}x = \frac{5}{6}x$. x (or $\frac{6}{6}x$) $- \frac{5}{6}x = \frac{1}{6}x = 3$. $\frac{1}{6} \times 18 = 3$, so the number of people on the task force is 18.

21. **The correct answer is (E).** The correct answer is not given. First, convert 2 hours and 12 minutes to 2.2 hours, and then set up a simple proportion: $\frac{22}{4} = \frac{x}{16}$. The number of hours it takes one filing clerk to do the job is $2.2 \times \frac{16}{4} = 8.8$ hours. If two clerks are filing 16 drawers, the job would be completed in half that time: 4.4 hours, or 4 hours and 24 minutes.

22. **The correct answer is (B).** The basic charge of \$40 applies to all patients (x); the additional average charge of \$20 applies to only 50% (or $\frac{1}{2}$) of them ($0.5x$). The combined charges—\$40 times the total number of patients ($40x$) plus \$20 times the total number of patients ($20 \times 0.5x$, or $10x$)—must equal \$60,000, the cost of maintaining the medical facility: $40x + 10x = 60{,}000$. Solve for x: $60{,}000 \div 50 = 1{,}200$, the number of patients who must be served per month.

23. **The correct answer is (C).** Obtain the correct answer by setting up a simple proportion: $\frac{110 \text{ km}}{60 \text{ min.}} = \frac{33 \text{ km}}{x \text{ min.}} = 33 \times \frac{60}{110} = 18$ min.

24. **The correct answer is (D).** The total number of eight-hour workdays of typing required for the two reports is 3 days $\times$ 2 typists $\times$ 2 reports = 12 eight-hour workdays of typing. If all of this had to be accomplished in one eight-hour work day, 12 typists would be needed to do the job.

25. **The correct answer is (B).** The clerk's net pay of \$6.97 per hour represents 82% of his gross pay (100% − 18% = 82%). The clerk's hourly salary before deductions is \$6.97 ÷ 82% = \$8.50. The total number of hours of work involved is 1,200 forms ÷ 40 forms per hour = 30 hours. The amount the government would have to pay for the work is 30 hours × \$8.50 = \$255.00.

Comparisons and Sequences

1.	E	9.	D	17.	E	25.	E	33. B
2.	B	10.	C	18.	B	26.	B	34. A
3.	D	11.	E	19.	E	27.	E	35. E
4.	D	12.	A	20.	C	28.	D	36. B
5.	C	13.	A	21.	D	29.	D	37. D
6.	A	14.	D	22.	A	30.	C	38. E
7.	A	15.	B	23.	E	31.	C	39. A
8.	B	16.	A	24.	C	32.	D	40. C

1. **The correct answer is (E).** In the first column, the first name differs from the first names in the other two columns. In the second and third columns, the last name differs.

2. **The correct answer is (B).** In the first two columns, the two names are identical, but in the third column, the last name is different.

3. **The correct answer is (D).** In the second and third columns, the two names are identical, but in the first column, the first name is different.

4. **The correct answer is (D).** In the second and third columns, the names are identical, but in the first column, the last name is different.

5. **The correct answer is (C).** In all three columns, the initial and last names are identical, but in the second column, the middle name differs from the middle name in the first and third columns.

6. **The correct answer is (A).** All three numbers are identical.

7. **The correct answer is (A).** All three numbers are identical.

8. **The correct answer is (B).** In the first two columns, the last three digits are 407, but in the third column, they are 047.

9. **The correct answer is (D).** The number in the first column ends with 88, while the other two columns end with 86.

10. **The correct answer is (C).** Again, the difference occurs in the ending of numbers. The numbers in the first and third columns end with 682, while the number in the second column ends with 862.

11. **The correct answer is (E).** In the first column, the last name differs from the last name in the other two columns. In the second column, the first name differs from that in the other two.

12. **The correct answer is (A).** All three names are identical.

13. **The correct answer is (A).** All three names are identical.

14. **The correct answer is (D).** The only difference is that, in the first column, the middle name differs from that in the other two columns.

15. **The correct answer is (B).** The names in the first two columns are identical, but in the third column, the second initial is different.

16. **The correct answer is (A).** All three numbers are identical.

17. **The correct answer is (E).** All the numbers differ from each other. In the first column, the last two digits are 41; in the second column, they are 47; in the third, they are 14.

18. **The correct answer is (B).** The first two columns end with 83, while the third ends with 38.

19. **The correct answer is (E).** There are differences in central digits and in final digits. The 66 in the middle of the number in the second column differs from the 56 in the middle of the other two. The 09 at the end of the number in the third column differs from the 90 at the end of the other two.

20. **The correct answer is (C).** The number in the second column ends with 936, while the numbers in the first and third columns end with 396.

21. **The correct answer is (D).** The last name is different in the first column.

22. **The correct answer is (A).** All three names are alike.

23. **The correct answer is (E).** All three names are different.

24. **The correct answer is (C).** The second number is different.

25. **The correct answer is (E).** All three names are different.

26. **The correct answer is (B).** The third number is different.

27. **The correct answer is (E).** All three names are different.

28. **The correct answer is (D).** The first name is different.

29. **The correct answer is (D).** The first number is different.

30. **The correct answer is (C).** The second name is different.

31. **The correct answer is (C).** The numbers in this series are increasing by 1. If the series were continued for two more numbers, the series would read: 1 2 3 4 5 6 7 8 9.

32. **The correct answer is (D).** The numbers in this series are decreasing by 1. If the series were continued for two more numbers, the series would read: 15 14 13 12 11 10 9 8 7.

33. **The correct answer is (B).** Each number in this series is repeated and then increased by 1. If the series were continued by two more number, the series would read: 20 20 21 21 22 22 23 23 24.

34. **The correct answer is (A).** This series is the number 17 repeated by numbers increasing by 1, beginning with the number 3. If the series were continued for two more numbers, the series would read: 17 3 17 4 17 5 17 6 17. Your answer must include the next number in the increasing series and the 17 that follows it.

35. **The correct answer is (E).** The numbers in this series are increasing first by 1 and then by 2. If the series were continued for two more numbers, the series would read: 1 2 4 5 7 8 10 11 13.

36. **The correct answer is (B).** In this series, the number repeats and then decreases by 1. If the series were continued for two more numbers, the series would read: 21 21 20 20 19 19 18 18 17.

37. **The correct answer is (D).** There are really two alternating series here. One series increases by 2, while the other alternating series decreases by 1. If the first series were continued, it would read: 1 3 5 7 9; the other series continued would read: 20 19 18 17. Combined as a single series, the series would continue: 1 20 3 19 5 18 7 17 9.

38. **The correct answer is (E).** This problem involves two alternating series. The first series decreases by 2, while the other alternating series increases by 2. Thus, one series would read: 30 28 26 24 22; the other series would read: 2 4 6 8. Together, the series would read: 30 2 28 4 26 6 24 8 22.

39. **The correct answer is (A).** This alternating series question follows a slightly different rhythm. The two alternating series are 5 6 7 8 9 10 and 20 19 18. Once you recognize the pattern, you can see that the continued series reads: 5 6 20 7 8 19 9 10 18.

40. **The correct answer is (C).** This series is familiar to that found in question 39. However, the two series begin at different points. Continued, it reads: 9 10 1 11 12 2 13 14 3.

Problems for Investigation

| 1. | C | 2. | E | 3. | E | 4. | D | 5. | B |

1. **The correct answer is (C).** The armored truck carriers had the greatest opportunity to substitute counterfeit bills for real ones during the transportation procedure. The scrap of material from an armored truck carrier's uniform caught in the seal of one of the satchels strongly links the carriers to the crime.

2. **The correct answer is (E).** Statement (1) establishes that eight satchels were missing from Greenville bank. Statement (6) identifies the satchels that arrived at the Belton Bank as the missing satchels.

3. **The correct answer is (E).** Statement (7) establishes that two stolen $10 bills were spent at Ferdinand's Restaurant. Statement (8) identifies a bank employee as a frequent diner at Ferdinand's Restaurant. This statement casts suspicion on the bank employee but does not prove complicity.

4. **The correct answer is (D).** The fact that the bank clerk saw the armored truck carriers talking secretively may cast some suspicion, but it would not be useful in proving the case. People who work together may very likely exchange private jokes or share personal information.

5. **The correct answer is (B).** The satchels were locked in the vault at 4:30 p.m. on one day and were not delivered until the following morning. Since we learn in statement (2) that the satchels were not checked after they were locked in the vault, the exchange could have taken place in the Greenville Bank.

answers

Judgment

1. A	3. B	5. D	7. A	9. E
2. C	4. D	6. D	8. B	10. B

1. **The correct answer is (A).** The inmate who repeatedly bangs his fists against the bars of his cell is in immediate danger of causing himself bodily harm. The inmate must be restrained.

2. **The correct answer is (C).** There are a number of points to take into consideration: Your own task is described as routine; the coworker's assignment is described as one that has top priority; and the coworker has asked for only a few minutes of your time. Under these circumstances, help get the priority work done.

3. **The correct answer is (B).** Without any knowledge of police rules, common sense dictates that saving lives is the number one priority. Lifesaving takes precedence over the desire for an uninterrupted parade, despite the officer's prior orders.

4. **The correct answer is (D).** The repeated complaints may be quite legitimate if the lighting problem has not been corrected. Do not dismiss the office worker as a "crank." The custodian should check out the fixtures personally before calling in an electrician. Costs can be held down by having in-house staff perform those tasks for which they are qualified.

5. **The correct answer is (D).** Where calm, reasoned explanation is offered as an answer choice, it is nearly always the correct answer. There is no need to be impolite or hostile to the neighbor. He may not even realize that he is asking you to do something that is not permitted. He will respect you for obeying the rules.

6. **The correct answer is (D).** A police officer is not a firefighter. Eliminate choices (A) and (C) immediately. It is the job of firefighters to ascertain if there is a fire and to extinguish it. Since the building is large and fires spread rapidly, the practical move is to call the fire department immediately rather than running through the building alone trying to rouse all the occupants.

7. **The correct answer is (A).** Leaking gas can ignite, causing a fire. If a large amount of gas collects in the basement and is ignited, an explosion and fire are likely. The broken sewer pipe and the water seepage can create health hazards and should be reported and repaired, but these hazards do not present the same emergency as the gas leak. An unlit basement is also a safety hazard, but is even less of an emergency.

8. **The correct answer is (B).** The most urgent hazard is the dangling wire. A quick call to the Police Department will get the area sealed off and a repair crew to attend to the wire. The Health Department could be notified of rodents in the building, but pest infestation is a chronic problem rather than an emergency. The parking enforcement agent can ticket the illegally parked car. The two men smoking marijuana pose no immediate threat.

9. **The correct answer is (E).** The chief advantage of familiarity with all types of ammunition for the worker in crime detection lies in the fact that such knowledge can be valuable aid in discovering and following up clues during the process of investigation. Choices (A) and (C) are untrue, and although choices (B) and (D) may be true in some cases, neither is the most important reason why acquaintance with ammunition is valuable to the worker in crime detection.

10. **The correct answer is (B).** The chief advantage of a properly administered parole system from the prisoners' standpoint is the opportunity it provides them for information and assistance concerning their reentry into society. A parole system cannot guarantee that released prisoners will never return to prison in the future, choice (A), that they will not be tempted to commit crime, choice (C), or that they will have the opportunity to save whatever they earn, choice (E), because these possibilities are largely in the hands of the prisoners themselves. Although choice (D) may be a result of the parole system, it is not the chief advantage from the standpoint of the prisoners.

answers

Logical Reasoning

| 1. | C | 2. | D | 3. | B |

1. **The correct answer is (C).** The most logical order of the five events is that first the man was shot (3); second, his body was discovered by the maid, and the police were called (1); third, the police questioned the maid and learned of the couple's argument from the night before (5); fourth, the police found Mary at her sister's home (2); and fifth, a gun was found in Mary's purse and was identified as the murder weapon (4). Choice (A) is not the answer because the maid could not have discovered the body (1) before the man was shot (3). Choice (B) is not the answer because the police could not have questioned the maid (5) before she called them (1). Choice (D) is not the answer because the first four events could not have taken place before the man was shot (3). Choice (E) is not the answer because the police could not have looked for Mary (2) before learning from the maid that she was the victim's wife (5).

2. **The correct answer is (D).** The most logical order of the five events is that first the inspector saw that Ms. Smith looked familiar (3); second, he decided to search her luggage (2); third, he found nothing in her luggage but identified her from her passport photograph as a suspected smuggler (5); fourth, he realized that she was wearing a wig and had her searched (1); and fifth, narcotics were found in her wig (4). Choice (A) is not the answer because the inspector would not have decided to search Ms. Smith's luggage (2) unless his suspicions were aroused by the fact that she looked familiar (3). Neither choice (B), (C), nor (E) is the answer because the inspector would not have realized Ms. Smith was wearing a wig (1) before seeing her passport photograph (5).

3. **The correct answer is (B).** The most logical order of the five events is that first Mr. Hayes was under surveillance (5); second, a detective saw him leave a printing shop with a large package (2); third, the shop owner said he had bought high-quality paper (4); fourth, a printing press and freshly printed bills were found in Mr. Hayes's basement along with the paper (1); and fifth, he was arrested for counterfeiting (3). Neither choice (A) nor (D) is the answer because the detective would not have seen Mr. Hayes leave the printing shop (2) if he had not been under surveillance (5). Neither choice (C) nor (E) is the answer because Mr. Hayes could not have been arrested for counterfeiting (3) before any evidence was discovered (1).

Tabular Completion

| 1. | E | 2. | C | 3. | C | 4. | C | 5. | D |

1. **The correct answer is (E).** The correct value is 650,228 (not given as an answer) and can be calculated by subtracting the value for "Charges and miscellaneous" from the value for "General" under "Revenue from own sources."

2. **The correct answer is (C).** It can be calculated by subtracting the value for "Intergovernmental" from the value for "Total revenue."

3. **The correct answer is (C).** Calculate the value of state revenues "From federal government" by subtracting the value of revenues "From state or local government" in the State column from the value of "Intergovernmental" revenues in the State column.

4. **The correct answer is (C).** Calculate the value of state revenues from "Employee and railroad retirement" by subtracting the combined values of "Unemployment compensation" and "Old age, disability, and health insurance" in the State column from the value of "Insurance trust."

5. **The correct answer is (D).** To calculate total local revenue, add together "Intergovernmental" revenue in the Local column and "Revenue from own sources" in the Local column.

answers

APPENDIXES

Federal Law Enforcement Training Facilities

No law enforcement agency will send a new recruit into the field without appropriate training. All law enforcement agents are trained in self-defense, use of weapons, rules and regulations of the department, and, of course, the specific duties of the job.

Most federal criminal investigators and uniformed police officers complete introductory basic and in-service training at the Federal Law Enforcement Training Center in Glynco, Georgia. Likewise, many federal law enforcement technicians, inspectors, specialists, general compliance investigators, and other support staff complete courses of study at the Center.

A few agencies operate independent academies specifically for the training of their own personnel (such as the FBI, DEA, Postal Inspection Service, and Air Force Officer of Special Investigations). These agencies operate programs to meet their own training requirements as well as to offer specialized courses related to their own particular areas of expertise.

FEDERAL LAW ENFORCEMENT TRAINING CENTER

The Federal Law Enforcement Training Center serves as an interagency law enforcement training organization for eighty-one federal agencies. The Center also provides services to state, local, and international law enforcement agencies.

Although the Federal Law Enforcement Training Center is headquartered in Glynco, Georgia, the Center also operates two other residential training sites in Artesia, New Mexico, and Charleston, South Carolina. The Center also operates an in-service requalification training facility in Cheltenham, Maryland, for use by agencies with large concentrations of personnel in the Washington, D.C. area. The Center also has oversight and program management responsibility for the International Law Enforcement Academy (ILEA) in Gaborne, Botswana, and supports training at other ILEAs in Hungary and Thailand.

Export training and technology-based distributed learning are increasingly important methods of training delivery. These methods are used when the programs being taught do not require specialized facilities and/or when a geographical concentration of personnel can be identified. In addition, the

appendix A

185

Federal Law Enforcement Training Center seeks and develops alternative training technologies, especially simulation and modeling to augment existing training delivery systems and methodologies.

Many of the Center's eighty-one Partner Organizations have transferred portions or all of their law enforcement training operations to one of the Center's permanent sites to coordinate the activities of their personnel and to conduct advanced and agency-specific programs.

Partner Organizations have input regarding training issues and functional aspects of the Center. Agencies take part in curriculum review and development conferences and help develop policies and directives. This relationship is characteristic of a "true partnership," responsive to the training mission.

Consolidation of law enforcement training permits the federal government to emphasize training excellence and cost effectiveness. Professional instruction and practical application provide students with the skills and knowledge to meet the demanding challenges of a federal law enforcement career. They learn not only the responsibilities of a law enforcement officer, but through interaction with students from many other agencies, they also become acquainted with the missions and duties of their colleagues. This interaction provides the foundation for a more cooperative federal law enforcement effort.

The Federal Law Enforcement Training Center's parent agency, the Department of Homeland Security (DHS), supervises its administrative and financial activities. The Center's Director serves under the authority of the Under Secretary for Border and Transportation Security. The Director is assisted with operational oversight and execution in the management of the Center by an executive team with unmatched breadth and depth of experience in training and administration.

Also, as an interagency training organization, the Federal Law Enforcement Training Center has assembled the finest professionals from diverse backgrounds to serve on its faculty and staff. Approximately one-third of the staff is permanent Center employees. The rest are federal officers and investigators on short-term assignment from their parent organizations or recently retired from the field. This mix of staff members provides a balance of experience and fresh insight from the field.

Basic Training Programs

- Criminal Investigator Training Program
- Mixed Basic Police Training Program
- Natural Resources Police Training Program

Advanced Training Programs

- Cyber Counterterrorism Investigations Training Program
- Critical Infrastructure Protection Training Program
- Anti-Terrorism Intelligence Awareness Training Program

Criminal Investigator Training Program

Length of Training: 55 training days

The Criminal Investigator Training Program (CITP) provides basic and fundamental training in the techniques, concepts, and methodologies of conducting criminal investigations. The CITP underwent a full Curriculum Review Conference in January 2003. As a result, the CITP was revised and changes were implemented in January 2004.

Throughout the program, trainees are mentored by Continuing Case Investigation Coordinators. Subjects in the training include interviewing, surveillance, computer-based case management, legal training, physical techniques and conditioning, tactical training, firearms precision shooting, emergency response driving, and other courses that provide the essential knowledge, skills, and abilities needed by the new federal criminal investigator.

Lectures, laboratories, practical exercises, and tests are used to ensure that each trainee acquires all of the critical knowledge, skills, and abilities required of new criminal investigators. Throughout the program, each trainee must participate as a member of a small task force team in a continuing case investigation. The investigation is sequentially structured, allowing each student to utilize new skills immediately. Interviewing of witnesses, surveillance, and undercover operations enable students to develop a case, write and execute search warrants, write a criminal complaint, obtain an indictment, arrest a defendant, and testify in a suppression hearing.

Prerequisites for Attendance: The training program is designed for full-time Criminal Investigators, GS-1811 series, from the Partner Organizations. However, a Partner Organization may request that a non-1811 law enforcement employee be permitted to attend the program if the agency believes that investigative training is essential for the employee. The Program Manager will review the request and determine whether the prospective student will be allowed to attend the training. All attendees must meet the employing agencies' recruitment standards and the Federal Law Enforcement Training Center's Practical Exercise Performance Requirements for the CITP prior to arriving for the training program.

Nonpartner federal agencies may send students on a space-available basis, and state and local law enforcement officers may attend if sponsored by a federal Partner Organization. Applications for attendance to all basic training programs must be submitted through supervisory channels to each agency's Center liaison/training officer.

Mixed Basic Police Training Program

Length of Training: 47 training days

The Mixed Basic Police Training Program (MBPTP) provides training in the basic law enforcement knowledge, skills, and abilities that a new federal officer must understand and/or be able to perform in the first two years on the job. Officers receive instruction in a number of areas including officer safety and survival, communications and interviewing, constitutional and federal criminal law, arrest techniques, defensive tactics, drugs of abuse, terrorism, VIP protection, physical security, firearms, physical conditioning, and driver training.

Prerequisites for Attendance: Each Partner Organization sets its standards in recruiting new employees. After the individuals have been selected, they are sent by that organization to the Center. Attendees must meet their agency's recruitment standards and the Center's Practical Exercise Performance Requirements for the MBPTP prior to arriving for the training program.

Natural Resources Police Training Program

Length of Training: 81 class days

The Natural Resources Police Training Program (NRPTP) provides entry-level training for federal land management law enforcement rangers who are assigned to patrol duties in urban, rural, or isolated areas. Agencies include the U.S. Forest Service, U.S. Fish and Wildlife Service, Tennessee Valley Authority, National Marine Fisheries, and Bureau of Land Management. Lectures, laboratory experiences, and practical exercises are oriented toward law enforcement rangers who work in a land management environment. Subjects include interviewing and communications, officer safety and survival, constitutional law, civil rights, firearms, physical techniques, driving, rural surveillance, drug investigations, natural resource violations, and other basic law enforcement subjects.

Personnel attending this program are employed primarily as cultural and natural resource protectors with law enforcement responsibilities and authority. Training is provided by the Federal Law Enforcement Training Center's staff personnel and instructors detailed from various land management Partner Organizations.

Prerequisites for Attendance: Each Partner Organization sets its standards in recruiting employees. After the individuals have been selected, they are sent by that organization to the Federal Law Enforcement Training Center. Students must be certified in Cardiopulmonary Resuscitation (CPR) by either the American Heart Association or the American Red Cross prior to being enrolled at the Center. Attendees must meet their agency's recruitment standards and the Center's Practical Exercise Performance Requirements for the NRPTP prior to arriving for the training program.

Cyber Counterterrorism Investigations Training Program

Length of Training: 5 class days

By the turn of the century virtually all known terrorist groups had a presence on the Internet. It is undisputed that terrorist groups utilize the Internet to engage in psychological warfare, propaganda, data mining, fund-raising, recruiting, networking, information sharing, and planning and coordination. The Cyber Counterterrorism Investigations Training Program (CCITP) focuses on investigations and operations centered on these uses of the Internet by terrorists.

The terrorists of today are highly sophisticated in their use of weapons, communications, and planning techniques. They operate in a highly decentralized manner that makes it difficult to locate and track more than a small cell of terrorists at any given time. They are using the Internet to collect large amounts of open source information to be used for the preparation and execution of their operations. Many of these terrorist organizations have recruited members with degrees in such highly sophisticated areas as computer science, biology, and chemistry. In order to effectively collect intelligence, conduct investigations, and run operations against these threats, we have to identify their methods and be able to operate within the same medium.

The CCITP provides criminal investigators with the training they need to begin conducting cyber-based investigations and operations against terrorist elements. Courses include:

- Understanding Terrorist Motivations, History, and Culture
- Cyber Capabilities of Terrorists
- Legal Aspects
- Internet Technology
- Task Force Collaboration Software
- E-mail Tracking and Tracing
- Cyber OPSEC
- Steganography
- Web-based Investigation Methodology and Tracking Tools
- Terrorists' Financing
- Practical Exercises

Prerequisites for Attendance: The target audience is criminal investigators (1811s), detectives, intelligence specialists, and intelligence analysts from the federal, state, and local law enforcement community who are tasked with performing intelligence gathering and analysis, investigations, and operations against known and unknown terrorist targets or threats. Students should possess a basic understanding of the DOS and Windows operating systems as well as a basic understanding of Internet functionality.

Critical Infrastructure Protection Training Program

Length of Training: $4\frac{1}{2}$ class days

The Critical Infrastructure Protection Training Program (CIPTP) is designed for the Security Manager or Senior Security Specialist. The program addresses protection of those physical and cyber-based systems essential to the operation of the economy and government, including telecommunications, energy, banking and finance, transportation, and water systems and emergency services. Courses include:

- Case Studies
- CIP Policy
- CIP Model
- Emergency Programs
- Information Security
- Matrix/Vulnerability Assessment
- OPSEC
- Personnel Security
- Physical Security
- Security and Contingency Planning P.E.
- Threat Assessment Process
- Threat Briefing

Prerequisites for Attendance: Generally, applicants should be mid-level managers; however, others assigned to duties directly related to the protection of physical and cyber-based systems against terrorist attacks can attend.

Anti-Terrorism Intelligence Awareness Training Program

Length of Training: 1 class day

The Anti-Terrorism Intelligence Awareness Training Program (AIATP) is an introductory awareness program designed to provide line officers and first-line supervisors with a working knowledge of the criminal intelligence process and applicable laws, guidelines, policies, tools, and techniques. Knowledge gained in this course aids in the detection of pre-incident indicators related to terrorist activity in the community that may be encountered during the course of their law enforcement duties. A portion of this training program is region-specific.

Prerequisites for Attendance: This training is open to any full-time law enforcement officer, especially as a first-line officer or supervisor. Courses include:

- Pre-Incident Indicators
- Terrorist Use of the Internet

- Intelligence Process
- Terrorism Overview
- Regional Update on Terrorism-Related Activity

Standard Daily Schedule at the Federal Law Enforcement Training Center

Morning Session*   7:30 A.M. to 11:30 A.M.

Lunch   11:30 A.M. to 12:30 P.M.

Afternoon Session*   12:30 P.M. to 4:30 P.M.

*Classes are 50 minutes in length with breaks scheduled according to the subject matter being presented and the status of practical exercise activity.

Student Evaluation

The Criminal Investigator Training Program cognitive testing system consists of five examinations: three legal examinations and two comprehensive examinations. In addition, students are expected to satisfactorily complete a series of practical exercises and/or homework assignments. Satisfactory completion of all examinations, practical exercises, and assignments is required for graduation from the Criminal Investigator Training Program.

Written Examinations

Students are required to achieve a score of at least 70 percent on each of the five written examinations. Students are allocated a total of one hour and 45 minutes to complete each examination. Immediately following each examination, a 15-minute examination review is conducted, allowing students to assess their performance on the examination. Official results are posted as soon as possible after the completion of the examination. Students' grades are maintained in confidentiality as far as fellow classmates are concerned. Student examination scores are available to the students' agencies through official channels.

In the event that a student fails to achieve a score of at least 70 percent on any written examination, he or she will be placed on probation. During this period, additional assistance will be made available to the student, upon request, in the form of counseling, out-of-class study assignments, and personal instructional sessions. The student will then take a remedial examination covering the same subjects as the original failed examination. The student must successfully pass this remedial examination to remain eligible for graduation.

A student may be placed on probation for failing a regularly scheduled examination on only two occasions. In the event that a student fails a third regularly scheduled examination (or fails to achieve a passing score on any remedial examination), he or she will not be eligible for graduation from the Criminal Investigator Training Program.

Practical Exercises

The second component of the CITP evaluation system is the measurement of physical skills acquired during training. Students must satisfactorily complete all phases of the practical exercises to successfully complete the training program.

The practical exercises are designed to provide students with as much individual attention and instruction as possible. This area involves the development of psychomotor skills and the basic knowledge needed to perform at least minimally in the occupational role. Each student is given a reasonable number of opportunities to meet the minimum standards of performance established by the learning objectives.

Evaluation of student performance is made during various practical exercises. Performance will be judged by the student's actual ability to satisfactorily complete the required tasks.

The Center encourages students to repeat the practical exercise portions of their training until mastery is achieved. Accordingly, students who do not achieve mastery in any of these tasks are not placed on probation. However, if a student cannot demonstrate the ability to satisfactorily perform the tasks prior to the completion of the program, a certificate will not be awarded.

In addition to practical exercises in many specific areas, students are required to successfully complete a final "single thread" practical exercise that lasts for three entire training days. Each student, assigned to an investigative team, will be assigned a particular problem in which the tasks learned in prior training will be tested. Once assigned the problem, each student will employ techniques acquired in interviewing, surveillance, execution of search and arrest warrants, crime scene investigation, and testifying at trial. Grades will be based on each student's performance. In addition, each team member must contribute to a written case report documenting each individual's actions as well as the actions of the team in acquiring evidence during the exercise. The case report will be used as the basis for the mock trial and related court hearings pursuant to the trial.

Firearms Training

Marksmanship is evaluated on a point system. Each student must qualify with a minimum of 70 percent on the Practical Pistol Course. A student who does not achieve a satisfactory level of proficiency on the Practical Pistol Course (210 points out of 300 points = 70 percent) will be offered the opportunity to participate in remedial training to correct the deficiency. The total amount of scheduled firearms remedial training offered to students will not exceed eight hours and two retests. Failure to qualify on this course will preclude students from successful completion of the training program.

FBI ACADEMY

The FBI Academy is considered one of the world's most respected law enforcement training centers. The Academy trains FBI Special Agents and professional support staff, as well as local, state, federal, and international law enforcement personnel.

New Agent Program

The New Agents' Training Unit (NATU) coordinates seventeen weeks of instruction at the FBI Academy in Quantico, Virginia. New Agent Trainees (NATS) are exposed to three components of curriculum involving the following areas:

- Investigative/Tactical
- Non-Investigative
- Administrative

The above three components total 643.5 hours of instruction spread over four major concentrations:

- Academics
- Firearms
- Operational Skills
- Integrated Case Scenario

NATs must pass nine academic examinations, with a score of 85 percent or better, in the following disciplines:

- Legal (2 exams)
- Behavioral Science
- Interviewing
- Ethics
- Basic and Advanced Investigative Techniques (2 Exams)
- Interrogation
- Forensic Science

A Physical Training (PT) test is administered to each NAT during the first, seventh, and fourteenth weeks of training. A minimum of 12 points (at least 1 point must be scored in each of the four events as well), out of a possible 40, is required to pass each PT test. The four events tested are:

1. Sit-ups
2. 300-meter run
3. Push-ups
4. One-and-a-half-mile run

NATs are also required to pass a Defensive Tactics (DT) test. The DT test focuses on grappling and boxing, handcuffing, control holds, searching subjects, weapon retention, and disarming techniques.

Each NAT must qualify twice with a Bureau-issued handgun and once with a shotgun. To qualify, NATs must shoot 80 percent or better on two of three qualification courses with the pistol, as well as a cumulative score of 80 percent on all three qualifications. NATs must also demonstrate familiarity with the Bureau submachine gun. NATs will fire between 3,000 and 5,000 rounds of ammunition during their seventeen weeks of training.

While engaged in the aforementioned training, NATs are given a case to investigate which will culminate in the arrest of multiple subjects. The investigation mirrors what they will experience in the field, since it is conducted at Hogan's Alley, a mock city built especially for practical exercises. NATs conduct interviews, perform surveillance, and put to use the street survival techniques taught by the instructors at Hogan's Alley.

NATU is staffed by Supervisory Special Agents who serve as class supervisors. They are assisted by 2 Special Agents, referred to as Field Counselors. These Field Counselors are Special Agents from the fifty-six Field Divisions throughout the Bureau, who have volunteered to spend seventeen weeks at the FBI Academy. During these seventeen weeks the NATU staff evaluates each NAT's suitability to be a Special Agent of the FBI.

DRUG ENFORCEMENT AGENCY TRAINING ACADEMY

The Drug Enforcement Agency (DEA) Training Academy is used for Basic Agent training, Basic Diversion Investigator training, Basic Intelligence Research Specialist training, Basic Forensic Science training, professional and executive development training, certification training, and specialized training. The Academy is also used to conduct drug law enforcement seminars for state and local law enforcement personnel, and through the use of specially equipped classrooms, international drug-training seminars for foreign law enforcement officials. The Academy's international classroom has the capacity to simultaneously translate an instructor's course of instruction into three different languages.

While trainees reside and attend class at the DEA Training Academy, firearms training, physical fitness and defensive tactics training, defensive driving training, and all practical application exercises continue to be held at the FBI Academy. The facilities required for these types of training are used jointly by both the DEA and FBI.

DEA Basic Agent Training

Over the past five years, the Office of Training has graduated more than 1,800 DEA Special Agents from the Basic Agent Training program. Typically, class sizes range from 40 to 50 Basic Agent trainees. The average age of these students is 30 years. Approximately 60 percent of all trainees arrive with prior law enforcement experience, while 30 percent come from a military background. Every student must possess a bachelor's degree and nearly 20 percent have some postgraduate educational experience.

The curriculum consists of a 16-week resident program that provides instruction in the basics of report writing, law, automated information systems, and drug recognition, as well as leadership and ethics. Underpinning the instruction is a rigorous 84-hour physical fitness and defensive tactics regimen designed to prepare new Special Agents to prevail in compliant and noncompliant arrest scenarios.

Students receive 120 hours of firearms training including basic marksmanship, weapons safety, tactical shooting, and deadly force decision training. An integral part of Basic Agent training is an emphasis on respect for human life, leadership and ethics, human dignity, and sound judgment in the use of deadly force. During the training, students are required to apply their classroom knowledge in a series of increasingly demanding practical exercises designed to test leadership, decisiveness, and knowledge of procedures and techniques that will be used in the field.

In order to graduate, students must maintain an academic average of 80 percent on academic examinations, pass the firearms qualification test, successfully demonstrate leadership and sound decision making in practical scenarios, and pass rigorous physical task tests. Upon graduation, students are sworn in as DEA Special Agents and assigned to DEA field offices located across the United States.

U.S. POSTAL INSPECTION SERVICE TRAINING ACADEMY

U.S. Postal Inspectors are federal law enforcement agents with investigative jurisdiction in all criminal matters involving the integrity and security of the U.S. Postal Service.

Postal Inspectors investigate criminal, civil, and administrative violations of postal-related laws, often using forensics and cutting-edge technologies. It is essential that Postal Inspectors be in sound physical condition and be capable of performing vigorous physical activities on a sustained basis.

The national academy for Postal Inspectors is located at the William F. Bolger Training Center in Potomac, Maryland. The facility contains a 525-bed complex co-located with the Postal Service Leadership Center that includes classrooms, a practical scenario building, an indoor firearms range, and exercise and dining facilities.

The training program mirrors Postal Inspection field operations, which minimizes lecture formats. Training modules focus on subjects such as postal inspection operations, ethics, team building, customer service, problem solving, mail processing and delivery, informants, controlled substances, crime scene management and processing, internal audits and accounting, search warrants, interviewing and interrogation, report writing, legal issues, civil fraud, computer hardware, officer survival, firearms proficiency, and physical conditioning.

U.S. AIR FORCE SPECIAL INVESTIGATIONS ACADEMY

Enlisted and civilian candidates attend a mandatory $10\frac{1}{2}$-week basic Special Investigator Course at the U.S. Air Force Special Investigations Academy in Washington, D.C.

The Basic Investigator course includes instruction in law, investigative theory, report writing, forensics, interview techniques, and other subjects designed to prepare Special Agents for the challenges of investigative duty. Upon graduation, new Special Agents spend a one-year probationary period in the field. Upon successful completion, the agents may return to Washington, D.C., for further specialized training in economic crime, antiterrorism service, counterintelligence, and other sophisticated criminal investigative capabilities.

Selected Special Agents attend ten weeks of technical training to acquire electronic, photographic, and other skills required to perform technical surveillance investigations. Experienced Agents selected for polygraph duties attend a 14-week Department of Defense course.

CANINE ENFORCEMENT TRAINING CENTER

The U.S. Customs Service's Canine Enforcement Training Center (CETC), located in Front Royal, Virginia, provides training for all Customs Enforcement Officer teams, and to federal, state, local, and foreign law enforcement agencies. The CETC maintains a staff consisting of instructors, animal caretakers, storage specialists, and administrative personnel. The Center's average canine population is between 100 and 150 dogs on a daily basis. On average, there is a yearly training completion of 120 canine enforcement teams.

Programs offered by the CETC staff include:

- Basic Narcotic Detection Course
- Passenger Processing Course
- Technical Training Course for Canine Team Leaders
- Basic Currency Detection Course

NATIONAL ENFORCEMENT TRAINING INSTITUTE

The National Enforcement Training Institute (NETI), located within the Environmental Protection Agency, is responsible for training tribal lawyers, inspectors, civil and criminal inspectors, and regulatory personnel in various aspects of environmental law enforcement. NETI courses and workshops focus on:

*   Environmental Crimes and Investigations
*   Statutes and Legal Issues
*   Solid and Hazardous Waste Identification
*   Enforcement of the Clean Water Act, Endangered Species Act, National Environmental Policy Act, Resource Conservation and Recovery Act, and National Historic Preservation Act
*   Wetlands and Flood Plains

Federal Agency Contacts

Air Force OSI Headquarters
500 Duncan Avenue
Bolling AFB
Washington, D.C. 20332
Phone: (202) 297-5352
Web site: wwwaf.mil

Board of Governors of the Federal Reserve System
Office of Inspector General
20th Street and Constitution Avenue NW
Washington, D.C. 20551
Web site: www.ignet.gov/ignet/internal/frb/oighome.html

Bureau of Alcohol, Tobacco and Firearms
Personnel Division
650 Massachusetts Avenue NW, Room 4100
Washington, D.C. 20226
Phone: (202) 927-8423
Web site: www.atf.treas.gov

Bureau of Diplomatic Security
Department of State
P.O. Box 9317
Arlington, VA 22219
Phone: (202) 663-0478
Web site: www.heroes.net

Bureau of Indian Affairs
Office of Personnel
1849 C Street NW
Washington, D.C. 20240
Phone: (202) 208-3710
Web site: www.doi.gov/bureau-indian-affairs.html

Bureau of Land Management
Office of Law Enforcement
Department of Interior
Washington, D.C. 20240
Phone: (202) 208-3710
Web site: www.blm.gov

Central Intelligence Agency
Office of Inspector General
Washington, D.C. 20505
Phone: (703) 874-2555
Web site: www.odci.gov/cia

Coast Guard Investigative Service
2100 Second Street SW
Washington, D.C. 20593
Phone (202) 267-2229
Web site: www.dot.gov/dotinfo/uscg

Department of Commerce
Office of Inspector General
14th Street and Constitution Avenue NW, Room 7616
Washington, D.C. 20230
Phone: (202) 482-0934
Web site: www.osec.doc.gov/oig

Department of Energy
Office of Inspector General
1000 Independence Avenue SW
Washington, D.C. 20585
Phone: (202) 586-5000
Web site: www.hr.doe.gov/ig

Department of Justice
Office of Inspector General
10th Street and Constitution NW
Washington, D.C. 20530
Phone: (202) 616-4500
Web site: www.usdoj.gov/oig

Department of State
Office of Inspector General
2201 C Street NW
Washington, D.C. 20520
Phone: (202) 647-4000
Web site: www.state.gov

Department of Transportation
Office of Inspector General
400 Seventh Street SW
Washington, D.C. 20590
Phone: (202) 366-2677
Web site: www.dot.gov/oig

Department of Veterans Affairs
Office of Security and Law Enforcement
810 Vermont Avenue NW
Washington, D.C. 20420
Phone: (202) 287-2499
Web site: www.va.gov

Division of Law Enforcement
U.S. Fish and Wildlife Service
P.O. Box 3247
Arlington, VA 22203
Phone: (703) 358-1949
Web site: www.fws.gov~r9dle/div_le.html

Drug Enforcement Administration
Agent Recruiting
Washington, D.C. 20537
Phone: (800) DEA-4288
Web site: www.usdoj.gov/dea

EPA Office of Criminal Enforcement
401 M Street SW
Washington, D.C. 20460
Phone: (202) 546-2480
Web site: www.es.epa.gov/oeca/oceft/cid

Federal Bureau of Investigation
Washington, D.C. 20535
Phone: (202) 324-2727
Web site: www.fbi.gov

Federal Deposit Insurance Corporation
Office of Inspector General
550 Seventeenth Street NW
Washington, D.C. 20429
Phone: (800) 695-8052
Web site: www.fdic.gov

Federal Protective Service
General Services Administration
18th and F Streets NW
Washington, D.C. 20405
Phone: (202) 501-0907
Web site: www.gsa.gov/pbs/fps/fps.htm

General Services Administration
Office of Inspector General
18th and F Streets NW
Washington, D.C. 20405
Phone: (202) 708-5082
Web site: www.gsa.gov

IRS Inspection Division
Department of the Treasury
1111 Constitution Avenue NW
Washington, D.C. 20224
Phone: (202) 622-5000
Web site: www.irs.treas.gov

National Park Service
Department of Interior
P.O. Box 37127
Washington, D.C. 20013
Phone: (202) 208-6843
Web site: www.nps.gov

Naval Air Systems Command Police Department
Washington Naval Yard, Building 111
901 M Street SE
Washington, D.C. 20388
Phone: (202) 433-8800
Web site: www.navy.mil

Naval Criminal Investigative Service
716 East Sicard Street SE, Building 111
Washington Navy Yard
Washington, D.C. 20388
Phone: (202) 433-9162
Web site: www.ncis.navy.mil

Office of Personnel Management
Office of Inspector General
1900 E Street NW, Room 6400
Washington, D.C. 20415
Phone: (202) 606-1200
Web site: www.opm.gov

Supreme Court of the United States
Personnel Office
1 First Street NE
Washington, D.C. 20543
Phone: (202) 479-3404
Web site: www.supremecourtus.gov

U.S. Army Criminal Investigation Command
5611 Columbia Pike
Falls Church, VA 22041
Phone: (703) 756-1232
Web site: www.belvoir.army.mil/cidc

U.S. Border Patrol, Immigration and Naturalization Service
425 I Street NW
Washington, D.C. 20536
Phone: (202) 616-1964
Web site: www.ins.usdoj.gov

U.S. Customs Service
Department of Treasury
1300 Pennsylvania Avenue NW
Washington, D.C. 20229
Phone: (202) 927-1250
Web site: www.customs.ustreas.gov

USDA Forest Service
P.O. Box 96090
Washington, D.C. 20090
Phone: (202) 720-3760
Web site: www.usda.gov/oig

U.S. Immigration and Naturalization Service
Department of Justice
425 I Street NW
Washington, D.C. 20536
Phone: (202) 514-4316
 Web site: www.ins.usdoj.gov

U.S. Marshals Service
Office of Human Resources
600 Army Navy Drive
Arlington, VA 22202
Phone: (202) 307-9000
Web site: www.usdoj.gov/marshals

U.S. Nuclear Regulatory Commission
Office of Personnel
Washington, D.C. 20555
Phone: (800) 952-9678
Web site: www.nrc.gov

U.S. Park Police
National Park Service
1100 Ohio Drive SW
Washington, D.C. 20240
Phone: (202) 208-3710
Web site: www.doi.gov/u.s.park.police

U.S. Postal Inspection Service
475 L'Enfant Plaza SW
Washington, D.C. 20260
Phone: (202) 268-4267
Web site: www.usps.gov/websites/depart/inspect

U.S. Secret Service
Uniformed Division
1800 G Street NW
Washington, D.C. 20223
Phone: (202) 435-5708
Web site: www.treas.gov/usss

Get a Résumé that Gets Results at...

ResumeEdge.com

Put Certified Professional Résumé Writers to Work for You!

In today's competitive job market, you need every advantage you can get. At **ResumeEdge.com**, certified professional résumé writers (CPRWs) help you focus on your strengths, better articulate your qualifications, and land more interviews. Whether you're a student entering the workforce for the first time or an experienced executive trying to reach the next level, you'll make a powerful first impression with a professionally written résumé.

Visit **www.ResumeEdge.com** today and give yourself an edge!

"Specializing in High-Impact Résumés for Executives and Professionals"
—The Wall Street Journal's CareerJournal

"The Net's Most Talented Résumé Experts"
—Lycos Careers

THOMSON
PETERSON'S

IHRE03